Latin American University Students: A Six Nation Study

Written under the auspices of The Center for International Affairs
Harvard University

Latin American University Students: A Six Nation Study

Arthur Liebman, Kenneth N. Walker, Myron Glazer

with an Introduction by Seymour Martin Lipset

Harvard University Press   Cambridge, Massachusetts   1972

For Our Children

> Katherine
> Judith
> Madeline
> Michael
> Lisa
> Amy
> Joshua

Preface

During the last two decades we have observed, participated in, and later studied student political activity in the Americas. Kenneth Walker's interest in student politics dates back to the Loyalty Oath controversy of 1950–1951 at the University of California. He observed the attempt of a small number of left student activists to mobilize a passive student body around an issue far more fraught with peril to academic freedom than the 1965 Free Speech issue at the same university. The shift from apathy to militant involvement between the two events tells much about the growth of a student movement in the interim.

Myron Glazer attended City College of New York in the mid-1950s and served as a member of the student government and as class president. McCarthyism had already exacted a heavy penalty from liberals as well as radicals. Glazer was among the last group of CCNY student activists as the college community succumbed to external threats and quietly, if only temporarily, joined the intimidated generation.

The Berkeley which Arthur Liebman found as a graduate student in the early 1960s was far different from the one which Walker had encountered only ten years earlier. The access routes into the university (on a narrow strip of sidewalk soon to become historic) were now marked by numerous tables bearing literature from a variety of political organizations. Liebman had come from Rutgers University where "left" meant the relatively inactive Americans for Democratic Action. In Berkeley, the label "left" was an imprecise designation covering a wide variety of active organizations. His interest in pursuing a study of student politics grew as the Free Speech Movement reached its high point and as he became a participant as well as an observer.

In 1963, a year prior to the open collision at Berkeley, Seymour M. Lipset had organized the comparative study of Latin American student politics. Walker, after several years of factory work, was now a graduate student and became involved in the earliest stages of planning and questionnaire construction. His concern with student politics was to deepen, first as a result of the Free Speech Movement, later with the formation of a teaching and research assistants' union fostered by the movement, and ultimately by his participation as a faculty member (at the University of Toronto) in the writing and enacting of a departmental constitution which put students on the executive committee and assembly which governed the department.

Liebman became associated with the project shortly afterwards in 1964 when Lipset invited him to use the comparative student data as the basis for his dissertation on Puerto Rican students. Liebman's first major field work experience resulted when he did follow-up interviews with students at the Rio Piedras Campus. He was surprised and disappointed by their lack of political zeal and was challenged to analyze the historical and social forces which constricted their political interest and effectiveness. After completing his dissertation on Puerto Rican students, Liebman next turned to the Mexican data and later travelled to Mexico City. Again, his exposure to the scholarly literature on Mexico, his analysis of the Mexican student data, and most important his interview with Mexican students forced him to alter his preconceived notions.

In Mexico, there was one political fact that every group including the students had to come to terms with – namely that the ruling Revolutionary Institutional Party or PRI completely dominated politics. Most students apparently had accommodated themselves to this fact despite their revolutionary or Marxist rhetoric. Nonetheless, their capacity to respond to oppression was vividly displayed when they challenged their seemingly omnipotent government in 1968. Many, unfortunately, lost their lives while others were placed in prison or exiled for their courageous political acts. Liebman has written and spoken on their behalf here as well as in Mexico. His Mexico experience has had a marked impact on his personal and scholarly life.

Glazer's participation in the project represents a continuation of his interest in the dual roles played by many Latin American university students. In 1960 he studied physics graduate students at Princeton University and analyzed the process by which they developed a professional self-concept. Shortly afterward, he decided that research on the professional training and political involvement of Latin American students could illuminate the tension which often confronts youth in developing nations, a tension which thousands of United States students and professors now also experience.

Glazer's doctoral research for Princeton University resulted in his spending fifteen months in Latin America, including two months in Mexico, several weeks in Peru, Argentina, and Uruguay, and a full year in Chile. During the

1964 presidential campaign he and his wife interviewed a carefully-drawn sample of Chilean students about their attitudes toward professional education, political commitment, and national problems. The Glazers gained first-hand experience with the challenges of pursuing field research during a period of heightened national tension when North Americans were particularly suspect.

In 1965, after Glazer had completed his dissertation, Lipset invited him to join the project. Glazer was eager to compare his Chilean data with the material collected elsewhere in Latin America. He found that the data tended to support his Chilean-based conclusions that the students were far more interested in learning and applying their knowledge than most analysts had stated. This view was reinforced when he and his wife returned to Santiago in 1969 to study the reform at the University at Chile. Students and young professors had joined forces to bring about major changes in the traditional and conservative university.

We have worked together on this project for the past six years. A division of labor was agreed upon: chapter 1, Liebman and Walker; chapter 2, Glazer and Liebman; chapter 3, Glazer with the assistance of Joel S. Migdal; chapter 4, Walker; chapter 5, Liebman; chapter 6, Liebman; chapter 7, Glazer, Liebman, and Walker.

We have placed our names on the title page in the order that makes sense to us. Liebman has done a considerable amount of the writing and rewriting and has also taken the responsibility for coordinating our efforts. Because he has assumed these and other major duties in seeing the book through to completion, his name is first. Walker has worked with the project longest and was directly involved in the important planning and development stages. Glazer did a disproportionate share of the editorial work and played a vital role in improving and revising the book along with Liebman in the spring and summer of 1971. We have all met on innumerable occasions to discuss, plan, read, criticize, and encourage each other in a variety of ways, particularly in the unpleasant task of rewriting drafts. These meetings and constant three-way communications helped to rekindle the motivation which is so essential in seeing so long-term a project as this to its successful conclusion. Each of us, then, feels personally identified with the entire volume and shares full responsibility for all of its contents.

Acknowledgements

This work is the product of the efforts of many people. We herein wish to acknowledge our indebtedness to the numerous individuals in Berkeley, Cambridge, Northampton, and Latin America who helped bring this volume into being. Early in the history of the project data collection was supervised by Glaucio Soares and Kenneth N. Walker, and data were collected by Edith Churchill, Brunhild Velez Heilbron, Mireya Suarez Soares, Jeanne Posada, Domingo Rivarola, and Cesar Moreno Perez. The coding and the processing of the questionnaires were completed by a staff from the Survey Research Center of the University of California at Berkeley under the direction of Elsa Turner. Margaret McIntyre assisted in the earlier stages of data collection and coordination. During the Berkeley phase of the project, all of the work on the project was done by members of the Survey Research Center and the Institute of International Studies. Among those on the staffs of these two research organizations who were especially helpful to the project were Charles Y. Glock, former Director of the Survey Research Center, David Apter, former Director of the Institute of International Studies, Neil Smelser, Associate Director, and Cleo Stoker, Administrative Assistant at the Institute.

At Harvard University, Karen Sapolsky of the Center for International Affairs was primarily responsible for coordinating computer work involved in the analyses reported in the book, as well as in various articles which were an outgrowth of the research. She also managed the files and correspondence with scholars in a number of countries who helped the project or used the data in their own research. Dr. Orlando Albórnoz of the Central University of Venezuela in Caracas spent over a year at the Harvard Center for International Affairs working on comparative aspects of student behavior in North and South America. He studied student activists in the United States, later publishing his results in two Spanish language books, while simultaneously advising us on our project and seeking assistance on his own. During our fruitful collaboration with Dr.

Albórnoz, we North Americans sought to explain Latin American students to our countrymen while he, a Latin American scholar, tried to interpret North American students to his compatriots. We believe that this is a unique example of cultural exchange. He is, of course, in no way responsible for our final analyses and interpretations nor are we, in turn, responsible for his.

Joel S. Migdal worked on the project during two summers and provided a great deal of assistance and insight in the development of chapter 3. We like to think that his research on students helped stimulate his doctoral study of peasants and revolution at Harvard University. David H. Smith gave us important methodological assistance as well as advice in the writing of the methodology appendix. William Creed proofread and graciously performed a myriad of minor functions before the manuscript was officially submitted to the publisher. Grace Watson did minor editing and a major portion of the typing. Elinore Kagan, Norma Lepine, and Agnes Shannon also did a great deal of the typing. Marina Finkelstein, the editor of the Center for International Affairs, was particularly helpful with respect to the final editing. The original draft improved considerably due to the skillfulness of her craft. Under her tutelage the manuscript was made more coherent and intelligible.

Penina Migdal Glazer and Edna Kirszner Liebman each criticized portions of the final manuscript, spent long hours at the typewriter, and provided crucial encouragement throughout and especially during the last stages of our work.

This volume appears as a product of the activities of the Center for International Affairs at Harvard University. It is an outgrowth of a program of comparative research on the role of the university and students in contemporary societies, both developed and underdeveloped, which is financed by the Hazen Foundation and the Ford Foundation. The monies which made the planning and data collection possible came largely from the general support funds given to the Institute of International Studies at Berkeley by the Ford Foundation and the Carnegie Corporation for comparative and international studies. Some of the early codification and analyses were fiananced by a basic research grant to the Institute of International Studies and Survey Research Center at Berkeley for methodological and substantive work on the application of survey (polling) techniques to problems of development from the Behavioral Sciences Division of the United States Air Force. Also, the Research Foundation of the State University of New York awarded a summer Faculty Fellowship to Arthur Liebman in 1968 for work on this volume.

Finally, this list of acknowledgments would not be complete without two more additions. This project could never have been completed without the enthusiastic support of Seymour Martin Lipset. During the long course of the project, he was a source of constant encouragement. We also acknowledge our intellectual debt to him. We have learned much and have been deeply stimulated by his prolific writings and insightful discussions.

The last and largest acknowledgment is, of course, reserved for the Latin American students who served as our respondents. We hope that this volume can help broaden the American public's understanding and appreciation of the students, their universities, and their countries.

Contents

Introduction by Seymour Martin Lipset

Diffusion of student political activism to most countries of the world, developed and underdeveloped, Communist and non-Communist, since 1964 has occasioned a massive literature. Every French bookstore now carries its equivalent of a five-foot bookcase of volumes discussing the "events" of May 1968. A seven-year-old Japanese bibliography of publications on student politics in Japanese includes some 1,700 items, while one dealing with literature on Japanese students in English contains 466 works.[1] Two American bibliographies, one covering the United States scene and the other the world have recently appeared and both are already dated.[2] There are now a number of publications which report on the political news of the university world.[3] And no one knows how many conferences are held each year to analyze the subject.

The phenomenon of university-based activism, of political conflict between radical groups in the academy and the rest of society, is clearly not a recent one. Throughout the world both intellectuals and youth have historically been disturbers of the peace, challengers of traditional verities, and critics of the status quo and established governments. As political philosophers sought to generalize about the causes of revolution, some located the sources of unrest in the universities. Thus, in *Behemoth*, Thomas Hobbes identified the universities as the "Trojan horse" responsible for rebellion.

1. Michiya Shimbori, "Bibliography of Student Movements in Japan," *Educational Studies of the Faculty of Higher Education*, II (Hiroshima University, 1963), 97–143; Herbert Passin, "Japanese Education: Guide to a Bibliography in the English Language," *Comparative Education Review*, 9 (February 1965), 81–101.

2. Philip G. Altbach, *Student Politics and Higher Education in the United States* (Cambridge, Mass., Harvard University, 1968); Philip G. Altbach, *A Select Bibliography on Students, Politics and Higher Education*, rev. ed. (Cambridge, Mass., Harvard University, 1970); Philip G. Altbach, *Higher Education in Developing Countries: A Select Bibliography* (Cambridge, Mass., Harvard University, 1970).

3. *Minerva*; Institute for International Youth Affairs, *News Features*; Institut International d'Etudes sur L'Education, *Bulletin*; *Student Mirror*; International Student Press Service, *SIPE*.

The Universities have been to this nation as the wooden horse was to the Trojans . . . . I despair of any lasting peace among ourselves, till the Universities here shall bend and direct their studies to the settling of it, that is, to the teaching of absolute obedience to the laws of the King . . .

The core of the rebellion, as you have seen by this and read of other rebellions, are the Universities, which nevertheless are not to be cast away, but to be better disciplined.[4]

Eighteenth and nineteenth century rebellions and revolutions lent support to Hobbes's dictum. As Richard Hofstadter noted: "In nationalist and colonialist revolutions college and university students have always played an aggressive part, and to this the American college students were no exception."[5] For a number of decades after the Revolution, American college students took part in many protest demonstrations, some quite violent, against orthodox theology, philosophical and political conservatism, and slavery.

In France, the center of revolution in the western world from 1789 to 1871, August Blanqui argued through the middle of the nineteenth century that the revolutionary classes were the students and the declassed intellectuals. They, rather than the masses, could see through the repression of the ruling class and had the intelligence and background with which to oppose the system. And he called on these revolutionary strata to set a revolutionary movement in motion through terroristic tactics, which would force authority to be repressive and to crack down on all potential dissent. Only through the use of what is today called confrontation tactics, could the revolutionary dynamic be set in motion.[6] Although Marxist leaders denounced the student-based Blanquists for their terrorist tactics, held to show their elitism, authoritarianism, and lack of faith in the political potential of the masses, these Marxists also recognized that all French revolutionary movements up to the Paris Commune of 1871 had drawn heavily on students, both for shock troops and for leadership. Thus, what is closest to an official Marxist history of the Paris Commune, Peter Lissagray's *History of the Commune of 1871* translated into English by Marx's daughter), stated unequivocally that "the students of the universities, till now [have been] the advanced guard of all our revolutions."[7]

This awareness of the students and universities as inhere   sources of social

4. Thomas Hobbes, *Behemoth* (New York, Burt Franklin, 1943) pp. 51, 71, 74.

5. Richard Hofstadter, *Academic Freedom in the Age of the College* (New York, Columbia University Press, 1961), p. 206.

6. Lewis S. Feuer, *The Conflict of Generations* (New York, Basic Books, 1969), pp. 266–267.

7. Prosper O. Lissagaray, *History of the Commune of 1871* (New York, Monthly Review Press, 1967), p. 91. This is a reprint of the edition first published in Great Britain in 1886, as translated by Eleanor Marx Aveling with an introduction by her.

criticism and unrest was not limited to political philosophers and radicals. In Japan, for example, in the late nineteenth century, Meiji reformers sought ways to restrain such behavior before they established Japan's first university. Thus, in a memorandum written in 1870, Arinori Mori, the first Meiji minister of education, argued that an effective modernizing Japan must have a first rate educational system. However, he acknowledged that the establishment of such a system would entail some political consequences. The schools, up to and including the level of the teachers' colleges, would be expected to produce skilled young Japanese for the economy who would at the same time be loyal to the emperor. But Mori also argued that a major industrial power had to have excellent universities as well. Unlike the schools, such institutions, he wrote, could not be expected to teach loyalty to the emperor and to the system. A major university must be a center of research and of new and critical ideas, its faculty and students must be exposed to the literature of the world and must be free to follow their beliefs. Hence, a good university would inevitably be a center of disloyalty, which, the education minister suggested, should be kept from contact with the rest of the society so as to avoid the spread of seditious ideas.[8]

Variants of the proposition that academic and intellectual life inevitably breed conflict with the powers, with established thought and values, have been advanced by many writers, both conservative and leftist, from the nineteenth century to the present. Since innovation and avant-gardism are inherent in the concept of the intellectual and scholar, the best and most creative among them, it is held, will inevitably find themselves at odds with the defenders of the status quo. Such opposition, of course, need not always have a leftist political implication. It could involve a nonpolitical or a conservative rejection of the dominant ethos. But, given the inherent role of the university as a physical center, a concentration point for scholars and students concerned with matters of the intellect, with ideal analysis and theory, these analysts and writers have repeatedly assumed that the university is more likely to be a source of unrest and of varying types of social criticism than any other part of society.

Writings which emphasize traits of intellectual and university life that result in critical outlooks and action by intellectuals and students are paralleled by those which also stress the inherent characteristics of youth. These characteristics also lead to critical outlooks and action and repeatedly contribute to the formation of "youth movements." Many of the more contemporary descrip-

---

8. Michio Nagai, "The Development of Intellectuals in the Meiji and Taisho Periods," *Journal of Social and Political Ideas in Japan*, 2 (April, 1964), 29.

tions reiterate characteristics found in the writings of the ancient Greeks, particularly of Aristotle:

> [Youth] have exalted notions, because they have not yet been humbled by life or learnt its necessary limitations; moreover their hopeful disposition makes them think themselves equal to great things — and that means having exalted notions. They would always rather do noble deeds than useful ones; their lives are regulated more by moral feelings than by reasoning . . . All their mistakes are in the direction of doing things excessively and vehemently . . . [They] love too much, hate too much, and the same with everything else. They think they know everything, and are quite sure about it; this, in fact, is why they overdo everything.[9]

Student youth have almost always been disproportionately attracted to movements and causes which seek to bring reality and ideals into harmony. As youth, they tend to look at social events from an absolutist ethical basis, as students they live in an environment which takes ideas seriously. In much of Europe during the nineteenth century, in the various revolutionary movements of France, in the efforts to bring democracy and a national state to Germany, in the attempts to overthrow Czarism and modernize Russia, in the struggles for democracy and national unification in Italy, the student rebels and young intellectuals were always in the forefront.

Student political activism has, of course, not only been on the side of those seeking to change society from a leftist or a more universalistic direction. While many student movements have been dedicated to incorporating the masses in the body politic, to eliminating particularistic prejudices against religious, ethnic, and racial minorities, and to fostering peace and internationalism, others have pressed idealistically for racial or national purity, for their own national supremacy, and for a manifest elitist system which barred the "incompetent" from a share in power. Japanese students demonstrated a considerable commitment to radical nationalism in the 1930s. French and Spanish students gave significant support to their national fascist movements in the 1920s and 1930s. Italian students formed a large part of the backbone of the Fascist party in the early 1920s. In fact, the party identified itself as a youth movement and its anthem was called *"Giovenezza,"* or "Youth." Most of its leaders were under thirty. The German Nazis also insisted that they were a youth movement. And by 1931 the party had won a majority in student council elections in most

9. *The Basic Works of Aristotle*, ed. Richard McJeon (New York, Random House, 1941), p. 1404.

German universities, before it had attained comparable strength in any other stratum.[10]

In the era after World War II, students and intellectuals continued to be in the vanguard of important social and political movements. A comparative perspective would suggest that these groups have been the most significant as agents of political change in developing societies. As Samuel Huntington put it, in modernizing societies "the city is the source of opposition within the country; the middle class is the focus of opposition within the city; the intelligensia is the most active oppositional group within the middle class; and the students are the most coherent and effective revolutionaries within the intelligensia."[11] This formulation is also applicable to the more developed and complex societies of the West and the Communist countries of Eastern Europe. Particularly in the post-Berkeley 1960s, students and younger intellectuals in these societies are the most ardent critics and most active challengers of entrenched interests as well as governments, often in the name of national ideals and values.

STUDENTS IN LATIN AMERICA

Of all national or regional student groups, the students of Latin America have been the most significant politically for the longest period of time. Although the European tradition of student-based revolutions goes back at least to Martin Luther's followers at the University of Wittenberg, student activism in Latin America has been the most continuous in modern history. Students played an important part in the events leading up to the attainment of independence in the early nineteenth century, and they continued to be active in succeeding decades. The origins of the contemporary student movements are located in the uprising at the University of Córdoba in Argentina in 1918 and the University Reform Movement which sprang from it and spread throughout

10. Daniel Guerin, *Fascism and Big Business* (New York, Pioneer, 1939), pp. 47–50, 62–63. Guido Martinotti, "The Positive Marginality: Notes on Italian Students in Periods of Political Mobilization," in Seymour Martin Lipset and Philip G. Altach, eds., *Students in Revolt* (Boston, Houghton Mifflin, 1969), pp. 173–175; Peter Gay, *Weimar Culture* (New York, Harper and Row, 1968), pp. 139–140; John Orr, "The Radical Right," in Julian Nagel, ed., *Student Power* (London, Merlin, 1969), pp. 73–90; Fritz Ringer, *The Decline of the German Mandarin* (Cambridge, Mass., Harvard University Press, 1969), pp. 250–251; Feuer, *Conflict of the Generations*, pp. 284–291.

11. Samuel Huntington, *Political Order in Changing Societies* (New Haven, Yale University Press, 1969), p. 290.

Latin America in the interwar period. In contrast, European and American student activism more resembles periodic political forays followed by years of relative political quiescence.

Latin American students have alternated in their concerns between the campus and the realm of national politics. In pursuit of their self-interest, they have achieved a considerable degree of *co-gobierno* or co-government with university faculty and administrators. They have also been able to cause curricular and administrative changes, some of which have served to reduce academic pressure on students while others have spurred educational innovations. To some observers it has seemed that student politics has been important in inhibiting the growth and development of first-rate universities in Latin America. This factor, however, is only one of several that have contributed to the existing situation. Others have been (1) the niggardly financial support given to the public universities, which results in the phenomenon of the part-time professor whose major interests must lie in his off-campus profession; and (2) the intrusion of politics onto the campus by nonstudents, which has led to the use of political criteria in the hiring, promotion, and removal of both faculty and administrative personnel.

The most significant role of the Latin American students remains their deep involvement in the political life of their countries. These students have been a major force in opposing and overthrowing rightist and military dictatorships throughout the region. This is not to say that Latin American student activists are always to be found on the left. This is not the case, for there are political divisions among these students as there are among student activists everywhere. However, with the exceptionof the latter 1930s and the early World War II years, when there was some visible flirtation with fascism and conservative nationalism, the bulk of student activists have been located on the left of the political spectrum. In the last two decades, it would perhaps be easier to list the Latin American countries in which student-based protest was politically insignificant than in those in which it played a prominent part in politics. In the 1950s, to cite a few cases, students played an important role in the events which led to the overthrow of the authoritarian regimes of Peŕon, Rojas Pinilla, and Peŕez Jimeńez in Argentina, Colombia, and Venezuela, respectively. The Castro movement had its origins and found much of its support among students recruited to the revolution while attending the university. In the past decade students have been among the more significant oppositional or revolutionary forces in Chile, Bolivia, Brazil, Uruguay, Guatemala, Mexico, Dominican Republic, Panama, Venezuela, and Argentina.

It may safely be predicted that Latin American students will continue to be a force for change both on and off the campus during the 1970s. It was no accident that among the earliest acts of the incoming military dictatorships in Brazil and Argentina were attacks upon student political rights and arrests of many students and faculty who were active in politics. The increase in the number of military regimes as well as the lack of meaningful social and economic progress in the last decade throughout Latin America indicate that the traditional factors motivating student political involvement will not be lacking in the present decade. It should also be noted in this regard that even the Castro regime has had difficulty with some of its youth and students but it has not yet been of as serious a political nature as in Brazil and Argentina.

CONTENT OF THE BOOK

The present volume is the most comprehensive comparative empirical study dealing with student political attitudes and behavior which has yet appeared. By concentrating on students in countries with similar religious, political, and cultural traditions whose universities derive from a common model, the authors have been able to narrow their focus to the sources of variation in student behavior which emanate from different political systems and levels of development.

It is important to note that within a common cultural and linguistic area such as Latin America, there are still considerable differences among countries within the region. This book deals with students in the extremely poor, traditionalist, and authoritarian society of Paraguay and with those attending university in Mexico, with its very high rate of economic growth and its special variant of a leftist authoritarian political system. The other four societies studied, Uruguay, Colombia, Panama, and Puerto Rico, offered an opportunity to deal with university political behavior in sharply different versions of competitive party systems. There is also variation with respect to university systems. Included in this study are public and private universities, secular and religious ones, as well as national and regional institutions of higher education. These variations also extend to differences in the proportions of college age youth attending university in the six societies included here. Puerto Rico has one of the world's highest percentages (19 percent) enrolled in higher education, while Paraguay has one of the lowest (3 percent) in Latin America. The inclusion of the University of Puerto Rico, the sole university in the study based on the North American model, affords further opportunity to specify potential sources of differences among students in different university systems.

The central theme of the study is: what is there about the interaction between

the children of the Latin American elite and an archaic, socially insulated institution – the Latin American university – that regularly produces a significant
number of students opposed to both their governments and the social structures that have and will so richly benefit them. In elaborating on this theme,
the authors focus on the tensions between reform and change on the one hand
and of tradition and status quo on the other. Since 1918, Latin American students have urged that their universities become more socially relevant, more
modern, and more democratic. Yet, despite the enactment of some of the stu-
dent-demanded reforms, Latin American universities do not appear to have
changed substantially, and present student criticisms seem similar to those
leveled by their counterparts half a century earlier. Students have alternately
been concerned with the university and the national politics in their attempt
to bring about political change and reform. They are cognizant of the interplay between the university and the government: to seriously change one is to
change or affect the other. Also, as this study makes clear, the leftists, the predominant source of the contemporary activists are a minority among the students – but a minority that has been able to seize the center of the stage within the university.

The organization of this book is designed to explore the major facets of the
basic theme. The first chapter provides a historic overview of the universities,
the movement for university reform, and student politics in Latin America. It
stresses the historical continuity of university issues and of student political
efforts, especially the constant dual emphases of the students – university and
societal reform. Chapters 2 and 3 deal with the processes of university recruitment or selection and the reactions of the students to their education as they
prepare for their respective careers. These two chapters illustrate the importance of both the structure of the university and the ways in which society
impinges upon it including the nature of the recruitment of students (4 percent
of the age cohort), the poor condition of the professorial staff, and nonuniversity or noneducational criteria and influences, particularly political, on staff
and students. These chapters make clear the deficiencies of the university and
of the educational experience of the Latin American students and the difficulties faced by the university in making the transition from a traditional status-
conferring institution to a genuine educational and research institution. Chapter
4 examines in detail the family and university-related factors underlying the
political attitudes and behavior of the students in the survey and particularly
focuses upon the relative importance of recruitment and socialization to student political attitudes. Chapter 5 consists of an in-depth analysis of the often
neglected "conservative" students who outnumber the "leftists" but are unable

to transform their numerical superiority into the political dominance of the campus. Chapter 6 is a detailed comparative case study of students in Puerto Rico and Mexico. Although both of these societies have recently experienced an upsurge of student activism, they have quite dissimilar political traditions. This chapter analyzes the way in which historical, structural, and political factors have shaped the political attitudes and behavior of students within these two settings. In the Conclusion (chapter 7) the authors stand back from the specifics of their data in order to generalize about the political role of the Latin American student and the seemingly inherent tension that exists between the students and their government in that region.

BACKGROUND OF THE STUDY

Although most of the writing of this book and the analyses which went into it were completed in the past four years, the study began in 1963 in a research program dealing with social and political development in the Institute of International Studies of the University of California at Berkeley, of which I was then director. An important aspect of this program dealt with the formation and role of elites in the third world. It was thought that comparative analyses of the attitudes and behavior of university students as the embryonic elite, the bulk of the future economic, political, and intellectual leadership of their countries, would shed considerable light on comparative prospects for development. Scholars conversant with various regions and countries were invited to undertake such research. The program dealing with universities and students ultimately resulted in a number of surveys of samples of students using comparable questionnaires. These surveys included the Latin American countries covered in this volume, the research being initiated by Glaucio Soares, currently Professor of Sociology at the University of Brasilia, assisted by Kenneth N. Walker, now Associate Professor at the University of Toronto; Yugoslavia, undertaken by Bogdan Denitch, a native Yugoslav, presently a Research Associate at Columbia University; Algeria, Morocco, and Tunisia, undertaken by Clement H. Moore and Arlie Hochschild, both of the University of California; and Iran, by Cyrus Manzoor, an Iranian now with the Ministry of Science and Higher Education in Iran and a doctoral candidate at Tufts University.

Over succeeding years, various scholars and graduate students have completed a variety of written work using data from these surveys. The Latin American data, for example, have been the bases for publications in English by Soares, Walker, and Liebman, as well as for articles and theses in Spanish and Portuguese by Soares and a number of his graduate students at FLACSO (The Latin

American Graduate School in the Social Sciences), Santiago, Chile. Arthur Liebman and Jeanne Posada have written dissertations using the Latin American data. Moore and Hochschild have published a major article dealing with North Africa and have another in press. Denitch and a group of Yugoslav scholars have written a book in Serbo-Croatian based on the material from the survey, which will, it is hoped, soon appear in English. Manzoor, in Iran, is now completing his doctoral thesis using the Iranian data for the Fletcher School of Law and Diplomacy, Tufts University.

The basic comparable research instrument containing the main items used in the surveys of the various countries was largely developed by Soares and Walker. Soares also supervised the collection of the data in the six Latin American countries. A report on the samples and data collection is contained in the methodological appendix. Although Soares had planned to be involved in the overall volume dealing with Latin America, he was offered, and accepted, the post of Director of FLACSO in 1965. The time-consuming tasks involved in this position forced him to curtail his involvement in this volume. Meanwhile, I encouraged Myron Glazer, Arthur Liebman, and Kenneth Walker, each of whom had written doctoral dissertations dealing with Latin American students, to continue their research on the subject, using the comparative questionnaire data. This volume, a part of the research program on the Socio-Cultural Aspects of Modernization which I developed at the Harvard Center for International Affairs, is the product of their joint efforts. Arthur Liebman undertook the task of overall supervision. In addition to the chapters he wrote himself, he planned the contents and did a considerable amount of the substantive and editorial revision of other chapters to make this volume a more unified work. He and Myron Glazer assumed responsibility for the arduous task of the final rewriting of the entire manuscript. Finally, in my opinion this is the best existing treatment of the situation of the Latin American university students.

1 Universities, University Reform, and Student Politics in Latin America: A Historical Overview

One cannot adequately comprehend the attitudes, values, and behavior of contemporary Latin American students, particularly in the political sphere, without first gaining some acquaintance with the history of their political and educational activities. Latin American student politics is characterized by a long and continuous history in which basic themes continually reappear. In this chapter we will briefly consider the history of Latin American universities emphasizing those integral features which have prompted generation after generation of students to launch political efforts toward reform and change. We will also examine the conditions under which the focus of student political efforts alternated between university and societal affairs. The central theme of this chapter as well as the entire book is that the attitudes, values, and behavior of the students, especially with reference to politics, are profoundly affected by the values and forces coexisting within their universities and societies as well as by the tensions emanating from the interrelationship between these two overlapping spheres.

THE UNIVERSITIES

The Colonial Era

In 1551 Charles V of Spain authorized the creation of the first two royal and pontifical universities in the New World, one to be located in Lima and the other in Mexico City. The charters and the organizational structures of these universities were modeled after those of the University of Salamanca in Spain. During the colonial era, Spain founded ten major universities and fifteen minor ones. The ten important ones were all royal and pontifical universities authorized by the Spansh crown while the others were run by the Catholic church or various Catholic orders, especially the Jesuits and the Dominicans. The church and the clergy were dominant in all of them. A very large proportion of the professors were clerics, and eventually all of the rectors of the colonial universities were drawn from the ranks of the clergy.

The universities generally consisted of a small number of quasi-independent faculties or schools. Four fields constituted the organizational core of these colonial institutions of higher education – theology, law, medicine, and the arts. The arts or philosophy and arts faculty was for a long period more of a preparatory school for the theology faculty and a normal school for secondary level teachers than co-equal with the other faculties. Deviating from the Salamancan model where law was the prime discipline, the most important and prestigious faculty in the colonial universities was theology. Prior to the Wars of Independence, the major function of these institutions of higher learning was the training of students for the clergy. Law was second in importance and provided the state with functionaries for its various offices. Throughout the colonial and postcolonial eras, the universities tended to prepare their students for the liberal professions.

The royal and pontifical universities in the Spanish colonies of Latin America were granted the privilege of autonomy, one of the few corporate bodies in the Spanish colonial world to be given this status. In actual practice, this autonomy was often violated by the viceroy and the civil and church authorities as well as by prominent citizens. This intervention generally took the form of interference in the selection of rectors and professors and pressure to grant degrees to unworthy students. With the passage of time national governments increasingly intervened in the affairs of the universities, violating their autonomy, until in many instances autonomy became more of a concept than a reality.

The governments of the universities were in the hands of the cloister, a body made up of the professors, degree holders living near the university, and, at various times and in varying numbers, representatives of the students. A committee, the "councillors," elected by the cloister was the administrative organ of the cloister. Its chief responsibility was the periodic election of the rector, the chief executive officer of the university. The rector had jurisdiction over the academic and civil conduct of all members of the university community.[1]

The role of the students in the governmental structure of the universities was not uniform. At the University of San Marcos in Lima, they apparently had their most significant formal influence. There, half of the councillors were students. More universal, particularly in the earlier years, however, was the participation of the students in the selection and election of *catedráticos* or chair holding professors. These and other governing rights and privileges over time

were withdrawn from the students at the same time as the powers and privileges of the catedráticos were on the rise.[2] Several centuries later, in the
twentieth century, the restoration of these prerogatives became a major impetus
underlying the University Reform Movement.

The universities in the colonial era, as through most of their history, were
inadequately financed. In the beginning they were dependent on the largesse
of royal patrons and then later on state funds. Libraries and other university
facilities were generally sparse and inadequate. Professors, primarily clerics,
but, especially later in the era, also judges and government officials, received
minimal salaries.

Despite some instances of intellectual vitality, particularly in the eighteenth
century, the colonial universities tended to be mediocre educational institutions
resistant to new ideas and modern forces. The dominant influence of a rigid
and conservative church within the universities caused them to adhere to an
antiquated status quo and eschew those philosophies and bodies of thought
which lacked the imprimatur of the church. Teaching methods, such as they
were, were predominantly syllogistic and deductive, generally failing to motivate the students to innovate or to come to grips with the real world about
them. For most professors, teaching was more of an avocation than a vocation;
they devoted only a few hours a week to professorial functions, spending the
bulk of their time in their nonuniversity positions. Often the chair was desired
more for the social honor associated with it rather than because of any inclination to teach or further the growth of knowledge. Generally professors did little
if any research, and in the classroom they were strict autocrats.[3]

The students reflected all of these negative inputs and in a sense constituted
the most significant indicator of the manifold deficiencies of the colonial universities. The products of these institutions were, according to John Tate
Lanning, "men of stupendous rote memory, along with imposing but inappro-
priate and artificial allusions to the ancients and to the myths. These had long
been the symbols of the 'compleat' intellectual, the proudest result of education
and the surest mark of the colonial scholar."[4]

The students during the colonial period were the children of the local elite.
There were also some, however, from poor families who managed to obtain
scholarships. In general, the pool from which prospective students were selected
was quite restricted. The vast majority of the colonial population was illiterate.
Although tuition fees were nominal, the cost of degrees was high, thereby
eliminating, except for the few scholarship students, all but those with some
wealth. Periodically throughout the colonial era other restrictions were formally
established. Negroes, mulattoes, and quadroons were excluded. At some univer-

sities candidates for admission and for degrees had to present certificates of racial purity. At times, illegitimate children were barred as were those whose fathers had engaged in trade.

In their essence, the colonial universities were creatures of and integral parts of their societies. The values and forces that were dominant in society were the same as those that predominated in the universities. The church and the aristocracy were the primary pillars in both spheres, and in both domains these two powers rigorously attempted to maintain the status quo. However, as independence for the colonies grew near, new ideas and social forces began to emerge in the universities and the society. In the forefront of these new developments were the younger intellectuals.

The Modern Era

Prior to the Wars of Independence which began about 1810, the clerical control of the universities and intellectual thought was vigorously challenged. The works and ideas of the French enlightenment and the English economists began to undermine the narrow scholasticism imposed by the church and sanctioned by the colonial viceroys. Science was increasingly and more openly discussed, and in some cases even clerics were instrumental in introducing new scientific approaches into the universities. Prior to independence new schools were established incorporating some of these new outlooks and bodies of thought.

These new ideas, primarily those emanating from the pens of the French *philosophes*, did not only undermine the clerical control of the universities, they also undermined the legitimacy of the colonial system and paved the way for the independence struggles. Throughout the hemisphere students and younger intellectuals who read or in other ways were exposed to Rousseau, Quesnay, Voltaire, Condillac and the other French philosophes and encyclopedists as well as to Locke and other British liberals were in the vanguard of the independence struggles. Various academies, schools, universities, and private study groups became seedbeds of revolutionary activity.[5]

After independence was achieved, the new republics soon concerned themselves with higher education. New universities proliferated throughout Latin America. The new governments also continued and accelerated the tendency toward secular control of their universities formally wresting them from church control. Clerics were purged from the professoriate and faculties of theology were either abolished or considerably reduced in importance. The state assumed sole power with respect to the universities. The separation of the church from the universities, however, was not permanent, and during the nineteenth and twentieth centuries the church's influence over higher education, public as well as private, periodically has provoked student opposition and major confrontattions.

In the post-independence period the faculties of law and medicine were elevated in prestige and importance and new ones were added. The new, independent governments rapidly expanded the numbers of universities, establishing 17 in the period from 1810 to 1847. The growth and proliferation of institutions of higher education became the most visible response which Latin America made to the modern era with respect to the universities. From 1538 until the end of the nineteenth century there were 36 universities in the entire hemisphere. In the first half of the twentieth century, 69 more were founded. From 1950 to 1966, however, an additional 116 institutions of higher education commenced operation. By the mid-1960s throughout all of Latin America there were slightly more than 1000 universities, teacher training schools, technical institutes, and colleges.[6]

However, despite the changes and growth in higher education that took place beginning in the early decades of the nineteenth century, certain aspects common to the colonial era persisted throughout the nineteenth and twentieth centuries. The history of the University Reform Movement and student politics in the twentieth century, is largely a chronicle of student efforts to eliminate from their universities the more negative features associated with the colonial era.

The early inroads made by science and humanism in the nineteenth century were not adequately followed up and broadened. Although there were some exceptions, the universities throughout the nineteenth and much of the twentieth centuries were not innovative institutions, and the study of science and the more applied fields was generally deficient. During this same period, again with some variations, most courses were and still appear to be highly theoretical in orientation, and many professors, like their colonial counterparts, tended and still tend to deliver authoritative lectures which are usually uninformed by either their own research or that current in their fields.

The more traditional fields have continued to attract the largest number of students and have retained their relative prestige and power within the universities. The primary function of the universities, albeit with some gestures in recent decades in the direction of the sciences and applied fields, remains the training of students for the liberal professions, particularly law and medicine.[7]

Power within the universities, with some exceptions and during certain periods of time, in the post-independence era has generally been in the hands of the catedráticos. This power was challenged by the students in the University Reform Movement which swept Latin America after World War I, but the gains registered by the students proved either not very significant or else did not last very long. More serious and more frequent have been the repeated interventions of the government and politicians into the affairs of the universities. When governments have chosen to act decisively, neither the students nor the professors have been able to bloc their efforts to reorder the universities. However, after the dramatic incursions of government forces and after student militancy has spent itself, the operational power within the universities gradually has returned to the senior professors. (See below and chapter 3 for further discussion.)

The university system of the nineteenth and to a somewhat lesser extent the twentieth century, resembles that of the colonial period in still another feature. Despite the proliferation of other types of institutions of higher education in very recent years, such as technical schools and science institutes, the older more traditional institutions, the universities, and primarily the public ones, continue to enjoy the highest social prestige. In the 1960s they enrolled approximately 90 percent of the post-secondary school students. Of those in universities, 80 percent attended public ones where the fees were minimal. Furthermore, among universities, as opposed to other types of institutions of higher learning, there is still a pronounced tendency for students in virtually every country to concentrate in one or two, usually the national universities located in the capital cities. In the mid-1960s there were approximately ten nations, primarily the smaller ones including Uruguay and Panama, where three-quarters or more of the students attended one university. In Argentina, Bolivia, Chile, Mexico, Ecuador, Paraguay, Puerto Rico, and Venezuela, approximately one to two thirds of the students were enrolled in one university.[8] Similar to the over-concentration in subject fields, the over-concentration of students in a very few universities again mirrors the situation found in the colonial era.

Also, very much like the colonial universities, those in the nineteenth and even the twentieth centuries have been elitists institutions. Although blood and caste barriers have been eliminated and although the numbers of students in higher education has grown, particularly during the period around World War I and after World War II, the students still are drawn from a small portion of the population, the middle and upper strata. In the mid-1960s, only 4 percent of the eligible age group in Latin America were in institutions of higher education. (See chapter 2 for more detailed discussion.)

UNIVERSITY REFORM

University reform has long been a central concern of Latin American university students. Since early in the twentieth century they have worked to democratize and modernize their universities in order to mold them into instruments for societal progress and development. In the process the students came to learn that significant university reform could not be brought about by restricting their efforts only to the confines of the university community. They realized that national political and social reform could not be separated from university reform. The history of the student university reform movement in Latin America reveals the constant alternation in concerns and efforts between the university and the national government. Indeed, the persistent interaction between the university community and political and social forces in the society did much to shape the student movement and affect the various directions in which it moved. As Gabriel del Mazo, the foremost historian of the student reform movement expressed it: "the University Reform movement was . . . affirming, with solid propositions, that only a major reform within a larger political and economic reform of the state, that is along with the solution of the entire national prob- lem, could resolve the educational and cultural difficulties which were especially to be considered: State, Society, University, Education were to be nourished by the same roots."[9]

The Early University Reform Movement and Its Historical Antecedents

Although students, intellectuals, academies, and universities had played an important role in the independence struggles of the early nineteenth century, there appeared to be a limited amount of political activity among the students during the rest of the century. The post-independence period was a chaotic one characterized by severe political and economic instability which unsettled vari- ous institutions, including the universities. The newly independent republics which had spawned a large number of universities during and immediately after the Wars of Independence tended to neglect them during the rest of the century. Several universities in different countries were even closed by their respective governments, ostensibly for economic reasons. In general, university reorgani- zation, consolidation, and development was severely hampered by the highly unstable political conditions throughout the hemisphere in the nineteenth cen- tury, beginning with the wars of liberation and then continuing with the large numbers of *coup d'états.*

Independence had slight affect on the social class composition of the Latin American university students. As in the colonial period they were predomi- nantly drawn from the aristocracy reflecting the still highly stratified nature of their societies. The major function of the university vis-à-vis its students during the period following independence appeared to be the certification of the status of its relatively few enrollees. Students did not seem overly concerned with the acquisition of skills since their future positions were generally guaranteed, based not upon their talents and knowledge but upon their family and class position.[10]

After the excitement and concern generated by the independence struggles had subsided, the students and the universities turned from national or regional affairs to a more traditional stance, a European orientation. The Latin of the clerics was replaced after independence by French as the language of the universities. Students tended to look to Europe for ideas and values and to adopt a European or cosmopolitan as opposed to a national or regional orientation, particularly the many who had studied or continued their education abroad.

Toward the end of the nineteenth century and in the beginning of the twentieth century, various changes began to take place among the students. University enrollments grew and increasing numbers began to attend their national universities as opposed to continental ones. These students began to develop more of a national outlook and a concern for the political and socioeconomic problems of their own societies.[11]

By the end of the nineteenth century, increased but sporadic political activity had started to take place among the Latin American university students. National and university issues were the foci of this activity. One of the university issues of concern to the students was that of student representation on faculty councils. This was destined to become a major concern of student politics throughout the twentieth century.

Student political activity increased during the first decade of the twentieth century. Reform of the university started to become a predominant interest of the activist students. At the same time university student organizations were founded in several countries. The capstone of the political and organizational activity of the students during this decade was the First International Congress of American Students held in Montevideo in 1909. It was attended by student representatives from Argentina, Bolivia, Brazil, Chile, Paraguay, Peru, and Uruguay.

This Congress proved to be the forerunner of other such international meetings of students throughout the hemisphere. It revealed the extent of international communication among Latin American students as well as their sense of common origins, problems, and destinies. The reform of Latin American universities was the central issue of the first student congress; the most important individual topic taken up by the Congress was student representation in the governing of the university. The Uruguayan resolution calling for student representation on the governing councils of universities through periodic elections was passed unanimously. Other reforms discussed at this Congress included changes in the examination system, five year terms for professors, student participation in the selection of professors, and voluntary classroom attendance. The statements of proposed university reforms were comprehensive and foreshadowed those of the Córdoba struggle of 1918.[12]

The Congress in Montevideo and those that followed it in 1910 (Buenos Aires) and 1912 (Lima) were not very militant. The delegates were primarily concerned with university-related matters. In these years prior to World War I, the politically concerned students did not yet fully appreciate the significance of the relationship between university and national politics. There was some vague concern for social justice outside of the university, but it did not become translated into active political efforts and proposals. Little sense of a revolutionary mission emanated from these conferences. The impact of major social changes taking place in their countries before World War I had not yet been felt on the national and international levels, and student dissatisfactions derived mainly from university problems.[13]

The Córdoba Movement and the Early Stages of University Reform

The Latin American University Reform Movement was officially inaugurated at the University of Córdoba in Córdoba, Argentina, in 1918. The protests of the Córdoba students and the reforms which they demanded ignited a movement for university reform which quickly spread to other Argentine universities and then to student bodies in other countries. Eventually, some or all of the reformers' or *Reformistas'* objectives were enacted into law in eighteen Latin American nations. The University Reform Movement's impact on Latin America was not limited to university students and their universities. It also became a significant force in Latin American politics.[14]

The specific impetus for the university reform movement at Córdoba was the closing of a student boarding house. The students, however, fired by more deeply seated grievances, quickly moved from this trivial issue to a major campaign for broad-scale university reform. They were disturbed by the archaic and oligarchic structure of their university. Contrary to the historic mandate of an institution of higher learning, the university did not devote its resources and energies to the pursuit of knowledge and the promotion of new ideas. Scant attention or support was given to new methods of teaching, original research, or the development of new fields of study. The students perceived their university to be one characterized by philosophical narrowness, nepotism, and faculty incompetence. There was little or no practical training, and all education was provided by formal lectures. The university appeared to be the personal fief of a self-selected, self-perpetuating governing council which demonstrated little interest in the lower status professors or the students. No concern was evidenced for the cultural needs or the practical problems of the nation.[15] It is crucial to emphasize that one of the primary reasons for the Reform Movement's quick and favorable reception outside of Córdoba and Argentina was that the conditions characterizing the University of Córdoba were typical of other universities throughout the hemisphere.[16]

The Córdoba students dramatically stated the case for university reform in the Córdoba Manifesto, the original and classic document of the University Reform Movement in Latin America:

Up to now the Universities have been the secular refuge of mediocrity, the salary of ignorance, the safe hospital for all intellectual invalids and — what is even worse — the place where all forms of tyranny and insensibility found the chair where they could be taught. The Universities have thus become faithful mirrors of these decadent societies . . . Our university regime . . . is anachronistic. It is based on a sort of divine right — that of the university staff. It is created by itself . . . The university youth of Córdoba . . . rebelled against an administrative regime, against an educational method, against a concept of authority. Public responsibilities were carried out for the benefit of a certain clique. There was no reform of curricula, and no reform of rules . . . The educational methods were corrupted by a narrow dogmatism, thus helping to keep the University cut off from science and from modern teachings. The University authorities, jealous guardians of dogma, tried to restrain the efforts of the youth . . . We then undertook a holy revolution . . . The student youth of Córdoba . . . salutes its colleagues all over the Americas and requests them to cooperate in the work of liberation which it is beginning.[19]

The goals first announced at Córdoba remained the principle ones of the University Reform Movement which spread throughout Latin America in the ensuing decades. These included student co-government or *cogobierno* of the universities, a governing role for alumni, selection of faculty through competitive examinations, periodic review of faculty competence, optional classroom attendance, free instruction, open enrollment to all academically qualified applicants, university extension courses for workers, university autonomy, and the orienting of the university toward the solution of national economic, social, and political problems.[18]

After the University of Córdoba officials refused to grant their demands, the students went out on strike, sought support from individuals and groups throughout Argentina, and requested the direct intervention of the President of the Republic, Hipólito Irigoyen. Student organizations throughout Argentina warmly endorsed their cause. The Córdoba movement served as the catalyst for the establishment of the first national student organization in Argentina, the University Federation of Argentina or Federación Universitaria Argentina (FUA). Student groups from outside the country also responded with messages of support. The Córdoba students' cause was endorsed by Argentine labor unions, leftist political parties, liberal groups, and important newspapers while opposition came from the church and conservative organizations.

After a careful assessment of the situation, President Irigoyen on October 7, 1918, decreed into law virtually all of the objectives desired by the student reformers at Córdoba. "The basic articles of the presidential declaration sanctioned student participation in university government through representatives on the administrative councils, approved electoral procedures which would permit periodic renewal and infusion of new blood among the members of these same councils, introduced the principle of free attendance at classes, granted professors more freedom in their choice of lecture materials, and permitted greater flexibility in examination procedures." In addition, the government obtained the resignation of administrators and professors opposed to the reform and replaced them with supporters, including two leading proponents who were appointed to professorial chairs. In the same year the reform statutes enacted into law at Córdoba were extended to the University of Buenos Aires and later to other Argentine universities.[19]

The major focus of the Argentine students during this period of struggle for University Reform was upon the university and matters internal to it. However, from the movement's very inception the students were aware of the relationship between the university and the national society. Reform, as they conceived it, would be a mechanism for severing Latin America's cultural dependence upon Europe and for turning their countrymen's attention to the problems and needs of the nation and hemisphere. An integral feature of the Reform Movement in Argentina and in other countries as well was the students' concern for the plight of the workers. Wherever possible, students attempted to ally themselves with workers' organizations and to establish schools and extension courses for the working population. This latter objective was invariably included in the list of student *reformista* demands.

Argentine students and, later, students from other nations involved in the Reform Movement were also cognizant of international forces which they felt were adversely affecting the progress and development of both their nations and their universities. These students publicly noted the dangers and evils of imperialism. In fact, the 1920 manifesto of the Argentine University Federation (FUA) condemning world imperialism was the first such public denunciation issued by an organized group in Latin America. This stand was later ratified and endorsed at the International Student Congress on University Reform held in Mexico City in 1921.[20]

Basically, the Reform Movement was a result of the interdependency and tensions between the university and other institutions and sectors of the nation. In Argentina and in other countries, particularly Uruguay and Chile, significant political, social, and economic changes were taking place during the first two decades of the twentieth century. Comparable changes did not take place within the universities, as they tended to maintain their traditional structures and orientations.[21] According to Richard J. Walter, a careful chronicler of the Argentine student movement;

the Reformistas of 1918 were seeking to modernize the Argentine university, to update the Republic's institutions of higher learning in correspondence with the larger national developments which had occurred in the past few decades. The Reformistas hoped to make the Argentine university an agent of, rather than an obstacle to change. If the university were modernized, they concluded, it could produce a national leadership capable of directing the development and modernization of the entire Republic.[22]

The growth of the University Reform Movement and the favorable response it received both inside and outside of Argentina reflected a number of significant developments which had occurred in Latin America during the first two decades of the twentieth century. For Argentina, Uruguay, Chile and Peru, the countries in which student politics seemed most significant during this period, the era had been one of peace, political stability, and economic growth. The major beneficiaries were the expanding middle classes in these countries. Political leaders and parties which reflected the growing strength and numbers of the middle classes were coming to power. The victories of Hipólito Irigoyen in Argentina, Jose Battle y Ordóñez in Uruguay, Arturo Allesandri in Chile, and to a lesser extent that of Jose Pardo and Augusto Leguía in Peru represented the triumph of reformist ideology in these nations. These men and their parties were based in the middle class and received considerable support from the urban working classes. It was an era of economic and social reform or at least dramatic attempts at significant reform. The universal franchise, a progressive income tax, shorter working hours, liberalized retirement benefits, the abolition of child labor and the formal separation of church and state were either advocated by these presidents and their parties or enacted into law. For the burgeoning urban middle class it was an era of optimism and progress.

The rising middle classes and their responsive governments in Argentina, Uruguay, Chile, and Peru also demonstrated a concern for education. This was reflected in the changing numbers and composition of the university students.

In Argentina, Chile, and Uruguay, in particular, there were dramatic increases in student enrollments as growing numbers of middle class students found their way into the universities. These students were to prove more dissatisfied with the status quo than their upper class peers and more open and receptive to new ideas as well.[23]

In Argentina and Uruguay, the two countries in which the Reform Movement started earliest and made the most significant impact, there was a vast expansion of the middle class, involving a great deal of upward mobility. In Argentina, more than two out of three members of the middle class in the years from 1890 to 1930, emanated from the working class. This mobility and growth of the middle classes led to the development of more egalitarian values and attitudes. These stratification and value changes politically resulted in support for reforms in a variety of institutional areas, including higher education.[24]

As similar, but less dramatic, changes took place in the stratification and value systems of other Latin American nations, clashes developed between the rising middle class and the traditional upper strata. Students were invariably in the vanguard of the middle class radical and reformist ranks. Gino Germani succinctly described this process:

> In Latin America, extremist or at least radical movements have been promoted by groups whose ascent was partially blocked by the persisting rigidities of the stratification system. The rising middle strata created by the first steps toward economic development and social modernization were led by their newly acquired class identification and their desire to gain political power and prestigeful positions to oppose the political and social order that gave the traditional elites a virtual monopoly on power and prestige.[25]

World War I and the Bolshevik Revolution were other large scale political and social developments that made major impacts upon the political and cultural attitudes and values of the students and young intellectuals of Latin America. The war caused them to turn away in disillusionment from the intellectual leadership of Europe and to become more concerned with their native lands and their regions. Richard J. Walter's remarks with respect to the Argentine students also seem relevant to other Latin American students. "For many intellectuals and students the war represented the culminating failure of nineteenth century ideas and institutions. Looking to their own country, young Argentines sought to eliminate European influences."[26]

In contrast to the despair of the war, the Bolshevik Revolution captured the imagination of many students. To them it represented the triumph of young intellectuals and workers over the traditional oligarchic exploitative forces of the decadent past. For the students it seemed to herald the dawn of a new age of democracy and social justice in which they as students and young persons would play leading roles. The revolution spurred their interest in socialism and radical ideas. The works of various socialist, anarchist, and radical writers were read with much interest. Latin American intellectuals such as José Ingenieros of Argentina expanded and amplified upon the radical themes emanating from the Marxist and revolutionary movements. These native writers deeply influenced students and young intellectuals, particularly because of the stress which they put on the leadership role of youth in bringing social progress to Latin America. It was a time, according to Frank Bonilla, in which "Anything that smacked of protest or attacked existing institutions was eagerly snapped up [by the students] ."[27]

Out of this maelstrom of change, progress, peace, and new ideas, the students emerged as a social and political force. They centered their energies and attention primarily upon their universities, which to them seemed so antithetical to all the developments transpiring about them. Concerned students desired to bring their universities into accord with the new social forces and to reshape them into democratic and modernizing institutions which would lead the way toward progress in their societies. There were some among the more radical students who contended that university reform was secondary to societal and political reform or revolution. But most, during the earlier years of the Reform Movement, while becoming increasingly aware of the interdependency between their nations and their universities, chose to focus their reformist efforts largely upon their schools of higher learning.

BEYOND CÓRDOBA: NATIONAL VARIATIONS IN THE DIRECTION OF STUDENT POLITICS

The success of the Reform Movement and the focus of student politics — university or national politics — varied among Latin American countries according to national conditions during the 1920s. The students seemed most likely to direct their political energies more toward university affairs in those nations where the government was relatively stable, democratic, and liberal in orientation. Where governments were not sympathetic to university reform or were authoritarian and unresponsive to the demands of the more progressive middle class or the needs of the poor, the students' major concern became national politics.

Peru

The case of Peru illustrates in dramatic fashion the impact of national politics upon a student movement as well as the importance of leadership in such a movement. The Peruvian students were the first to emulate the example of the protesting Argentine students. Shortly after Córboda, in the beginning of 1919, the students at the University of San Marcos in Lima organized a strike to enhance their demands for university reform. Their principle demands were similar to those of their Argentine peers as were their university problems. Like the University of Córdoba, the University of San Marcos was the oldest university in the country; in fact, having been founded in 1551, it was the oldest on the continent. It, too, appeared to the students to be dominated by antiquated rules and procedures and to be unresponsive to the changes taking place in Peruvian society and to the needs of the lower strata. In their strike demands, the students focused on university issues. They called for academic freedom, modernization of university regulations, student participation in the governing councils, open competition for the selection of professors, and the removal of the influence of the church from the affairs of the university. After striking for four months, the students, aided by the support of Lima workers, were victorious; the Peruvian legislature enacted into law university reform legislation incorporating many of their demands.

In the following year, 1920, the Peruvian students turned their attention to other matters. The first Peruvian congress of students met to discuss mutual problems and coordinate future activities. The congress organized evening schools for workers. It also resolved to study national problems and to proclaim social justice to be the goal of Peruvian students.

Despite the apparent change in orientation revealed at the 1920 congress, the Peruvian student activists did not turn to national political action. They continued to believe until 1923 that education was the key to social change and social justice. In their view, the reform, democratization, and modernization of educational institutions would bring in its wake similar changes in other societal institutions and sectors of the society. However, in 1923 their position changed, and they turned to political action in order to obtain their desired goals. They inaugurated the first indigeneous Latin American reformist political movement, Popular Revolutionary Alliance for America or *Alianza Popular Revolucionaria Americana* (APRA), a movement which would have a significant impact in many Latin American countries.

Factors outside the university and the realm of education, particularly national political ones, were the cause of the political metamorphis of the Peruvian students. Similar to their Argentine peers, the Peruvians were also stirred by the Bolshevik Revolution and World War I. They, too, had their critical intellectuals like Manuel González Prada, who called into question tradition and established norms and who advocated the need for widesweeping reforms. González Prada had an immediate and direct influence upon the ideology and action of the Peruvian student leaders.

In the years immediately prior to and after World War I, Peru, again like Argentina, experienced political stability and economic growth. It was also a period of reformist nationalist governments led by Presidents José Pardo (1904–1908, 1915–1919) and Augusto Leguía (1908–1912). Both tried to initiate reforms to better working conditions and improve the living standards of the Peruvian workers. Leguía, when re-elected in 1919, appeared to represent a break in this liberal, democratic trend when he seized power prior to his inauguration. However, in the first years of his second administration, he did in fact adhere to a liberal and reformist position. He recognized the right of labor to organize in unions. He consciously sought the support of middle class intellectuals and the middle strata as opposed to the traditional upper class. Leguía concerned himself with education, built many new schools, and imported teachers from the United States. He officially ended the serfdom of the Indians. In 1920, Leguía was instrumental in incorporating into the new Constitution extended franchise to all literate males over the age of 21 and the direct election of both the president and the congress.

However, despite Leguía's generous intentions and self-proclaimed humanism, the dictatorial aspects of his regime came increasingly into focus. The press was censored, opponents indiscriminately jailed, corruption intensified, and the Constitution flouted. By 1923, it became clear that Leguía intended to remain as chief of state by any means necessary. The students organized against him and demanded an end to dictatorship and a return to constitutional rule. On May 23, 1923, government troops attacked a student-worker anti-Leguía demonstration, killing one student and one worker. Immediately thereafter the University of San Marcos, the base of the students' opposition, was closed and many student leaders jailed or exiled. Among them was the President of the Federation of Students of Peru and of the National Council of Peruvian Students, Victor Raul Haya de la Torre, the founder-to-be of APRA.

The dictatorship of August Leguía and the repression of the students in 1923 turned the Peruvian students from educational and university concerns to political action, a position to which they would adhere for decades. The Peruvian students in exile began to organize a mass political party, APRA, as their primary vehicle of opposition to the Leguía regime.[28]

APRA was founded by Haya de la Torre in Mexico City in 1924. Its doctrine, *Aprismo*, was an amalgamation of humanism, Russian Communism, the Mexican revolutionary doctrines, and European socialism. The five basic planks of the organization were designed to promote continental unity and democracy:

1. Action against Yankee imperialism
2. For the political unity of Latin America

3. For the nationalization of land and industry
4. For the internationalization of the Panama Canal
5. For solidarity with all peoples and oppressed classes.[29]

APRA subsequently inspired the organization of like-minded parties throughout Latin America, including Venezuela, Cuba, Guatemala, and Paraguay.

APRA, however, had its greatest strength in Peru. There, in addition to the aforementioned five points, it stressed the integration of the Indians into society and the necessity for an elected government which would guarantee personal liberties. The Apristas received their most significant support from the small but growing middle class which was attracted by the idealism and some of the proposed reforms of APRA and at the same time repelled by the corrupt Leguía dictatorship and the growing North American dominance of the Peruvian economy. Finally, it is important to note that in the subsequent development of its program, the Apristas, primarily students and former students, continued to place university matters in a distinctly subordinate position, giving their greatest emphasis to politics.[30]

Cuba

In Cuba during the 1920s was another situation in which an authoritarian government influenced the focus of student politics. From 1920 to 1927, the Cuban students seemed concerned with both the state of their only university, the University of Havana, as well as with national political conditions. The University was plagued with the typical problems of financial shortages, the lack of a competent full-time professoriate, a low level of instruction, and interference by the government. Education within the university was for the most part divorced from the needs and problems of Cuban society. Nationally, the period after 1917 was characterized by a fragile parliamentary democracy infused with widespread corruption. It was also an era of economic crises and various forms of North American intervention. Under President Gerardo Machado, who came into office in 1925, there was a brief period of economic recovery, limited prosperity, and a respite from brazen governmental dishonesty.

From 1923 to 1927, the Cuban university students were primarily occupied with university reform. However, reform, as they envisioned it, would mean the transformation of the University of Havana into a modern university whose attention would be directed to solving the nation's problems. After a visit to the University of Havana by the Rector of the University of Buenos Aires, José Arce, the Cuban students, inspired by Arce's account of university reform in Argentina, actively began their own struggle. In 1923 after a series of short-lived strikes and occupations of university buildings, some of their demands were granted and government subsidies to the university were increased. The government, nonetheless, refused to accede to the students' call for university autonomy.

By 1927, the primary emphasis of the Cuban students had shifted from university related matters to the national political arena. The precipitating factor was President Machado's announcement that he would stand for re-election and that he desired to see the presidential term expanded from four to six years. His unopposed re-election in 1928, his increasingly dictatorial tactics, and the growth in graft and corruption fired the students' oppositional activities. For the next five years until his overthrow in 1933, the Cuban students' principle efforts were devoted to overthrowing the Machado regime. His closing of the University in 1930 prompted many more students to devote their energies to defeating Machado. The University re-opened in 1933 following Machado's flight from Cuba. For a short time afterward the students through their University Student Directorate or *Directorio Estudantil Universitario*, the organization that had led and coordinated the struggle against Machado, became the most influential force in Cuban politics.[31]

Venezuela

As in Peru and Cuba, student politics in Venezuela after Córdoba were deeply influenced and shaped by authoritarian rule. At the same time, Venezuelan students were also affected by forces similar to those which had aroused their counterparts throughout the hemisphere. The Mexican Revolution, World War I, and the Bolshevik Revolution stirred and stimulated them. They, too, were a leading part of an increasing number of middle strata professional and business groups who called for more political and social power commensurate with their growing economic importance. In pursuit of their own self interest, these middle groups, like their counterparts in Argentina and Uruguay, expressed their desires for greater democratization and modernization of the country. But in Venezuela, unlike Argentina, Uruguay, Chile, or even Peru, their political aspirations and those of the Venezuelan students were effectively denied by a ruthless dictator, Juan Vincente Gómez, who ruled from 1908 to 1935.

Gómez ruled Venezuela as if it were his personal property and, indeed, much of it literally did belong to him, as the nation's biggest landowner. Supported by a reorganized and modernized army, he achieved a virtual monopoly of organized and effective violence for his government. An expansion of revenues during his rule due largely to oil profits and royalties allowed him to lavish monies and goods on his family, retinue, military officers, and bureaucratic elites, assuring Gómez their long-term allegiance. He identified with the traditional Venezuelan upper classes and gave them strong support for the maintenance of their power and prerogatives.

Gómez, during his long reign, brutally and effectively prevented the formation of any organized political groups, friendly or unfriendly. The Venezuelan middle status groups never had the opportunity to politically interact or organize. Consequently they did not develop a finely articulated set of political demands or much of a political consciousness. The only source of organized opposition during much of Gómez's rule came from the Venezuelan university students.

As a result of their antiregime activities, Gómez closed Venezuela's major university, the Central University in Caracas, from 1912 to 1923. After it was reopened, the students finally organized the *Federación de Estudiantes de Venezuela* (FEV) in 1927. Twice before they had attempted to organize the FEV but it had been prohibited and dissolved by the government. During the period after the reopening of the Central University as well as in the time when it had been shut, the students' primary and almost total political efforts were devoted to the overthrow of the dictator.

Led by the newly organized FEV, the students' anti-governmental activities reached their height in 1928. Utilizing the cultural activities of the supposedly non-political Student Week as a cover, the FEV dispatched student speakers to denounce the regime and issue public calls for liberty. Gómez responded in traditional fashion by arresting the leadership of the FEV. This in turn touched off major student demonstrations leading to the arrest of several hundred students. At this point, surprising both Gómez and the student activists, thousands of Caracans took to the streets in support of the students. Gómez was so shocked and impressed by this popular reaction that he ordered the arrested students released.

The activist students, after their initial shock, realized that they had been pursuing an elitist political policy. Although they mouthed the abstract phrases of liberty and freedom, in actual practice there had been no attempt to work with, much less on behalf of, groups which were more suppressed and exploited than the students. Rómulo Betancourt then a student leader and later president of Venezuela commented: "I had the first concrete revelation that the popular mass was beginning to intervene in Venezuelan history as a new factor. The student movement had initially been wrapped in its own pride. We students considered ourselves . . . as chosen to transform the country. Then our people suddenly made known their presence; and without leaders, without action committees or strike funds, the people organized a massive demonstration in Caracas."[32]

After the popular outpouring, motivated by the population's own grievances as well as their concern for the students, Betancourt and the other student leaders were determined to forge a coalition between the students and the masses.

After the Student Week disturbances, some of the more radical student leaders joined with some military cadets and young army officers in an attempted coup. They were crushed by loyalist forces and many students were arrested, sent to forced labor projects, or forced into exile. From then until Gómez died in 1935, Venezuelan students in exile and underground within the country concentrated in earnest on bringing down the regime. To this end they launched several unsuccessful military operations. Also, applying the lesson learned during Student Week in 1928, they organized the first mass-oriented political parties in Venezuelan history. In 1936, it is interesting to note, joint student-worker demonstrations proved instrumental in forcing Gómez' successor, General Eleazar López Contreras, to restore the political rights which he had suspended after assuming office. Venezuelan students throughout the Gómez years (and until the present) subordinated university and student affairs to national political struggles.[33]

Colombia

The impact of national political conditions and socio-economic problems upon student politics and university reform was particularly acute in Colombia. The initial focus of the Colombian students throughout the post-World War I years until the latter 1920s was primarily upon university related matters. Like their counterparts throughout Latin America, they, too, were stirred by the events at Córdoba and the University Reform Movement emanating from Argentina.

The first two national student congresses in Colombia's history, held in 1922 and 1924, were reactions to the Argentine developments. The congresses gave birth to the first national student organization in Colombia, the Federation of Colombian Students or *Federación de Estudiantes Colombianos* (FEC). It is interesting to note that prior to Córdoba in 1911 an initial attempt to create such an organization had failed.

The two congresses and FEC concentrated on the university-related aspects of reform. The major objectives of these students were student representation in the governance of the university, the upgrading of the curriculum and teaching methods, and better professors. In addition, some consideration was given to nonuniversity political issues. Generally, these interests were phrased in broad and abstract terms, such as defining the students' future role in the statutes of FEC as a vanguard force in the affairs of Colombia. Students also publicly declared themselves to be the national and social renovators of their society. Even when they became more specific, for instance, with respect to imperialism or the role of the United States in Colombian affairs, it was not a very divisive issue as almost all Colombians were united in their negative attitude toward the United States because of its machinations in the separation of Panama from Colombia in 1903. The major objective of the two national congresses and FEC during the early and mid-1920s appeared to be the building of a united student movement in Colombia. They did not want Colombian students to become divided by taking positions on controversial national issues before such a unified movement could be developed.

In the four years following the second congress, the Colombian students were not able to develop a strong and vigorous student movement. The government also consistently refused their demands for university reform. By the time of the third national student congress a definite shift in approach and emphasis from the earlier years was discernible. FEC and the third congress delegates adopted a more activist orientation. Unlike the two earlier conferences, the 1928 congress devoted considerable attention to national political issues. The delegates were explicit and specific in their discussion of controversial matters. The congress advocated nationalization of the petroleum industry. Dictatorships and imperialism were denounced in direct terms.

In order to understand the weakness of the Colombian student movement as well as its change in orientation from essentially nondivisive university problems to controversial national political issues, it is again necessary to examine national politics and the socioeconomic conditions which together served as the context in which the Colombian student movement developed. Colombian students in contrast to their Argentine, Uruguayan, and Chilean counterparts at the end of World War I lacked the supportive political and structural features which would have enabled them to launch and sustain a significant student movement capable of gaining university reforms from their government. Whereas liberal reformist governments were either in power or had come to power in Argentina, Uruguay, and Chile in the years after the war, the situation was starkly different in Colombia. From 1886 to 1930, Colombia was ruled by a traditionalist Conservative Party which was unsympathetic to reform in any area. Thus the Colombian students unlike their aforementioned peers could hope for and, indeed, found little governmental support for university reform.

In those countries with vigorous student movements and in which university reform came earliest, the student activists benefitted by the direct and indirect support of an energetic and rapidly expanding middle class. This rising class represented, at the time, a liberalizing political force. Support for university reform from this class was enhanced by the apparent predominance of its sons within the ranks of the student reformers. There was no such class in Colombia in the years preceding World War I nor in the decade following it. In these years social, economic, and political power were monopolized by a very small self-perpetuating elite. The existent Colombian middle class lacked class consciousness and did not agitate for political reforms either for itself or any other stratum. On the contrary, this class strongly supported the party of the status quo, the Conservative Party. Vernon Lee Fluharty's concise summary statement aptly states the case: "the Colombian middle class acts neither as a liberalizing nor a stabilizing element in the nation's social struggle. It has gained no political competence of its own, for it has traditionally equated its interests with those of the oligarchy."[34]

Colombia, however, did experience some of the same forces for change that were found in Argentina, Uruguay, and Chile. Yet in Colombia these forces were either weaker and or later in coming. In the wake of World War I, the Mexican Revolution, and the Bolshevik Revolution, there was some political turbulence in Colombia. This ferment was primarily expressed by young intellectuals who spoke out for political and economic reform. They also organized various discussion groups, political clubs, and small parties. These organizations, however, had brief life spans. With the passage of time the youthful political innovators of the 1920s joined the traditional parties and the oligarchic system against which they had railed so vehemently.

Nevertheless, during the time in which they were active, pressures for change in the country also began to emanate from other sources. The mid-1920s was a period of rapid economic growth for Colombia. The benefits of this growth, however, did not extend beyond the small upper class and its retinue. In fact, the economic conditions of the workers actually deteriorated, and their real wages actually declined during these years, The frequency of strikes, land seizures, and protests increased. In response, the Conservative government became increasingly repressive and used the army to clear squatters from seized land and to break strikes. In 1928 the army brutally suppressed a strike of banana workers against the United Fruit Company, killing 1400 strikers and peasants. This massacre horrified the nation and weakened support for the Conservative Party. A year later, depression came suddenly to Colombia principally because of the sharp drop in the price of coffee, the country's main export. Business ground to a standstill, and the Conservative Party was further discredited. Disorders, tensions, and fears began to mount. Even sectors of the Conservative Party realized that unless some reforms and orderly political change were forthcoming, it would be exceedingly difficult to avoid a rebellion or increased revolutionary activity. In such a political climate, a portion of the Conservative Party joined with the Liberal Party to elect a Liberal president in 1930, Enrique Olaya Herrera. This marked the first time in forty-four years that the Conservatives no longer held national executive power in Colombia. For students, it was these factors — the outspoken youthful intellectuals, the economic disparities and crises, the repression and the decline in the legitimization of the Conservative government, and the increasing domestic strife — that tended to predispose them to activism and a concern for national politics during the period of the latter 1920s and early 1930s.

The nature of the university reform law in Colombia and the conditions under which it was enacted in 1935 some seventeen years after Córdoba are pertinent. The reform itself was a moderate one compared to similar legislation passed years earlier in Argentina, Uruguay, and Chile. The major features dealt with student representation in the governance of the National University in Bogotá. However, student participation was circumscribed, as their representatives were limited both in number and scope. In addition, the National University was granted a restricted condition of autonomy.

The reform itself became law during the administration of Alfonso López Pumajero (1934–38), the Liberal successor to President Olaya. It was under his aegis that liberal reforms, albeit largely quite moderate, reached their height in Colombia. He borrowed from the ideas of the Mexican Revolution, Marxism, the Peruvian *Apristas*, and Franklin D. Roosevelt's New Deal. In addition to university reform, he introduced labor, land, and tax reforms. He dramatically increased federal expenditures, expanded the suffrage and tried to reduce the influence of the Catholic church. The general political profile of López and his administration bore striking resemblance to that of Argentina's Hipólito Irigoyen and Uruguay's José Battle y Ordóñez during their reformist administrations more than seventeen years earlier. There were important distinctions, however, which in large part explain why university reform was moderate and why the other López reforms tended to be limited as well.

The major explanatory factor appears to be the social composition of the groups supporting President López. Unlike the supporters of reform during comparable periods in Argentina, Uruguay, and Chile, the Colombians were primarily members of the upper class. López drew his backing from the liberal wing of the Liberal Party from those members of the upper class who were the more modern, urban, and industrialized. They were more sympathetic to the need for change than the more traditional members of their class. However, unlike the middle-class reformists of Argentina, Uruguay, and Chile, the Colombian upper-class reformists were not as interested in making significant transformations in the system. They wished to modernize Colombia and stave off more basic changes. Reform for the middle class of Argentina, Uruguay, and Chile was much more a direct expression of a rising class desirous of renovating traditional institutions and changing power relationships in order to reflect their emergence into the power-wielding circles of their society. It was their children who struggled for commensurate changes in the universities. In Colombia an analogous middle-class group of students who were united behind a vigorous reformist program was absent for the most part. Thus, university reform as well as reforms in other arenas came not as the result of the efforts of a significant self-interested constituency demanding such change. Instead reform came to Colombia as the result of the decisions of a sector of the oligarchy concerned with its own future and the forestalling of more basic changes.[35]

THE ERA OF DICTATORS: 1930s TO THE 1950s

Country after country in Latin America succumbed to dictatorships in the 1930s as the world-wide depression spread through the hemisphere. Once in power, these authoritarian governments soon came into direct confrontation with the universities and their student bodies, which became the earliest and more significant bases of opposition to these regimes. Writing in 1966, one observer of Latin American students politics noted, "In fact in the last 20 years almost all political movements posing a radical alternative to repressive or unrepresentative governments have originated in the universities and have found their first expression through student organizations."[36]

The era of dictatorships and authoritarian governments from the 1930s through the mid-1950s was one of retrogression for the university in Latin America. Students witnessed the successive loss of reform after reform which their predecessors had struggled so ardently to obtain in the optimistic years after World War I. University autonomy was violated. Professors and students were purged and their replacements selected on the basis of political loyalty rather than academic competence. Deans and rectors were chosen by the governments on the basis of their political credentials. In general, the quality of education deteriorated as the universities either fell under the political control of the dictatorships or were severely weakened by the constant political struggle.

The students' response to the dictators and to government intervention in the universities was to turn even more to political action. They devoted their energies to attacking and attempting to overthrow their dictatorial regimes.

The struggle against the dictators of the 1930s, according to Gabriel Del Mazo, educated the students to political realities. They learned that they should never again restrict their reforming activities primarily to the universities as they had done prior to advent of the dictators.[37]

The students also learned the extent of their own limitations. They discovered that without allies in other sectors of the society they could neither topple their authoritarian regimes nor even defend their own bastion, the university, from governmental forays. Sheer necessity demanded that the activist students join together in coalitions with other groups. As the Latin American nations became more industrialized, urbanized, and complex, the students' relative power position declined. Increasingly, in such situations the students found that they could articulate issues, assume vanguard positions, and take great risks, but in order to overthrow authoritarian governments in the 1930s, 1940s, and 1950s coalitions were necessary.[38]

Ironically, it was in Argentina, the home of the Reform Movement, that the students were given the earliest and one of the longest object lessons concerning both their power limitations and their dependence upon outside political forces. The inauguration of President Marcelo T. de Alvear in October 1922 marked the beginning of the successful movement against university reform. Unlike his predecessor, Hipólito Irigoyen, who had hand picked him for the position, Alvear proved to be no friend of the Reform Movement. During his administration (1922–1928), the government militarily intervened in several universities, including Córdoba, violating, among other things, their autonomy. The Alvear regime gave its support to counter-reformists within the Argentine universities, who proceeded to nullify or render ineffective many of the reforms passed during the 1918–1922 period. The students, politically fragmented and bereft of significant support, were generally incapable of resisting the attacks made on university reform.

The situation did not improve when Irigoyen returned to the presidency in 1928. He was seventy-eight at the time of his re-election, and his administration was marked by widespread corruption and inefficiency as well as by his failure to cope with the depression which arrived in Argentina during his term of office. The students vehemently demonstrated against Irigoyen, particularly for his inability to deal with the large scale unemployment. By arousing public opinion, they encouraged the army to implement its long-held plans to overthrow the Irigoyen government, which it did in 1930.

The new government headed by General José F. Uriburu moved quickly and decisively against the students and the universities. After only three months in office he seized control of the University of Buenos Aires. This was soon followed by the government's intervention in other universities. Reformist professors and students were purged and the selection of professors and administrators began to be guided by political criteria. The students organized to oppose the Uriburu government, but their actions whether legal or illegal made little impact upon governmental policies, especially with respect to institutions of higher education. From 1930 to 1943, the students in conjunction with the workers actively opposed the authoritarian and corrupt regimes which held power in Argentina, but even with considerable worker support, they were unable to oust the governments or protect their universities and reforms from governmental and Conservative incursions.

The situation of the students and the Argentine universities deteriorated even further with the rise to power of Juan Domingo Perón in 1943 and 1944. Until his ouster in 1955 he ruthlessly intervened in and purged the universities of any oppositional or potentially oppositional elements. Seventy percent of the Argentine professoriate were forced from their positions by Perón. Hundreds of students were also ousted. In addition, under new regulations, prior to admission at the university and prior to examinations students were required to obtain cards from the police testifying to the fact that they had not engaged in anti-regime activity. Extensive files were kept on almost every student and professor by the secret police. Perón also intervened to assure that the contents of university courses and texts were politically reliable. The regime required that classes in Perónist political philosophy be made mandatory for students in all universities. In general, through his chosen rectors, deans, and secret police, Perón attempted to maintain thorough control over the students and universities.

Despite all of these efforts, student oppositional activities continued throughout his years in power. Argentine students continued to risk arrest and exile as well as expulsion from the universities in order to oppose Perón. In 1951 and 1954 they launched strikes against the government for the restoration of university and national liberties. Although the students were united, articulate, innovative, and courageous in their long years of opposition to Perón, it was not until he successively alienated the Church, the military, and prominent sectors of the business community that he was overthrown in 1955.[39]

From the 1930s through the 1950s, whenever dictators and authoritarian governments came to power throughout the hemisphere, students invariably appeared at the forefront of the opposition. In Cuba, they fought against President Gerardo Machado (1925–1933) and against Fulgencio Batista during the years in which he dominated the Cuban government (1934–1959). In the process many were punished by arrest, exile, and expulsion. As in the case of the Argentine universities under Perón, the quality of higher education in Cuba suffered due to the government's intervention and the continuing struggle between the authoritarian regimes and the students. Often the universities were closed by the government for political reasons as in the years from 1931 to 1934, 1935 to 1937, and 1956 to 1959.[40] In Brazil, Venezuela, Colombia, Peru, Bolivia, and Guatemala as well as in Argentina and Cuba, whenever dictatorial regimes were overthrown from the 1930s through the 1950s the students of these respective countries played a significant role. But in every case, they required the assistance of other groups.

During the depression and in their struggles against dictators, the students became acutely sensitive to their own limitations. Increasingly, they turned from their universities and sought approaches and answers to important national problems from political organizations and ideologies. They became progressively politicized and oriented to national and international problems and politics. Students were instrumental in founding or organizing broad based reformist national political parties and movements, including the aforementioned APRA in Peru and its offshoots in other countries: *Acción Democrática* (AD) in Venezuela, the National Revolutionary Movement (MNR) in Bolivia, and the Christian Democratic Party in Chile, all of which eventually played major national political roles. Increasingly, students became exposed to and adherents of varying political ideologies. Marxism and various strains of socialism seemed to be the most popular of these ideologies. Fascism, particularly during the 1930s, also appealed to the students. The *Tacuara* in Argentina and the *Falange* in Bolivia were the most noted examples of student fascistic organizations. As students were moving off campus to participate in national politics and pursue various ideologies, national political parties and ideologues more and more looked to and became involved in student politics. Elections for student offices came to be conflicts between the opponents and supporters of competing national parties and ideologies.[41]

The student activists did not turn their backs on the university. Their basic position, however, was quite different from that of the early Reformistas. From the 1930s through the 1950s, student politicians argued that the restructuring and the reforming of the nation took precedence over the restructuring and reforming of the university. A democratic university, they contended, could not exist in a nondemocratic polity. University reform, although important, was deemed a part of the larger struggle for basic structural change. These ideas were concisely expressed in a leaflet distributed by a Chilean political student organization in the 1930s, the United Anti-Fascist Group: "It is evident that an integral transformation of the system of public education presupposes a profound and radical transformation of society; but the University Reform encompassing those well known postulates for which we are again ready to fight, requires no other change than the establishment of a true democracy."[42]

The demise of the dictators and the return of elected constitutional governments in the 1950s did not bring an end to student political activity oriented to the national scene, nor did it herald a new era of concern primarily with university affairs. In actuality, it ushered in a period of flux, search for new orientations, and stock taking. There was little consensus as to the direction of future activities. The students were deeply divided along political party and ideological lines. Militants wished to utilize the university as a base from which to attack bourgeois governments resistant to significant structural change. Other activists wished to stress university reform issues and concentrate on student related needs and interests, a student syndicalist position. Many students, wearied and frustrated by the constant political machinations of the various student political groups, wanted little to do with any politics, student or national.

Basically, concerned students were torn between their desire to democratize, reform, and modernize their universities on the one hand and their commitment to foster democracy, social justice, and progress in their societies on the other. Often it became difficult to separate the two orientations. One example of this situation took place in Brazil in 1962. The Brazilian National Union of Students chose to focus student political efforts upon university reform, specifically upon the demand for one-third student representation in the governing bodies of Brazilian universities. A strike was called in support of this demand. The strike, however, was ended by student political leaders apparently at the request of the government which feared the military might use it as a pretext to launch a coup.[43]

In general, the students by the latter 1950s were cognizant of the need to reform and modernize both their universities and their societies. The resolutions passed at the Third Latin American Student Congress (LASC) in 1959 reflect these dual concerns. They also indicate the permanence of the conditions that originally motivated the early Reformistas, as these resolutions were almost identical to the demands made by student reformers some forty years earlier: university autonomy, open enrollment, student participation in university government, selection of professors through competitive examinations, non-compulsory attendance, and no tuition. There was, however, more emphasis at the 1959 LASC in linking the university to national needs and problems. This can be seen in the LASC's formulation of the main purposes and mission of the Latin American University. "To give professional and technical training, ensuring the complete humanistic and democratic education of the students, without any discrimination and with a view to the needs of our countries. To offer the benefits of culture and techniques and to propogate the Latin American revolutionary idea in the service of the interest of our peoples . . . [is] the proper mission of the University in the education of the peoples, this being the foundation of democracy in its indefatigable struggle for the attainment of justice."[44]

By the end of the 1950s, there seemed to be a sense of disillusionment and disappointment prevailing among the more concerned students. In most of the major public national universities in Latin America, they had won representation in the governing bodies of these institutions. On the average their representation in these organs is about one-fourth to one-third of that of the professors. At the University of Honduras and the University of San Andres in La Paz, Bolivia, the students have equal representation with the professors, but in Chile, Brazil, and Colombia, their proportional representation is less than average. Many of these same universities were also guaranteed their autonomy by laws which the students had been instrumental in getting enacted. Yet, despite these gains, relatively little within the universities had changed, as vested interests, particularly the catedráticos, proved adept at blocking democratizing and modernizing reforms.[45]

Similarly, after suffering hardships and risks to overthrow dictators, the students saw that the parliamentary governments for which they had fought were slow to act on the major societal and university problems. The new governments did not seem to mirror the students' sense of urgency about these conditions nor the students' concern with the growing influence of foreign capitalists, primarily North Americans. Again, in the national sphere as in the university sphere, vested interests and power elites were able to resist the implementation of effective democratizing and modernizing reforms. There appeared to be an absence of significant leadership within both the universities and the national governments. Among their own ranks, opportunists and self-serving individuals were becoming more numerous. All of this was happening while the societies and the universities seemed in such dire need of major reform.

THE IMPACT OF FIDEL CASTRO AND THE CUBAN REVOLUTION

The victory of Fidel Castro and the Cuban Revolution in 1959 had a major impact upon Latin American students. Given the romantic, heroic image of Castro as a radical-intellectual, a former student leader triumphing over a corrupt military dictatorship, gaining the support of the masses, and standing alone against the colossus of the north, Latin American students admired and sought to emulate the Cuban Revolution. It offered the students a vivid model for social reconstruction. The message was effectively spread by the Cuban leader, who spoke before enthusiastic audiences in Venezuela and elsewhere, and by demonstrations and meetings organized throughout Latin America.

The Cuban Revolution had a broad radicalizing and polarizing effect on both national and student politics in Latin America. It challenged the radical claims of the Aprista parties and other representatives of liberal, democratic, and quasi-socialist tendencies as well as the various Communist parties. In Peru, Bolivia, Colombia, Venezuela, and elsewhere, student and other young adherents of Communist, Socialist, Aprista and liberal-centrist parties defected and joined or formed Fidelista organizations. Where they did not defect, they rebelled against the older leaders of their parties, attacking them for collaborating with dictators and oligarchies and for lacking ideological militancy. The Cuban Revolution also served as a radicalizing stimulus for Christian Democracy especially in Chile. For many politicized Catholic youth, the development of a reformist and progressive Christian Democratic movement offered a vehicle which allowed them to remain devoted to the faith and at the same time be politically liberal or radical.[46]

The Cuban Revolution also inspired the growth of student-led guerrilla movements, particularly in the period from 1959 to 1961. The earliest and most prominent development in this direction occurred in Venezuela, where the Central University in Caracas served as an armed fortress from which student militants carried out attacks against the Venezuelan government. Venezuelan students also formed an important part of the Armed Forces of National Liberation (FALN), a guerrilla force which operated in the rural areas. In Venezuela, Guatemala, Colombia, and Peru students were prominently involved in guerrilla activities, either as direct participants or as suppliers of information, funds, and material.[47]

David Spencer, in summarizing the impact of the Cuban Revolution upon Latin American students, delimits four major areas:

First, it greatly radicalized the student movement and further politicized the university. Second, it enhanced the importance of ideology, increasing the impact and prestige of Marxism in its different forms, and contributing to the development of Christian Democracy in Latin America. Thirdly, as ideological movements became more and more important, structures such as student government institutions and National Unions of Students became relatively less important. Fourthly, national political parties became more involved in university politics, and student leaders often became activists in the youth sections of the political parties.[48]

No successful revolutions, however, followed in the wake of Castro's triumph in Cuba. Guerrilla warfare and urban terrorism in the 1960s proved to be unsuccessful political tactics. No reformist, radical, or revolutionary government came to power in Latin America after Castro's victory due to such tactics. When a socialist government did come to power in Chile in 1970, it was through the electoral process rather than political violence.

As the exhiliration over the Cuban Revolution subsided and as it became clear that no other countries would quickly follow the revolutionary route, the sense of urgency and militancy that had characterized Latin American student politics immediately after Castro's triumph declined. This disappointment was heightened by the military take-overs in Peru (1962), Guatemala, Honduras, and the Dominican Republic (1963), Brazil and Bolivia (1964) and Argentina (1966), and by the repression of the universities and students in these countries after the military was in power. It is instructive, at this juncture, to turn our attention to the Brazilian and Argentine students and briefly examine how they coped with their military regimes and how these students apportioned their energies between university and national problems under a dictatorship in the 1960s.

In 1964, the government of President João Goulart was overthrown by a military coup d'état. The army immediately seized control of the universities, abolished the national student organization, the National Union of Students, and prohibited the students from engaging in student politics or strikes. The students were unprepared to cope with the coup or with the repressive acts of the military regime. This was, in part, due to the fact that under the administration of the populist and sympathetic Goulart, they had concentrated upon university reform.

By 1966, under the aegis of an illicit National Union of Students, a response to the military rulers was formulated. A two pronged policy was constructed. The student leaders decided to actively organize against the regime and at the same time energetically work for student interests and rights. In theory, it was acknowledged that the struggle against the government took precedence over the defense of student interests but the leaders felt that it was necessary to operate effectively in this arena in order to retain the support of the mass of students for actions in opposition to the national authorities. Wherever possible, the activists hoped to tie these two issues together and thus clearly demonstrate to the rest of the students the nature of the relationship between university reforms, student interests, and authoritarian military rule.

Two years later, in 1968, this dual approach was suspended. Numerous student demonstrations and other political activities had failed to arouse the active support of the Brazilian populace or a large proportion of the students. The student actions against the government had led to the arrest and torture of many students and student cadres without substantially weakening the regime. Further calls for immediate revolution, the student leaders opined, would be opportunistic and costly in terms of resources and future actions. Instead they agreed to concentrate their energies on university and student issues in order to maintain and develop a student base for future and hopefully more successful forays against the government.

The student issues to which the movement then directed itself were both general and specific. The leadership called for a more modern and rational university structure, student participation in the governance of the universities, better professors, and upgraded and more relevant curriculums. Also, they actively opposed the government's proposals to institute tuition increases, university budget cuts, and limitations upon student enrollments. The National Union of Students, still the primary political vehicle of the Brazilian students, did not, however launch a major campaign for total university reform in the tradition of the Reformistas.[49] The organization reasoned that such a goal was "impossible in the present structure. A university oriented toward the interests of the people is possible only with a government of the majority of the people."[50] Thus, for tactical reasons, the Brazilian student movement, confronted by a powerful authoritarian government, temporarily but not totally turned its energies from combatting the regime toward building a significant student constituency. In 1969 and 1970, however, in response to an increasingly "hard line" military regime which continued to utilize brutal, repressive measures against any form of dissidence, particularly if it was associated with the universities, the students took to the streets in "instant" protest demonstrations and resorted to guerrilla warfare as well.[51]

In Argentina, even prior to the military coup of July 28, 1966, the military and business interests exerted strong pressure on President Arturo Illia to intervene in the Argentine universities. They were concerned about the Marxist influences in the universities and the student political agitation. After seizing power, the military government promulgated the Law of 16,912 which in effect abolished the major accomplishments of the Reform Movement: university autonomy, academic freedom, and student participation in the governance of the universities. The military also came onto campuses where they set upon students and professors. In the wake of this intervention many professors from the larger and more advanced universities and scientific institutes resigned, a large number leaving the country.

The Argentine students' response to the military domination of their governments and universities was similar to that of the Brazilian students. On the one hand, they have attempted to organize and work with other oppositional elements to overthrow the regime. This policy, most closely associated with the Communist Youth Federation, places a priority on direct action and confrontation with government authorities. The other major policy position is to continue defending and working to reform the universities. The reforming and democratizing of the university and its various aspects, however, by 1966 and 1967 were no longer considered ends in themselves. For the students who promoted these goals, the underlying rationale was to utilize the university, once its autonomy had been restored and they had gained or regained an influential role, as a lever with which to democratize and bring progress to their society. Few Argentine students or for that matter few students elsewhere in the hemisphere by the latter 1960s could comfortably harbor the concept of the university as a special institution, an "ivory tower," existing apart from influences and values of other institutions and societal and military elites.[52]

In general the mid-1960s, the period in which our six nation student survey was taken (1964-1965), was again a period of reassessment and a search for new and better ways of dealing with old and seemingly lasting national and university problems. The students alternated the focus of their concerns between the university and the national political arena. At the same time, national political parties and ideologues, particularly leftists, maintained their interest and involvement with the students and became increasingly a part of university and student politics. The students level of participation in and commitment to national politics, however, was not as high as in the years immediately following Castro's victory in 1959.

Interest in university and student affairs which had waned during this period was rekindled in the mid-1960s. The students realized that there were important problems to be addressed within their immediate environment. Many of these proved to be very similar to those which their predecessors had confronted in the years after World War I. Half a century after Córdoba, Latin American students still considered important the issues of an archaic, oligarchic university structure, the lack of professorial accountability, poor quality of instruction, inadequate student participation in the governance of the university, a narrow class-biased enrollment, and the absence of a commitment to deal with the pressing needs of the nation.

The students were aware of the history of the University Reform Movement and student politics in Latin America. They realized that the university could not be democratized and modernized in a social vacuum. Societal and political reform, from their perspective, had to accompany university reform. They also knew from history and experience that alone they could not accomplish either objective. But, in the mid-1960s, no one seemed to have new or positive answers as to how best to avoid the mistakes of the past and how best to proceed with the task of modernizing and democratizing the universities and the societies.

Furthermore, during the same period time, there was little of the aura of immediacy and optimism surrounding the students that there had been during the early years of the Reform Movement or in the victorious battles with the dictators. The Cuban Revolution had not been successfully emulated, and there seemed little likelihood that the United States would passively allow such an eventuality to occur elsewhere in the region. A new wave of dictatorships appeared to be rising succeeding those that the students had helped to defeat in the 1950s. Those constitutional, elected, and parliamentary governments for which their predecessors had fought fell far short of student expectations. Although the leaders of these governments voiced their concern for such pressing national problems as poverty, hunger, illiteracy, and land reform, elitist power groups, vested interests, and bureaucratic inefficiency effectively blocked any concerted efforts to deal with them. Marxist and traditional radical parties, while continuing to use their oppositional and revolutionary rhetoric, appeared to have accomodated themselves to the existing system. Within the universities approximately fifty years of student efforts have had mixed results as the same battles seem to be fought over and over again. Indeed, in Argentina, the place where the University Reform Movement was born, from 1966, the time of the military take over until the present (1971), the universities have been stripped of their autonomy and the students barred from effectively participating in the governance of their universities, thus in effect turning back the calendar to 1918 as far as those aspects are concerned.[53] Many of the politically active students in the middle of the 1960s, unlike their predecessors, did not represent the moral vanguard of the student bodies of Latin America. Instead, it appeared that for considerable numbers, student politics has become either an end in itself or a vehicle for future social mobility.

Nonetheless, despite all of these disillusioning factors, Latin American university students and particularly talented minorities among them continued to be actively concerned about the quality of their universities and societies. This was revealed by our survey findings and by the continual emergence of new and splinter student political organizations devoted to reforming or radicalizing their schools and nations. This concern was also indicated by the courageous actions of students in the most adverse circumstances who risked their careers and lives for the sake of their ideals of what constitutes the "good society" and the "good university." Various social scientists, including ourselves, while admitting to the complexities in the motives and behavior of Latin American students, contend that the idealistic component has been a primary motivating force in the historic and seemingly omnipresent readiness of elements within this strata to fight for more democratic and progressive universities and societies.[54] The students themselves expressed it in somewhat exaggerated terms in the Córdoba Manifesto: "Youth is always surrounded by heroism. It is disinterested: it is pure. It has not yet had time to contaminate itself."[55]

2 Social Characteristics and Career Orientations of Contemporary University Students in Latin America

The political and social behavior and attitudes of contemporary Latin American students are related to their socioeconomic backgrounds and their socioeconomic destinations as well as to the institutional and historical contexts in which they are located. Our major concerns in this chapter will be the social origins and career choices of those students fortunate enough to have hurdled the variety of barriers to higher education in Latin America. Our discussion will shed further light on the workings of the Latin American social structure as well as provide a more comprehensive basis for the analysis of student behavior and attitudes in the chapters which follow.

THE STUDENTS

The most striking fact to emerge from the study of Latin American university students in the middle 1960s is that they were so few in number. Despite considerable expansion in both institutions of higher learning and in their enrollments, only 4 percent of those 20–24 years of age attend an institution of higher education in Latin America.[1] The data in Table 1 indicate the enrollment percentages of the university age cohort for the societies in the region, including the United States and its associated Commonwealth, Puerto Rico. As might be expected, the United States, with 44 percent, has the highest proportion in attendance both in the region and in the world. Puerto Rico, reflecting the educational influence of the United States, was next with 19 percent. If the United States and Puerto Rico were to be excluded from the table, there would not be much variation in enrollment percentages. Except for Argentina's 14 percent, there is no country in which the percentage exceeds 8 percent. Furthermore, in only seven countries including Argentina, is the enrollment percentage higher than 4 percent. Thus, despite differences in the levels of economic development, the Latin American countries are strikingly similar

Table 1. Percentages of age group 20-24 enrolled (university and higher learning) by country, 1966

Country	Percent
Argentina	14
Panama	8
Venezuela	7
Peru	7
Uruguay	7
Chile	6
Costa Rica	5
Mexico	4
Colombia	3
Paraguay	3
Ecuador	3
Bolivia	3
Brazil	2
Dominican Republic	2
Guatemala	2
Nicaragua	2
El Salvador	2
Honduras	1
Trinidad Tobago	1
Haiti	0.4
Latin America (total)	4
Puerto Rico	19
United States	44

with respect to the low percentage of the student age cohort in the universities. This can also be seen as a reflection of their educational heritage and models — the elitist European systems. In this regard, it is interesting to note that Spain, Italy, and France, the countries which have made the biggest cultural impact upon Latin America, had in the mid-1960s an average percentage enrollment in higher education of about 5 percent.[2]

Another means of gaining a perspective on the quantitative aspects of student enrollment is to compare Latin America and the United States in absolute numbers of university students. In 1966 Latin America, with a total population of 237 million, had a university population of 880,000, as compared with approximately 6,000,000 for the United States, which in that year had a population of only 196 million. It should be noted, however, that the figure of 880,000 in

1966 is more than double the total enrollment in 1956. In fact, during the decade from 1955 to 1965, the average annual rate of increase for the Latin American university population was higher than that for the United States, or 7.9 and 7.6 percent respectively.[3] However, despite the rapid growth in the number of Latin American students, the basic fact remains — higher education is the province of the few.

The vast majority of Latin American youth does not complete elementary and secondary school. The base upon which the universities draw is extremely small. In 1960, 78 percent of the primary school population were enrolled in school. About 17 percent of the students who started primary school completed it, with a majority dropping out by the third grade. Only 15 percent of the appropriate age group attended secondary school. Of those who began, 22 percent finished the entire course.[4] Thus, out of every hundred students who started elementary school, only eight completed their secondary education. While the retention rate grew in the mid-1960's, it is apparent that most Latin American children never receive more than a few years of primary school education.[5] In the United States, the retention rate from the beginning of elementary school to the end of secondary school is about 70 percent, or about 900 percent larger than that for Latin America.[6] The Latin American educational system is a reflection of the region's social structure — a steep pyramid with a tiny minority at the top.

Determinants of the Selection Process: Place of Residence

One major determinant of whether a Latin American reaches the university is place of residence. Latin Americans who reside in rural zones are less likely to attend a university than their counterparts in the urban areas of the same country. In fact, urban youth are more likely to attend a school at any level. Thus, in Latin America, as of 1960, 25 percent of all rural children in the age group from 7 to 14 attended school, compared to 56 percent of urban youth in the same age group.[7]

To a large extent, the urban-rural educational discrepancy within any given country repeats the picture for the region as a whole. In Guatemala 84 percent of the rural children did not complete the first year of school, compared to 43 percent of the urban youth. In Cuba, in 1953, 50 percent of the eligible age group attended primary and secondary schools in rural areas compared to 80 percent of those in the urban parts of the country.[8] In Colombia, during the period from 1960 to 1964, 33 percent of the urban youth who started elementary school finished, compared to 2 percent of their rural counterparts.[9] In

Buenos Aires 62 percent completed elementary school whereas the comparable figure for those in the rural northeastern part of Argentina was 14.[10] The situation is the same for Puerto Rico, the most advanced Latin American society according to standard economic indicators. There, 96 out of every 100 children who started primary school in the urban zones graduated, as opposed to 58 out of every 100 in the rural zones.[11] This discrepancy between educational opportunities in the urban and rural areas of Latin America takes on a significant dimension, since approximately half of the hemisphere's population lives in the countryside.

As is to be expected, the educational differences between rural and urban youth at the preuniversity level are also very much in evidence in the universities. According to our data, both proportionately and absolutely, very few university students were drawn from the countryside. Among the students in our study, one percent of the Uruguayans, 2 percent of the Paraguayans, 6 percent of the Colombians, 7 percent of the Panamanians, and 13 percent of the Puerto Ricans came from nonurban areas. At the University of Buenos Aires, the largest university in Latin America (and not part of our sample), only 2 percent of the entire student body came from towns of less than 2,000 population.[12] The evidence, then, strongly shows that rural residence in Latin America, and in all likelihood most other parts of the world, effectively bars the road to education from the earliest to the highest levels.

A variety of factors underlies this state of affairs. A major aspect is the pronounced tendency of both governments and private businesses to concentrate their resources, including educational resources, in the major urban areas, particularly in the capital cities. In essence, both the quantity and quality of texts, teachers, and schools deteriorate as one moves from the urban to the rural regions.[13] The higher the level of education, the more this feature is accentuated. There are simply not enough schools and trained teachers to serve the needs of the primary school population in the countryside. The situation is much worse at the secondary school level. Furthermore, very often, even when a primary school is available in a rural area, it will not offer the full six years required for secondary school.[14] In Venezuela rural education is so poor as to be virtually nonexistent.[15] In Mexico secondary schools do not, in effect, exist in the countryside.[16] In Brazil half of the counties lack a secondary school, and in only 800, or 28 percent, of the counties is there a secondary school which offers the grades necessary for entrance into a university.[17] Even in Puerto Rico, accessibility of schools is regarded as an important determinant of school attendance, with Puerto Rican parents in rural areas citing the distance between home and school as the major reason for their children's failure to continue in school.[18]

As Aldo Solari asserts, to all intents and purposes, "secondary education is largely an urban phenomenon."[19]

Qualitatively, there are also problems which further lessen the probabilities that youth outside the metropolitan areas and cities will attend secondary school or a university. The large majority of teachers in areas outside the cities lack appropriate training. Many of the rural primary school teachers have barely completed their own secondary education. Qualified teachers are reluctant to go to the rural areas or to stay for any length of time. Salaries are low. In many rural areas, teachers are often appointed at the whim of the local politician.[20] Thus, the teachers whom children in rural areas meet are, more often than not, unqualified and uninspired. They frequently serve as barriers rather than channels to higher education.

In addition, the curricula in the rural schools are, for the most part, irrelevant to the experiences of the students as well as to the needs of their communities. The rural classroom is often a poor imitation of the urban one. Even the academic calendar is frequently not coordinated with the need of agricultural families to have their children help with the harvests.[21]

Under these circumstances, both students and their parents have difficulty relating investment in education to future rewards. There is little associated with the school to engender a sense of support or identity on the part of the students, their parents, or the rural community in general. If, after three years of education, the school has produced quasi literates in areas where literacy is not thought to be very important, and if the school has also taught few of the skills needed by rural communities, why should rural parents continue to forgo the income and labor of their children? Absence of indigenous and structural support for continued education makes postprimary education (even when schools are available) a rarity in the rural areas.

It is not surprising that attending the university is not a very realistic goal in rural areas where so few go on to secondary school. If secondary schools are an urban phenomenon the same is even more true of universities. Universities throughout Latin America are located in the larger cities, particularly in the capitals. Although in recent years there has been some tendency to locate universities outside the major urban areas, this has not yet greatly changed the situation. As of 1966 higher education in Latin America was still a major-city or capital-city phenomenon. In 50 percent of the countries more than three-quarters of the students attended the principal university of that country, located in the capital. In over 85 percent of the countries, one-third or more of the students attended the country's major university located in the capital, while many of the remaining students attended other universities in the same city.[22]

The accompanying tendency to draw students disproportionately from the capital city can be seen most clearly in the cases of the National Autonomous University of Mexico and the University of Buenos Aires. In the former university 59 percent of the students were natives of Mexico City even though the population of Mexico City represented only 14 percent of the country's population.[23] At the University of Buenos Aires, 75 percent of the student body were natives of Greater Buenos Aires though only 35 percent of the country's population lived in this area.[24] In Puerto Rico, where over 60 percent of the university students on the island attend the University of Puerto Rico in San Juan, the issue of the location of the universities and particularly of the junior colleges has become political, with politicians throughout the island appealing for votes on the basis of their ability to attract a junior college to their particular area.[25]

In Latin America, at each successive level of education the institutional location is further from the potential rural student's home. For those who reside far from the major cities, whether in distance or in travel time, the university is not only actually far, it is sociologically distant as well. In essence, to the people of the Latin American countryside, the university is a foreign institution which many of them will probably never see and to which they will not strive to send their children.

Social Class

Whereas rural residence virtually rules out the possibility of attending a university, urban residence is by itself no guarantee of such attendance. A crucial factor which cuts across residence is social class. In Latin America as in other areas, there is an integral relationship between social class and education. This is particularly so in higher education. As a prominent sociologist of education, A. H. Halsey, has observed, "universities always play a role in stratification because, controlling access to highly valued cultural elements, they are always intrinsically inegalitarian."[26]

The fact that only 4 percent of the appropriate age group in Latin America attend a university is a strong indication that the university population is selected according to social class. Such a low figure virtually insures that higher education will be limited to the upper and middle strata. Even in the United States, where the percentage of the age cohort attending college is approximately 44 percent, social class remains a crucial factor. Only about 18 percent of the college age group were from families earning less than $5,000 a year in 1967, whereas more than three-quarters of their age peers in college were from families whose incomes were $15,000 or more per year.[27] Another way of examining the influence of class is to relate the proportion of an occupational group among students to the proportion of that occupational group in the labor force. In the United States in 1966, 37 percent of the students were drawn from the ranks of blue collar, service, and farm worker families, though their parents represented approximately 55 percent of the labor force.[28]

What is the class composition of the university student population in Latin America? This is difficult to estimate, and there are no reliable data for the entire region. But, utilizing the available information (primarily university censuses), it is evident that very few students come from the lower strata. In 1964 students from working class backgrounds at the University of Buenos Aires constituted about 8 percent of the school's enrollment.[29] At the National Autonomous University of Mexico in the same year, the comparable figure was approximately 14 percent.[30] In Uruguay, 12 percent of the students were from the working class.[31] At the University of Puerto Rico, the percentage of students whose parents were workers or agricultural laborers was about 28 percent in 1961.[32] Again the contrast between Puerto Rico and Latin America appears, reflecting the North American influence on higher education in the Commonwealth and the European influence in the Latin American republics. This observation is reinforced when the working class origins of European university students during the latter 1950s and early 1960s are compared to the figures previously presented for various Latin American schools. In Germany, working-class students were 5 percent of the university enrollment; in France, 7 percent; in Italy, 11 percent; and in Spain, 5 percent.[33] For Latin America as a whole, it has been estimated that approximately 10 percent of the university students are of working class origins.[34]

The nature of the under-representation of the lower strata at the Latin American universities is brought more sharply into focus when the proportion of these strata in the labor force is considered. In Argentina they form approximately two-thirds of the labor force, while in Mexico approximately four out of five people are workers, peasants, or low-service workers. In Uruguay the comparable figure is about two-thirds, and in Puerto Rico somewhat more than half of the labor force is in this category. In the entire region approximately 80 percent of the labor force are manual workers, service personnel, and farm workers.[35] An examination of the distribution of the labor force shows quite clearly that the working class in Latin America is far from having an "equitable" representation in the universities.

As previously discussed, the narrow class-biased enrollments within Latin American universities have been an object of student concern since Córdoba.

In the post World War II era, various governments, including Perón's in Argentina and the military regime in Brazil in the mid-1960s, have also become more aware of this problem and have made some gestures to broaden the social base of the student bodies.[36] However, the most radical measures to recruit members of the lower strata into the universities have been taken by the Castro government in Cuba. Programs were established by which factory workers aged 18 through 40 were selected for admission to the universities. Also, the number of scholarships to students from poorer homes was greatly increased.[37] It is doubtful whether other Latin American governments, particularly nonsocialist ones, will follow the Cuban example. But the very fact that the Cuban model exists undoubtedly will increase the pressures throughout Latin America for more broadly based university student bodies.

What is the distribution of students who are not of working class or peasant origin? Again, the data are such that it is difficult to give a firm response, particularly when dealing with divisions within the middle and higher strata. However, from the data that are available it would appear that the children of small businessmen and white collar employees have been quite successful in gaining access to higher education. In Uruguay children from families of small businessmen and low level officials constituted 33 percent of the student body, the largest from any occupational strata both in absolute and proportional terms.[38] At the University of Puerto Rico in 1961, 40 percent of the freshmen were the children of white collar workers and small buinessmen, although these strata constituted only 16 percent of the labor force on the island. Here, too, the percentage was highest both in absolute and proportional terms.[39] In Mexico's major university, 40 percent of the student body were white collar dependents, the largest number of students from any stratum. However, in their proportion vis-à-vis their size in the labor force, they were not as disproportionately over-represented as the students from professional families, who constituted 15 percent of the student body.[40] At the University of Buenos Aires, 38 percent of the students had parents who owned their own firms, and 23 percent were the offspring of white collar employees, which meant that more than 60 percent of the students at the university were from these backgrounds.[41] Although it is interesting to note the differential representation of the various sections of the middle and upper strata, the major import of the data is in the fact that, proportionately, the 80 percent of the Latin American population who are the workers, peasants, and low-level service workers are virtually excluded from higher education.

What are the factors contributing to this state of affairs? Poverty is the single major reason why the lower strata are underrepresented in the university. The

importance of this factor increases at each successive level of education.[42]
Many families simply cannot afford to send their children from primary school
through a university. The cost of foregoing income from the child, in addition
to the expenditure for school supplies and clothing, becomes too big a burden
over a period of years. There are also other factors associated with poverty
which inhibit school attendance. Sickness and disease rates are high, and impro-
per diet frequently affects ability to concentrate on studies. Learning potential
is also often negatively affected by such factors as large family size and overcrowded conditions.

This does not mean that the lower strata do not value education. Some
appear to have a type of mystic faith in its power. According to William Mangin,
the low income residents of the "squatter settlements" in the cities of Latin
America have a deep concern for the education of their children. "Without
exception," he writes, "education ranks near the top of the list of the desiderata
for children in every country."[43] Melvin Tumin asserts that Puerto Ricans in
the lower strata are quite aware of the importance of education. More than 90
percent of the two lowest status groups in his study responded in the affirma-
tive to the proposition that, "Persons of my social status can improve their
positions in life only by increasing the amount of schooling they get."[44] Oscar
Lewis in *The Children of Sánchez* vividly describes the responsiveness of the
father, despite his poverty, to the educational needs of his child. Consuela, the
daughter, described her father's reaction to her requests for school as follows:
"as long as it was for school. All I had to do was show my father the list of
school supplies and the next day I had everything I needed. It was the same with
clothing; as long as it was needed for school, we had it almost before we asked
him for it."[45]

This interest in education is not limited to the poor and the lower strata.
During the last decade growth in enrollments at all levels has exceeded the
growth of the school age population during the same time period.[46] According
to Solari's calculations, however, the major beneficiaries of the expanded
enrollments, particularly on the postprimary level, have been the middle
strata.[47] This situation is analagous to that in the United States with respect
to the expansion of higher education. The growth of the percentage of the university age cohort attending university in the United States, from 22 percent
in 1946 to 44 percent in 1964 was accounted for mainly by the increase in the
numbers of middle class adolescents enrolling in colleges and universities during
this time period.[48] This pattern was replicated in Puerto Rico.[49]

Ironically, increased enrollments, particularly the disproportionate growth
of secondary education in relation to higher education, have had negative con-

sequences in the access to the university by the lower strata. Because of their slower rate of growth, Latin American universities increasingly have more applicants than vacancies. Therefore, graduation from secondary school can no longer be a sufficient prerequisite for admission. Increased utilization of examinations has correlated with an expansion of private secondary schools whose graduates are believed to have a better chance for admission to universities.[50] This process can be seen at the University of Puerto Rico where the number of students coming from private schools has grown, with approximately one-third of the recent Puerto Rican university students being graduates of private high schools; twenty years earlier the comparable percentage was 16. In Puerto Rico, private school enrollments account for 10 percent of secondary school students, which implies that they contribute proportionately three and a half times their numbers to the student body of the University of Puerto Rico.[51] In Latin America as a whole the percentage of secondary students in private schools is much higher than it is in Puerto Rico, with approximately two-thirds of the secondary students attending private schools which charge tuition.[52] In Brazil the disparity between the number of secondary school graduates and places available in higher education has reached such proportions that even attendance at private schools is not regarded as a guarantee of admission to a university. Consequently, there has been a growth of private preparatory courses for secondary school graduates desiring high scores on the all important admission examination.[53] This tendency toward private secondary schools and private preparatory courses has put the lower or poorer strata at a further disadvantage by degrading public secondary education as a key step toward higher education. Tuition payments now present these strata with yet another financial barrier on the route to higher education.

At present, secondary schools in Latin America serve many of the same functions as do American colleges and universities. The secondary schools of Latin America are thought to provide their students with the same mobility and status as do the colleges and universities of the United States. Aldo Solari indicates that graduation from academic high school is still regarded as a minimal requirement for the preservation of high status in Latin America. Lower white collar parents look upon secondary school as a means of ensuring upward mobility for their sons while working class parents feel that graduation from secondary school is the only way by which their sons can move into the ranks of nonmanual workers.[54]

That there has been movement on the Latin American educational scene is most vividly indicated by the increase, both in numbers and proportions, of the school age children attending school at all levels. As primary school attendance becomes universal and as secondary schools enroll increasing proportions of the appropriate age cohort, it appears highly probable that the mobility and status-conferring functions of higher education will be transferred to the universities in the same manner as occurred in the United States. However, if the United States experience is to be the model, the major beneficiaries will not be the working and lower classes but the middle classes of Latin America.

At the present juncture there are many obstacles which limit access of the lower strata to secondary and, particularly, to higher education. As discussed previously, low income is a crucial factor. The nature of the schools is, and will continue to be, a significant problem as well. Despite the growth of secondary education, most of it has been along the lines of academic schools which function primarily to prepare students for entrance into colleges.[55] The universities remain predominantly traditional, status-conferring institutions, and there has been no widespread growth of junior and technical colleges. Institutions of higher learning tend not to be dispersed throughout the countryside or the smaller urban areas.[56] There is little in the organizational structure and nature of university education (and to some extent of secondary education as well) to induce large segments of the working and lower classes to identify such education as an attainable goal for themselves or their children. Many parents in both these groups evaluate education positively as indicated above. Yet it is doubtful whether this has a strong effect on either secondary school completion or on enrollment at a university since these accomplishments are far removed from the working- and lower-class way of life. The nature of their class position, as well as the vague image of future rewards, would perforce limit their motivation. In his discussion of lower-status Puerto Ricans, Melvin Tumin phrases the issue in the following manner:

education of children must be valued highly before the necessary sacrifices are likely to be undertaken. A type of providential thinking – planning for the future and delaying gratifications now for oneself in preference for latter gratifications from one's children – must precede any consideration of these sacrifices. But this type of thinking is hard to acquire unless one has some good reason to approach life this way. And good reasons of this kind are themsevles hard to come by unless one has somehow experienced the benefits of thinking in these terms.[57]

Sex

Sex is another social factor which differentiates between those who attend college and those who do not. This is true for Latin America and for the rest of the world as well. At each successive level of education, the proportion of females declines; it is lowest at the university level. Latin America approximates this pattern. In 1963 females accounted for nearly half the enrollments at both the primary and the secondary levels. However, in higher education, females represented 34 percent or about one-third of the total enrollment. Curiously, despite the differences in stages of development, values, and traditions, the proportions of females at each level in the United States are approximately the same as in Latin America.[58]

It is also interesting to note the close correlation between the percentage of the university age cohort enrolled and the proportion of female students in any given country. In those countries where the cohort enrollment ratio is high, the proportion of female university students is also high. In Puerto Rico, the percentage of female students is slightly higher than 50 percent, and in Panama, Uruguay, Argentina, and Chile, female students average about 40 percent of the total.[59] When the proportion of the appropriate age group attending university increases, females are prominent beneficiaries of that increase.

It is evident that there are at least three major determinants to enrollment in higher education in Latin America — place of residence, social class, and sex. Those in the appropriate age cohort who live in the urbanized areas, who are from the middle and upper strata, and who are male have the best chance of gaining access to the university. They represent the fortunate few, the 4 percent of the university age cohort who are assured of attaining or maintaining high status and obtaining high-level positions in government, business, education, and science.

Barriers Confronting Secondary School Graduates

Until recent decades, graduation from a secondary school was a virtual guarantee of admission to a public university in Latin America. However, in recent decades despite the growth in the number and size of universities, the diploma from a secondary school has tended to lose this important quality. Universities have erected additional barriers and screening mechanisms, all of which function to limit access by secondary school graduates. These impediments usually take the form of entrance examinations or in some instances an additional year of secondary school or more courses at a university supervised preparatory school. Some countries have also utilized the secondary grade point average as a selection filter. In Uruguay, there are no entrance examinations nor are there any at several Argentine public universities, in both cases because of students opposition to them.[60]

One important reason for the shortage of places in higher education in a region where universities accomodate only 4 percent of the appropriate age group is the disparate rates of growth between secondary school and university enrollments in the post World War II era. Although enrollments in higher education have grown considerably in the last decade, their rate of increase has been less than those of secondary schools. It is estimated that secondary school enrollment has increased at a rate twice that of higher education. This problem has been compounded by the increased demand for higher education. The difficulties have been further intensified by the failure of most Latin American governments to plan systematically for the expansion of higher education. Thus, throughout the hemisphere less than half of the applicants, generally graduates of secondary schools, succeed in gaining admission to higher education.[61] In Brazil, where the problem is most acute, two-thirds of the applicants were denied entrance into institutions of higher education in 1960.[62]

Paradoxically, despite the pressure for admissions, many faculties or schools have vacancies in their freshmen classes. The educators and administrators explain this by citing the necessity of maintaining standards in the face of the rising number of secondary school graduates and applicants to the universities. This position has been challenged by UNESCO-sponsored studies of access to higher education in Chile and Brazil. These studies reported that there was little if any relationship between entrance examination scores and intellectual ability or capability of doing work at a university level.[63] Although there has undoubtedly been some deterioration of standards in secondary schools given their rapid growth, it appears that this is not a very significant factor in limiting the size of enrollments in universities.

One reason for the coexistence of vacancies and an excess of applicants is that Latin Americans tend to overlook opportunities at regional or state universities in favor of the major public universities in the larger cities, particularly the prestigious national ones located in the capitals. In addition, prospective students tend to overselect the more traditional fields, leaving vacancies in the new or lesser status-conferring faculties such as dentistry and veterinary medicine. Thus, tradition and prestige appear to be the intervening variables which produce a distorted academic market situation.[64]

There are also other reasons for this state of affairs which do not involve the decisions of students or prospective students. In some cases, best exemplified by Brazil, various faculties and universities have simply decided not to expand beyond a certain size. The imposition of enrollment ceilings can be viewed, in part, as a device to maintain the favorable market advantage of certain professions by limiting the number of future practitioners. Since most of the Latin American professors are full-time professionals or practioners and part-time instructors, the professions have their interests well protected in the universities. The restriction of the number of candidates seems most evident in the more prestigious and lucrative fields of medicine and engineering.[65]

A good illustration of some of the factors involved in the admissions policies of Latin American universities can be seen in the case of the Faculty of Philosophy, Science, and Letters at the University of São Paulo in Brazil in 1968.[66] In 1968, the number of applicants greatly exceeded the number of places available in the Faculty. Responding to this situation, the administration instituted an objective examination in order to filter out the excess. However, this exacerbated the problem as the number who passed the examination still remained larger than the number of openings. When this was revealed, a student crisis ensued, eventually leading to a boycott of classes.

The university authorities turned to the state and federal ministries of education in the hope that additional funds from these agencies would resolve the crisis. This quest, however, proved fruitless. In fact, the money which these same education ministries had promised for the *excedentes* admitted in 1967 was never sent to the universities.

The administration of the Faculty also raised the issue of the lowering of standards should the excedentes be admitted. The excedentes and their student supporters responded by pointing out that even those who presumably qualified for university work on the basis of the Faculty's own entrance examination were denied admission. Furthermore, most students in the Faculty felt that the issue of academic quality was a false one. They "argued that the standards were so low that they could not become appreciably worse."[67]

The issue was eventually made the responsibility of the senior or chair holding professors of the Faculty. The administration asked them to decide how many additional students each chair, the functional equivalent of a department in a North American university, could adequately handle. In the ensuing discussions, in which junior professors also participated, it became apparent that the professors' positions on the issue were motivated by more than academic universalistic criteria. Although many voiced their concern about the lowering of educational quality, the major determinant of a professor's stance on whether or not to admit more students seemed to be the political ideology of the faculty member. Political conservatives did not want to admit additional students while political liberals and especially radicals were in favor of enlarging the enrollments. This political division reflected a split between the junior or younger professors and the senior or older ones. The younger, who were also more left, tended to favor the admission of the excedentes while the converse was the case for the elder professors. In addition to political ideology, it seemed that the senior men who had established their own niches and privileged positions were resistant to any changes which even potentially could disturb or threaten their interests. Eventually, a compromise solution was worked out allowing more than 150 excedentes to enroll.

The growth of the Latin American universities to date, then, has not matched the increased demand for access to higher education. The problem of the excess of applicants and the shortages of places in the universities is not solely a technical problem of the educational market. Its locus is to be found in the relationship between the university and the society. The problem itself mirrors and highlights the tensions that emerge when persons and institutions with traditional values and outlooks are continually confronted with changing situations challenging their values, prestige, and power. As Latin America becomes increasingly bureaucratized, industrialized, and urbanized — in short "modernized" — traditional institutions such as the universities will more and more be challenged to adapt to their modernizing environments. A more open and equitable admissions policy is only one facet of this confrontation.

SOCIAL DESTINATION OF STUDENTS

After the fortunate few gain access to the university, what are their social destinations or career choices? One way of answering this question is to determine the distribution of Latin American students according to field of study. Although there is no certainty that they will enter careers directly relevant to this field, the probabilities appear fairly high. Our student survey data indicate that approximately three-quarters believe they will enter occupations in their field of specialization.

It is evident from Table 2 that the more traditional fields continue to attract Latin American students. Law and medicine account for nearly a third of the total enrollees, and, if humanities and education are added, enrollments in these four fields come to approximately one-half of the total. In the United States in 1967 the comparable figure for law and medicine was less than 5 percent. There are, however, a substantial proportion studying in the more "modern" fields in Latin America. Thirty percent are studying engineering (which in Latin America is primarily civil engineering), administration, accounting, economics, and statistics, but only an additional 7 percent are occupied with the natural and agricultural sciences. The students in these fields do represent an increase over the proportion during the previous decade, but, particularly in the more scientific areas, the increase is not very significant. In the mid-1950s, 16 percent of the students were enrolled in engineering and the natural and

Table 2. Distribution of Latin American students by fields of study

Field	Percent
Administration, economics, accounting, and statistics	17
Law	15
Social and political fields	5
Medical and health sciences	17
Physical, chemical, and mathematical sciences	3
Agricultural sciences	4
Engineering	13
Architecture	3
Visual arts and music	1
Humanities and education	17
Other careers	4
Total	100

agricultural sciences, as compared to 20 percent in those same categories ten years later. There was also a diminution in the proportion studying medicine and law, but again the shift was slight — from 38 to 32 percent.[68]

If we focus once more on Argentina, the country with the largest number of students in Latin America, the change from the traditional to the more modern fields over a period of sixty years is quite noticeable. From 1901 to 1905, doctors and lawyers accounted for 86 percent of all Argentinian graduates. A quarter of a century later, during the period from 1926 to 1930, the proportion of graduates in medicine and law was approximately half of the total, and, in the period from 1956 to 1960, it was about 38 percent. As the proportion of graduates in these fields declined, there was an increase in the proportions of graduates in the fields of engineering, dentistry, accounting, and pharmacy — the more modern fields.[69]

A report of the Inter-American Development Bank estimates that, during the 1930s for Latin America as a whole, enrollments in the more modern fields such as agronomy, natural sciences, accounting, and the social sciences were almost zero.[70] Therefore, although law and medicine still account for a plurality of the university students in Latin America, changes in enrollment distributions have occurred. Over time, as Latin America has become more industrialized and urbanized and as it has developed new and different occupational needs, changes in enrollments in fields of specialization have also taken place.

Still, overconcentration in fields of study, particularly the more traditional ones, has been an object of concern to governments throughout the hemisphere. To further their industrialization and development plans, they feel that it is necessary to increase the numbers of scientists, engineers, administrators, and technicians graduating from the national universities. For a variety of reasons, student and professorial resistance coupled with university autonomy have generally blocked governmental attempts to significantly change the curriculum or shift enrollments. The students' objections appear to stem from a variety of sources including their traditional suspicion of governments intervening in university affairs, anxiety over employment prospects in relatively new fields located outside of the familial employment network, and concern with prestige considerations.

Latin American governments have resorted to various methods in order to surmount student and university related obstacles. In some countries such as Venezuela, new nonautonomous or limited autonomy schools whose orientation is primarily scientific and technical have been established.[71] But it has been in Castro's Cuba that the most radical measures have been applied. In Cuba, prior to Batista's closing of the universities in 1956, most university courses were theoretical. Only about 8 percent of the students were enrolled in science and agricultural courses while the vast majority studied in the more traditional fields such as humanities and law. Fidel Castro, upon reopening the universities, abolished their autonomy in order to integrate them into the revolutionary political and economic structure his government was creating in Cuba. The numbers of students in each field of study were planned so that they would be more in accord with the needs of the economy as envisioned by the Cuban state. Scientific and technical fields were emphasized while the others were accorded a low priority. In 1962, the first year of the new educational plan at the University of Havana, no first year students were accepted in philosophy and no scholarships offered in that field. The situation was different in the more applied fields. Forty-three percent of those studying mechanical engineering received scholarships as well as approximately 25 percent of those in medicine and technology. Through such means the number and proportion of students in the scientific, technical and applied fields have increased significantly.[72] Other governments, including the military dominated one in Brazil, have openly voiced their desire to reorient their educational system in the Castro manner.[73]

Students' Assessment of Professional Opportunities

Considerable attention has been devoted to the issue of career opportunities for university students as these relate to other facets of their lives and behavior. One would expect that in highly elitist educational systems such an issue would not be very problematical. Given the fact that only 4 percent of the age cohort attend universities in Latin America, such a system could be described as elitist. However, in recent years, there has been a growth in the number of students as well as a broadening of the social base from which they are recruited. How, then, do the Latin American students assess their futures?

Almost all of the students in our sample believed that a university education, regardless of its quality, would enable them to secure a position of high prestige. Student responses to questions concerning future salary and professional opportunities were, however, deeply affected by national background.

Puerto Rican students, despite the fact that Puerto Rico has the largest percentage of the appropriate age group in universities of any society in Latin America, were the most optimistic about the availability of professional opportunities. This attitude reflected the very substantial economic development that had taken place on the Island during the previous twenty-five years. Industry had grown, the importance of agriculture had been reduced, and the provision of welfare services had greatly expanded. Per capita income had risen substantially. This transformation had changed not only the physical landscape of Puerto Rico but also its cultural climate. American values, imported along with huge doses of American capital, had become paramount.[74] The emphasis on ambition, accumulation, consumption, and achievement had had an impact. More than three-quarters of the Puerto Rican students in our sample were convinced that competence was essential to their success.

Thus, when Puerto Rican students predicted the future, in general, they tended to be quite sanguine. They were less optimistic, however, about their *personal* economic position than about their assessment of general opportunities. Apparently they realized that there were many competitors for available positions. They believed that a university graduate would have to demonstrate the competence which is a prerequisite for success. Such a definition of their personal future increased their concern about their ability to reach their own goals.

Mexican students, on the other hand, believed their university experience would almost automatically provide them with a financially secure and highly prestigious social position. While a majority of Mexican students did not foresee "many opportunities" for themselves, they were nonetheless relatively confident about the abundance of future rewards. In addition, two-thirds of the Mexican students surveyed believed that such rewards could be attained primarily through professional *competence*. Only in Puerto Rico did a higher percentage of students think their society was operating according to the modern norms of success through competence and achievement. The importance of personal contacts will be discussed further in chapter 6.

Table 3. Percentages of students who anticipate success and their evaluation of influences on success

Country	Expectations				Key to success		
	Higher social class in 10 years	Many opportunities	Much higher economic status than family	High salary	Competence	Family	Luck
Mexico	95	23	38	23	66	30	4
Colombia	86	55	27	22	54	40	6
Paraguay	84	54	37	9	54	38	8
Puerto Rico	83	72	31	6	79	19	2
Uruguay	79	46	21	_a	51	31	18
Panama	63	49	43	6	42	46	13

a_ indicates less than 0.5 percent.

Students in less developed countries, such as Paraguay, had been less challenged by the incessant and everchanging needs of an industrializing society. The more restricted recruitment to higher education and the attenuated demands for professional expertise or innovation provided a more secure future for those who received a university title. Although Paraguayan students were the most critical of the quality of their training, they were, at the same time, quite confident about existing career opportunities. Their views apparently reflected the major role of government or political patronage in Paraguay. (See chapter 5 for further discussion on this point.) Students apparently believed that deficiencies in professional education need not directly affect career opportunities. Competence was obviously only one, and perhaps not the most important, factor in attaining professional success.

In Panama the growth of secondary and higher education had far outpaced other sectors of national development. The large sums invested in Panamian education by the government had opened the university to large numbers of students from modest backgrounds. Students were not, however, unaware of the restricted nature of their future opportunities. The Panamanian educational system was capable of producing greater numbers of professionals than could readily be absorbed by the economic system.[75] Students were thus very restrained when they predicted their future salary or their social class position as it would be in ten years. They were also far more dubious than their peers in other countries about the extent to which competence would be a determining factor in their professional success. Indeed, most of them emphasized the importance of family contacts and were no doubt aware that their upper-class peers would eventually return from overseas study to command many of the more desirable jobs. Only in comparison to their families' present social position, did many students believe they would fare quite well in the labor market.

The severe economic and political problems which plagued Uruguay in the years prior to and during our data collection were accurately reflected in the students' pessimism about their future situations. Over 50 percent were negative in evaluating professional opportunities. Only one-fifth of the students believed that they would attain a higher economic status than that of their parents. In general, they foresaw a much gloomier future for themselves than did their peers in other countries. The Uruguayan students' evaluation of the key to professional success was consistent with their general pessimism about the lack of professional opportunities. The direct relationship between the level of national development and emphasis on achievement criteria, which we observed in Puerto Rico and Mexico, broke down in the Uruguayan situation. Only 51 percent of the Uruguayan students chose competence as the primary factor in attaining professional success. However, unlike their peers in the less developed countries, they did not focus on the importance of ascriptive characteristics. Indeed, in both Uruguay and Mexico less than one-third of the students believed family factors to be the most significant key to professional success. Only in Puerto Rico did the students mention family less frequently. Uruguayan students were, however, notable for their belief that luck was a key variable in future professional success. Fully 18 percent of them, compared to 4 percent of the Mexican and less than 2 percent of the Puerto Rican students, emphasized luck. This designation by the Uruguayans clearly expressed a lack of confidence on the part of many students in the predictability of the health of their nation's economic and social system. [76]

Mark Van Aken's study of Uruguayan university students conducted during the same period as our own corroborated our findings. The Uruguayan students, he stated, showed little confidence in the system that must eventually accommodate them. According to Van Aken, 80 percent of the students regarded the government as corrupt and over 90 percent thought that the government had allowed the country to slip into a "deep and grave crisis." [77]

Social Status and Career Choice

Having ascertained the overall distribution of Latin American students in different career fields and the significance of national factors upon their choices, we now turn our attention to the social determinants of career selection. The data in Table 4 reveal which fields in each of the six countries in our survey are most likely to be chosen by students according to varying social status backgrounds. [78] The findings in Table 4 indicate that medicine is usually selected by students from high status backgrounds, while education and economics are fields disproportionately chosen by students from the lower strata. Architecture is disproportionately comprised of high status students in Colombia and Paraguay, although not in Uruguay and Panama (the only other countries where architecture students were included in the sample.)

Another method of approaching the association between socioeconomic status and career is to ascertain whether or not there is a relationship between the institutional context of the occupation and status rather than between the particular occupation and social status. In Latin America as elsewhere, where one works is often more important than the particular job one holds. The sharpest distinction is between employment in the private sector and employment in the public sector or government. Nepotism is a prominent feature of business life. Familial ties often count far more than expertise, and businesses tend to keep

Table 4. Field of study most frequently chosen by high and low status students

Country	High Status	Low Status
Uruguay	Engineering Law Dentistry	Humanities Economics Veterinary
Colombia	Architecture Humanities Engineering	Education Law Exact science
Puerto Rico	Medicine Law	Education Engineering
Mexico	Medicine Philosophy Science	Economics Law Engineering
Panama	Medicine	Humanities Science
Paraguay	Architecture Engineering	Dentistry Social service Economics

their important positions in the hands of family members.[79] Those in government are not as able as businessmen to allocate employment to relatives. If governments were to try to restrict employment in this manner, they would run a high risk of revolution. The government, in its employment policies, has to pay attention to nonascriptive factors such as party loyalty and expertise.[80] Therefore, it seems likely that there should be a difference in the social class patterns of private and government employment. Because of their family background and contacts, students of higher status would appear to be more likely than lower-status students to gain access to the business world. Students from backgrounds of lower status, experiencing intergenerational social mobility and thus less reliant upon their families for important positions in business, should be comparatively more likely to avail themselves of channels of mobility that are relatively more open, namely, the government.

The data support the contention regarding differential recruitment or selectivity by class for government and business employment. In every country (except Uruguay where the question was not asked) there was a linear relation-

Table 5. Percentages of students planning careers in government and business by social status and by country[a]

Country and career		Social Status		
		Low	Middle	High
Paraguay				
	Government	39	30	11
	Business	61	70	89
	N	(236)	(106)	(66)
Panama				
	Government	66	56	43
	Business	34	44	57
	N	(658)	(193)	(56)
Mexico				
	Government	37	35	28
	Business	63	65	72
	N	(334)	(196)	(160)
Puerto Rico				
	Government	67	48	38
	Business	33	52	62
	N	(220)	(145)	(143)
Colombia				
	Government	38	25	17
	Business	62	75	83
	N	(384)	(443)	(515)

[a]Question regarding employment was not asked in Uruguay.

ship between class and nature of employment. The lower the status of the student, the more likely he was to plan to work for the government and, conversely, the higher the status background of the student, the more likely he was to be planning a career in business. Upwardly mobile students from the lower strata hope to avail themselves of employment opportunities in government.

To what extent is sex a determinant of career choice? It is generally felt that women disproportionately select or are disproportionately recruited to certain career fields. Specifically, humanities and education are often thought of as the fields most likely to be chosen by female university students. This is true for the United States and for many other countries as well.[81] In Latin America this is also the case, as women are overrepresented in these fields. A close third choice, however, is pharmacy. In every major Latin American university, including the University of Puerto Rico, pharmacy ranks close to education and humanities in the percentages of females in the field, and in most of the major universities the majority of the students in pharmacy are women. Dentistry is the next most popular field.

What accounts for the overrepresentation of women in pharmacy and dentistry? Unfortunately, the nature of the data, either from official government sources or social science surveys, precludes an analysis along these lines. One could, however, hypothesize that these two fields might be considered in the purview of women because of their "helping" characteristics and could thus be considered in the same dimension as nursing. One might also argue that in neither dentistry nor pharmacy is the female incumbent likely to be able to wield "undue" authority over men. One could also contend that pharmacy and dentistry are available to women because men have channeled their attention to the older and more traditional status-conferring fields of medicine, law, architecture, business, and engineering and are reluctant to forsake status ambitions associated with these professions for other and newer fields even when the employment prospects might be better.

3 University Problems and Students' Attitudes Toward Higher Education

Many planners and social scientists concerned with Latin America and other developing regions define education as a central component of modernization. As industries are planned and as services are mapped, the need for skilled manpower becomes ever more significant. Notwithstanding the debate over the relative importance of investing in primary, secondary, or higher education, there can be no doubt that developing countries desperately need the contributions of citizens trained in medicine, teaching, physical science, engineering, administration, and the social sciences.[1] These professionals have a major responsibility in leading their countries in building industrial plants, in training citizens to operate them, in providing for the health and other needs of expanding urban centers, and in broadening current knowledge by engaging in research. This chapter will emphasize the possibilities and problems involved in training these professionals by analyzing the attitudes of the student respondents toward the type and quality of their educational experience and by exploring the impact of the structure of the university on this experience. The focus will be on the education and professional socialization of young adults within the Latin American university setting.

In developing societies professional socialization is particularly complicated, for university education often is provided in an institutional environment where both traditional and modern norms toward professional work exist. Administrators, professors, and students oriented toward modern definitions of the function of the university are constantly challenged by powerful contemporaries who are committed to a more traditional approach. In such instances there is no one set of professional norms to which the student can easily relate. Uncertainty shrouds the outcome of the contemporary university struggle as the new view of professional education is not yet completely accepted and not always rewarded.[2]

STRUCTURAL PROBLEMS OF THE UNIVERSITY

The organizational structure of the Latin American university, generally rooted in the past, often impedes educational innovations and contributes to the dissipation and maldistribution of scarce educational resources. One of the university's most serious organizational problems has been the relative independence of the various component faculties or schools. Despite the existence of a single rector and governing bodies drawn from representatives of all the faculties, many Latin American universities are poorly integrated institutions. Loyalties of staff and students are generally restricted to their particular schools, which lead to conflicts over the allocation of institutional resources as well as other issues. Quality education and efficient use of limited funds become the major casualties in such struggles.

Both educational quality and resources are debilitated by the fragmentation and duplication that stem from another aspect of this state of affairs. Students in one school rarely take courses in another school within the same university or, if they do, cannot receive credit for them. Professors teach only in their own separate schools. Regardless of the importance or universality of a particular course, it is taught only in one school with enrollment limited to the students of that school, even if it is virtually identical to courses offered in other faculties. Thus, for example, there may be several basic mathematics or chemistry courses offered in different schools of the same university. The sparse communication between the professors and the students teaching or enrolled in courses in the same or even identical subject matter further compounds this negative situation. While there have been some attempts made in recent years to alleviate certain aspects of this fragmentation and duplication, these have been met with great resistance. One informed observer, commenting on the prevailing structural malintegration of the Latin American universities, stated: "This leads to a proliferation of undernourished departments and to a useless multiplication of labor and expense. Efforts toward unification are viewed with suspicion as an infringement on acquired privileges."[3]

The situation at the school or *facultad* level in many ways parallels that of the entire university. The basic unit within the facultad is the *cátedra* or chair, which is somewhat analogous to a department in a North American university. Each *catedrático* or chair holding professor has the responsibility for one major subject area. Any other person holding an academic appointment in this area, from associate professor to lab assistant, works under his supervision. Their careers are dependent upon him. The catedrático decides which courses in his area shall be taught as well as their content.

Traditionally, there were few, if any limitations on the power of the catedrático. After passing a competitive examination for his chair and then confirmed in an election by the governing board of the university, he would be assured of his position until his retirement. Once ensconced in his chair, his position was that of a sovereign ruler. No one could officially challenge his academic performance or his competency. This lack of accountability often led to abuses of the system by the professors. It has been a cardinal demand of student reformers that catedráticos be periodically reconfirmed in their positions so as to motivate the chair holders to perform their academic tasks conscientiously.

The autonomy and sovereignty of the chair has come under increasing attack in recent years as others beside the students have become aware of and concerned about the abuses engendered by the situation. In a number of countries and in various universities, life tenure has been abolished. In its stead, professors are appointed to fixed terms of office subject to reappointment after consideration of their performance and achievements. In addition, there have been numerous attempts to weaken the power of the catedrático and systematically integrate educational endeavors in a field through the establishment of a departmental system modeled after that of the North American universities. However, the autonomy of the chair still persists, albeit in a more limited form than in the past, and it has even managed to maintain itself within newly organized departmental structures. The catedráticos historically have been resourceful in resisting structural or curricular changes or reforms which they have interpreted as challenging their prerogatives.[4]

Another associated problem derives from the administration of the university. Latin American universities function, for the most part, without trained or professional administrators. Rectors, the chief executive officers of the universities, are usually drawn from the ranks of the professoriate, but their terms are generally short as many in the university community are fearful that the rectors will establish independent bases of power. Most of the administrative burden is carried by professors, often in addition to their professorial duties. Latin American universities have grown too large and too complex to be effectively administered by a part time or constantly revolving administrative staff lacking appropriate training in administration.[5]

Compounding and exacerbating all of these structural problems is the chronic problem of the inadequate financing of the universities. Almost all universities in Latin America, public and private, are dependent in varying degrees on the public purse. The support from this source is rarely sufficient to operate an efficient, large, complex institution of higher education capable of undertaking meaningful and innovative research and public service programs in a variety of fields. The problems of the universities, however, transcend the monetary shortage. Even with substantial funding, such problems as the basic structure of the university, the cátedra system, and an inadequately trained and revolving administrative staff would still remain. These structural difficulties reflect basic tensions concerning the definition and the mission of the Latin American universities. Significant forces in and out of the universities are supportive of the traditional model and resist changes designed to modernize or to democratize these institutions.

Reforms and changes, however, are taking place in the institutions of higher education in Latin America. There are now a variety of groups and strata, including an expanding and more educated middle class, which realize that the development of modern, complex, and self-sustaining economies and societies are closely related to the organization of more modern and instrumentally oriented universities. Even among these more modernizing forces, however, there is no clear consensus about the structure and mission of the universities. Invariably the struggles of all of these varying groups enter into the political arena, becoming linked to governmental policies as well as to different partisan groups and ideologies. As a result of all these different levels of conflicts present in, as well as interjected into the universities, these institutions lack stability and the various reforms and modifications that do occur are often piecemeal, unsystematic, and not firmly established. Naturally, such an environment has a significant impact upon the nature and quality of the education the students receive as well as upon their attitudes and values concerning their education and future professional roles.

THE EDUCATION OF UNIVERSITY STUDENTS

The education of students in Latin American universities varies by university and facultad. The educational process can be conceptualized along a continuum from modern to traditional. At the modern end, the students are involved in a process of professional socialization in which, according to one researcher, "The first task [is] . . . the transformation of the lay conception of the outsider into the technical orientations of the insider . . . this transformation [is accomplished] by emphasizing the mastery of technical skills and knowledge as a prerequisite for professional status."[6] At the traditional end of the continuum, the students experience attenuated demands to master professional knowledge, and there is a lack of opportunity and facilities to implement newly acquired professional skills. Instead of emphasis on the acquisition of knowledge and the practice of tasks, these students are exposed to a learning process which merely emphasizes the ritualistic aspects of education. Under such conditions, they enroll in prescribed courses which they may possibly never attend, take examinations requiring rote memorization, and spend a certain amount of years *in* the university without really ever being part *of* it. An increasing number of professors, institutes, and universities have adopted a more modern and instrumentalist approach to education as opposed to the more traditional and symbolic orientations. However, low standards and traditional values and methods still appear to be prevalent throughout Latin America.[7]

Many observers and commentators have placed a large part of the responsibility for this state of affairs upon the students. They are portrayed in the most sweeping terms as ritualists, uninterested in quality education and unconcerned with acquiring meaningful professional skills. In fact, they are characterized as being the major obstacle to genuine reform and modernization of their universities. One of the foremost proponents of this position, Rudolph Atcon, has argued:

[He] . . . is by no means interested in *real learning*. The university to him is but an obstacle course of anywhere from five to seven years, excluding repetitions, which society has placed between him and the title. Once he has become a "doctor" — especially if fortunate enough to make it as a "medical doctor" — he has become a count or baron in the new social order. Whether he also knows something about medicine is quite beside the point, just as it would have been for the medieval baron. Because chances are anyway that many of these doctors never will practice their profession. Those who do, will just have to learn things as they go along, or go abroad for further study . . . . students no longer consider the university a place to study but only a mere place to be. They are not at the university to acquire knowledge, to receive discipline and to be educated academically, scientifically and civically . . . Like all children, they abhor discipline and dislike effort."[8]

This contention, however, and others similar to it are not supported by most of the recent research on Latin American students. In Chile, a survey of four diverse careers in 1964 found that the majority of students studying medicine, engineering, history, and science designated the acquisition of professional knowledge as the most important aspect of a university education. The percentage of students taking this position ranged from slightly more than half in the school for secondary school teachers of history to 80 percent in the highly innovative Institute of Science. The percentage whose primary desire was simply to acquire a degree was appreciably smaller. In science, none of the thirty respondents placed the primary emphasis on the degree. In the three other careers studied, less than 10 percent felt that merely acquiring the degree was most important; student responses to a variety of other questions consistently supported these findings.[9]

In the course of a similar investigation in Argentina, also conducted in the mid-1960s, David Nasatir found that almost half of a sample (43 percent) of students enrolled at the University of Buenos Aires stated that the most important reason for seeking a higher education was to obtain professional training and to develop abilities directly applicable to a career.[10] This result compared quite favorably, Nasatir observed, with the responses of a sample of North American students. Among the latter, 36 percent emphasized the simple acquisition of a degree.[11] Only 23 percent of the Argentine students indicated the same motivation.

A study Kalman Silvert conducted in the late 1950s found that Argentine students were concerned with both the instrumental and innovative aspects of their professional training. In medicine two-thirds of the students were preoccupied with the practical and vocational aspects of their education. These students also tended to be both upwardly mobile and among those who were most concerned with modernization. Silvert reported similar findings in his studies in the fields of economics and the exact sciences: "It is only reasonable that technological change, the necessity for a high degree of specialization, and emphasis on economic development should lead modernizing Argentines to insist upon improvement of vocational training at the university level, even if at the apparent expense of some cherished notions of the popular university."[12]

These studies are supported by E. Wight Bakke's research on Colombian and Mexican students. "In the cases of all the students I interviewed the motivation to realize this vocational aspect of the image of the student was high; indeed it was clearly, for many and perhaps a majority, their primary motivation."[13]

The student responses in our own comparative study confirm these findings. As indicated in Table 6, in every case, except Puerto Rico, more than 80 percent of the respondents indicated that the most important function of a university education was to prepare students for a professional life. Although, given the structure of university education, the intense emphasis on professional training might have been predicted, the significance of these findings was reinforced by student responses to other questions.

When asked what single major change in the university they would advocate, the students in our sample proved especially interested in introducing a greater variety of courses geared to the practical application of their skills (Table 7). In three of the five cases — Mexico, Colombia, and Puerto Rico — more students

Table 6. Percentages of students indicating a particular function of the university as most important

Function of university	Colombia	Mexico	Puerto Rico	Panama	Uruguay	Paraguay
Provide general education	11	9	37	13	18	19
Prepare student for professional life	85	87	61	84	82	81
Reject[a]	4	4	2	3	_[b]	–
Total	100 (1495)	100 (830)	100 (577)	100 (1027)	100 (469)	100 (417)

[a]Respondent did not answer question.
[b]_ indicates less than 0.5 percent.

expressed a desire for an increase in practical courses than for any other change. In Panama and Paraguay, where students' primary attention focused on the lack of facilities, more practical training ranked as the second most frequent response. Many other respondents in Mexico, Colombia, and Puerto Rico were most concerned about the dearth of libraries and laboratories which plagued their schools. Student emphasis on the need to reorient courses directly toward practical application and to improve educational facilities indicated the type of concern most prevalent among the majority of Latin American university students.

Many students seemed to be aware that the professional skills they sought depended upon thorough training. They were obviously critical of traditional "prefabricated instruction" and were demanding that more time, money, and resources go into instrumentally-oriented education. It is highly significant that such factors as greater participation in university government or the necessity for more academic freedom, which many observers believe are the major concerns of these students, received relatively little attention. Modification of curriculum and improvement of facilities seemed at least as important to the students as they are to other critics of university education in Latin America.[14]

This observation is readily suppported by previous Chilean research. When asked to specify the major problems of the school, as many as half of the respondents in a given school criticized the degree or quality of student politics. Many students were obviously chagrined that political concerns, often instigated

Table 7. Percentages of students indicating a particular change in the university as most important[a]

Change	Colombia	Mexico	Puerto Rico	Panama	Paraguay
Improve recreational facilities (cultural sport)	9	3	5	4	11
Improve educational facilities (labs and libraries)	23	23	19	25	51
More courses oriented to practical application	30	42	33	15	22
More academic freedom	5	3	3	6	4
More student participation in school and university government	8	5	24	4	12
Improve social services	0	0	0	13	0
Establish university press and radio	0	0	0	3	0
Reject	25	24	16	30	0
Total	100 (1495)	100 (830)	100 (577)	100 (1027)	100 (417)

[a]Questions not asked in Uruguay.

by nonuniversity events, had such a direct and devastating effect on their studies. The majority of the students in every career sampled felt that commitment to instrumental and innovative professional endeavors would make a more important contribution than would involvement with political activities geared toward achieving more immediate results.[15]

The Impact of Career Choice

Engineering, science, medicine, and education students in our six nation study generally tended to be oriented toward the educational and practical aspects of their role. A greater degree of interest in nonacademic matters was found among law and social science students. It appears, as Glaucio Soares has observed, that students preparing for technical fields were quicker to develop a more specialized role-definition. In contrast, their peers in the humanistic fields had a more amorphous definition of their future roles.[16]

Student responses were, no doubt, affected by the stage of national development and the prestige of a particular career in a given nation. The more highly developed the country, the greater is the degree of occupational specialization and the more intense the pressure to increase pre-employment training so as to insure a steady flow of practitioners able to maintain the ever-rising standards of professional importance. As Silvert has argued,

the needs of Latin America's new industries have already impelled curricular revision and expansion in many Latin American universities in such fields as business administration and the sciences. But at least as important have been the effects of governmental commitments to partially planned procedures of economic growth, which are now given formal approval as an announced requirement of the Alliance for Progress, but which have been a long-standing administrative practice in such countries as Uruguay, Costa Rica, Mexico, and Chile. Economic planning has naturally force-fed the growth of faculties and departments of economics, but has also been felt in engineering, sociology, and public administration.[17]

The Impact of "Year"

In all the countries surveyed, students in the upper years indicated the greatest concern with improving the practical application of their learning (Table 8). Students in the earlier stages of their university careers were somewhat less interested in this. Because of the very high dropout rates of students in institutions of higher education in Latin America, propositions about the effect of length of time spent in the university must be made with great caution. It is not possible to know whether the surviving students had special characteristics which from the start separated them from their less successful peers.

Table 8. Percentages of students in different years in the university desiring professional changes

Country[a]	1st–2nd year	3rd–4th year	5th–7th year
Colombia	69	72	88
Mexico	81	90	96
Puerto Rico	59	57	72
Panama	54	62	63
Paraguay	63	81	86

[a]Question not asked Uruguay.

It is clear, however, that students in their more advanced years knew that it was only a matter of time before they attained the credentials necessary for professional practice. They had faced and overcome major problems in their university training. As they prepared to leave the university, the students – quite normally – expressed concern about the quality of their professional competence.

THE QUALITY OF HIGHER EDUCATION

The issue of the quality of higher education in Latin America is neither new nor unique to that hemisphere. Latin Americans, especially the students, have long been concerned about this problem. By the latter part of the colonial era, it became evident that the universities were not functioning effectively as genuine learning institutions. In 1786 the University of San Fulgencio in Quito, Ecuador was closed for academic inefficiency. Concern over the problem of educational quality persisted after independence. The Royal and Pontifical University of Mexico, one of the oldest universities in the region, was closed from 1865 to 1910, in part because of its shallow educational standards. The growth and spread of the University Reform Movement, as pointed out earlier, was largely inspired by the low educational standards of the universities throughout the hemisphere. During the depression and the era of dictators, academic quality in the institutions of higher education suffered. In the post-World War II decades, efforts were made to study and to deal with the task of upgrading the universities. Official university and governmental bodies continually cited the pressing need to improve the standards of learning in higher education. The problem of the lack of quality education is, in the 1960s and early 1970s, a hemispheric one, troubling societies at all levels of socioeconomic development.[18] One gross measure of the problem is the high student dropout rate. Between 50 to 80 percent of the students in Argentina, Colombia, Chile, Mexico, Uruguay, and Puerto Rico do not complete their university studies.[19] These rates are especially disturbing given the fact that so few in the hemisphere are even able to qualify for admission to the universities.

The general description of the university situation in Peru offered by R. Ames Cobián can be considered as illustrative of the problems of universities throughout the region. "Our university exists, in reality, virtually isolated from its inherent purpose. The professionals that it trains receive, in the greatest number of cases, a mediocre technical preparation and an insignificant cultural orientation. Research is hardly carried on. The exercise of memory instead of intelligence is promoted."[20]

Facilities and Curricula

The inadequacy of research, learning, and teaching facilities in the Latin American universities has been a characteristic for centures. One of the basic reasons for this state of affairs is the lack of sufficient funds to operate and maintain universities with adequate or above adequate standards. Libraries in contemporary universities, with a few notable exceptions, are inadequate for both research and learning purposes. In terms of both quantity and quality of available books and journals, students and professors are deprived of a vital mainstay of an institution of higher learning. Laboratories as well as other research, teaching, and learning facilities are also in short supply or when available are often poorly equipped or maintained. Many universities and institutes must rely on funds from foreign governments and foundations for needed equipment.[21]

In addition to a shortage of facilities and resources, the universities lack other vital components necessary to function as effective institutions of higher education. There is a dearth of proper counselling for students throughout the hemisphere. David Nasatir has observed that at one of the better universities in the region, the University of Buenos Aires, incoming students often experienced a sense of disorientation upon entering a large and impersonal facultad.[22] This feeling was an important contributing factor in the extremely high dropout rate in Argentine universities. It is worth pointing out that the School of Engineering at the University of Chile, which had an extremely high failure and dropout rate despite stringent admissions requirements, instituted a new program in 1965 whereby each fifty students were assigned to a faculty counselor. It was hoped that student problems would in this way be overcome before they were manifested in failure to complete the six-year training program.[23]

William Knowles, writing about Puerto Rico, has observed that deficiencies in the counseling procedure have resulted in a lack of correlation between university output and the demands of the labor market. He believed that proper counselling could reduce the imbalance in the output for the various careers.[24] This imbalance, nonetheless, continues to be a primary characteristic of all Latin American countries.

The curricula of Latin American universities has attracted much critical comment. Most universities, facultades, and courses are oriented to traditional subject matter. As previously noted, the universities generally continue to have as their central function the preparation of students for the liberal professions. In addition, education within the facultades tends to be restricted in scope, emphasizing professional aspects of the particular field. Students graduate from the universities with little exposure to a general or a liberal arts education.

Ameliorative steps are being taken to deal with these curricula and curricula-related problems. More scientific and technical courses are being added to the offerings of various universities. New schools with such orientations are being founded, either as separate entities or as parts of existing universities, while already functioning technical and scientific schools and institutes are attracting more support. Oriente University in Venezuela, the National Polytechnical Institute and the Institute of Technological and Higher Studies of Monterrey in Mexico, the Universities of America, Gran Colombia, and Bogotá and the Andes in Colombia as well as the University of Havana, as discussed earlier, represent examples of these developments.

Other reforms have been aimed at strengthening the liberal arts aspect of higher education and the avoidance of duplication of courses. Various universities, such as the Technological Institute of Monterrey and the University of Puerto Rico, have schools of general studies in which all incoming students are enrolled prior to entering their professional schools. At the University of the Andes, students are also required to take liberal arts courses in the Faculty of Arts and Sciences upon admission, and even when pursuing professional education they continue to take such courses. The Faculty of Arts and Science is not another separate school as is the case at other universities. It provides a common link among students from all fields and, in addition, provides services to other schools within the University of the Andes. Many other universities throughout the continent have established *Escuelas de Idiomas* or language schools in which students from various faculties are enrolled. Similar models are being instituted with basic science courses. The University of Concepción in Chile leads the way in this respect.

In Central America, five small nations have established the Consejo Superior Universitario Centroamericano, the High Council of Central American Universities (CSUCA), in large part, as an attempt to centralize their resources, liberalize the curricula within their universities, and avoid unnecessary duplication. The CSUCA has proposed the institutionalization of a two year general studies program prior to specialization as well as a system which will allow a certain number of electives. Another innovation introduced by several Latin American universities is the credit system. Under this plan students would not have to take all required courses or electives within their own schools. Instead, each course would be assigned a certain amount of points and students could obtain their degrees by amassing a specified number of credits within a structure established by the university. Overall, despite these various changes, reforms and attempts at modernization, traditional curricula and approaches still predominate throughout the institutions of higher education in Latin America.[25]

The Impact of Nonuniversity Factors

The situation has been complicated by political and social factors which influence the distribution of resources, the extent of academic freedom, and the creation of a relatively stable working environment. The interdependence of major social institutions has been nowhere better illustrated than in the attempt to establish new institutes of training for new careers which can contribute to national development.

The history of the Institute of Science at the University of Chile and the development of the exact sciences in Argentina and Brazil can serve as case studies indicating the tremendous problems inherent in attempts to create new and needed specialists in even the more advanced nations of Latin America. There are substantial numbers of professors and students who are committed to pioneering in new fields. A close examination of their efforts demonstrates both support for and resistance to changing professional role-definitions.

The Institute of Science at the University of Chile was established in the early 1960s to train undergraduates in modern physics, biology, chemistry, and mathematics. Professionals trained in the new Institute of Science would, it was hoped, augment the nation's small core of qualified scientists and pass their skills on to others so as to modernize the teaching of science at all levels of the educational system. In addition, it was predicted that the research they would undertake could contribute to the nation's industrialization process.

The majority of the staff of the Institute was full time, and many of the professors had received doctorates in the United States and England. These men were cosmopolitan in their outlook and identified strongly with the goals and values of the international scientific community. While many could have taken lucrative and prestigious positions abroad, they chose instead to help develop Chilean science. Their attempts to realize this goal were given the strongest support in the national press and in the reports of various government agencies. Most Chilean educators knew that their students suffered from poor science and mathematics instruction in the secondary schools. Deficiencies in preuniversity preparation presented severe problems to those who went on to study in the sciences and related technical fields. In the School of Engineering, for example, high failure and repeat rates have often been attributed to such inadequate preparation.

Widespread verbal recognition and apparent encouragement of scientific progress, however, obscured the tremendous problems encountered in this pioneering effort. The scientists suffered, as did other Chilean full-time professors, from relatively poor salaries and from the chronic financial insecurity resulting from serious inflation. Furthermore, expensive equipment was not easily acquired and high-level scientific research and training were often impeded by the meager resources provided for the university and particularly for the Institute of Science. Direct grants from international agencies were resisted by university officials who were committed to controlling distribution of funds to various faculties. The Institute was relatively powerless in influencing budget decisions and in attracting favors from the university administration. The scientists found it difficult to compete with their colleagues from the traditional and better endowed faculties of medicine and engineering.

These difficulties resulted in a near crisis in the mid-sixties, when the Institute failed to acquire desperately needed equipment. A direct grant had been offered to it by a North American foundation but was rejected by university officials. As a result, a number of science professors reluctantly gave very serious consideration to leaving the country and eventually did so. Others felt it a national and professional duty to remain in Chile to lead the struggle to educate the needed scientists. They refused to be forced out of the university and were determined to seek a more equitable share of the limited resources available to the various faculties.

The inadequate support for new scientific careers was aggravated by a lack of appreciation of the usefulness of advanced scientific research in national development. In spite of favorable newspaper coverage, many Chileans, including those in high university circles, strongly questioned the value of basic scientific research to the country. They believe that a nation with so many fundamental problems could not afford the long-term investment necessary to support advanced scientific investigation. In addition, Chilean industrialists who often held a monopoly in the market, did not encourage the application of scientific discoveries to their production problems.

The obstacles of pursuing a scientific career made it difficult to recruit desirable students to the Institute. Those well trained in mathematics were reluctant to risk their professional futures in uncharted waters when they were able to enter the established and prestigious engineering profession. Indeed, the Institute's professors continually cautioned both incoming and advanced students about the problems and challenges of working in a new career. Training for frustration and flexibility was an integral part of science education at the Institute.[26]

These problems have not been confined to Chile. One eminent Brazilian scientist has, for example, indicated that poor resources, both financial and moral, have led to a situation in which, "any junior scientist who achieves distinction will seek and find appointment under preferable conditions in the United States."[27] These difficulties are further aggravated by political instability. One observer has stated that "certainly it is difficult for a public university in Latin America to attain a much higher level of stability than the society and government of which it is a part."[28]

Unstable as well as politically oppressive environments are not conducive to the development of knowledge and the proper functioning of professors and universities. This is especially true in the case of dictatorships. These governments make the university community a special object of their attention which generally results in negative, if not disastrous, consequences for quality education. In Paraguay, after the rise to power of General Alfredo Stroessner in 1954, the University of Paraguay was thoroughly purged, and political criteria were made dominant in the selection and retention of faculty members and administrative staff.[29]

Argentina has also experienced severe political intervention in the affairs of its universities. In 1946, shortly after General Juan Perón became president, he assumed personal control of all of Argentina's universities. The Peronists then purged these universities of more than 70 percent of their faculty. Others were forced into early retirement or resigned in protest or because they were unable to function in such an environment. The men who left their positions due to the intervention of Perón were among the finest scholars of Argentina and Latin America. In their stead, professors were appointed primarily on the basis of their loyalty to the regime.[30]

After the overthrow of the Perón regime in 1955, university autonomy was restored, academically qualified professors returned or were recruited, and the universities began once again to function as true centers of education. In 1966, unfortunately, the situation appeared to revert back to that of 1946. The new military dictator, General Juan Carlos Onganía, came to power in June 1966 and by the end of July, a month later, university autonomy was revoked and purges of faculty members began anew. For more than a few, this represented the second time in twenty years that they had been politically fired.

In the process of ending autonomy and intervening in the universities, the Faculty of Exact and Natural Sciences of the University of Buenos Aires appeared to be selected for special consideration. A day after the decree ending university autonomy was promulgated, police entered the building housing this Faculty in force and brutally attacked unarmed teachers and students. No quarter was given because of age, sex, or scholarly reputation. Severe wounds were inflicted, as the victims, including a visiting professor from the Massachusetts Institute of Technology, were first struck at random and then forced to run a police gauntlet.

By the end of the summer more than two-thirds of the professors had resigned from the faculty. This figure eventually rose to over 90 percent. Since most of these men had held full-time positions in the university, they were in difficult economic straits, and a special committee of North American professors was established to help them find jobs outside Argentina.[31] The consequent mass emigration of physical and natural scientists from Argentina left numerous students without guidance in their training.

In Brazil, the military dictatorship of Humberto Castelo Branco came to power in April 1964 and immediately proceeded to intervene in the universities. The regime issued an *Acto Institucional* which allowed for the dismissal or detention of all state employees, including professors, subject to the judgment of investigatory commissions established by the armed forces. Among those dismissed by these commissions were scientists, research workers, professors, and teachers. Many scholars were imprisoned or physically abused; others were interrogated. The apprehension and panic which ensued led a number of trained researchers and scholars to seek employment abroad. Forty-two professors or research workers in physics, chemistry, sociology, economics, medicine, and other fields left by the end of the year. Twenty who were abroad decided to remain out of the country. By December 1964 approximately 31 university teachers had been dismissed or "retired," and about 130 intellectuals were known to be in prison. Others declared that their research was no longer free but directed and censored by political considerations. This situation has persisted into the 1970s. In April 1970 Brazilian science suffered a particularly severe setback as 10 distinguished scientists were dismissed, by order of the government, from the Oswaldo Cruz Institute, Brazil's oldest and most respected research laboratory. In addition to the actions of the government, local animosities and unauthorized decisions by institutional or area "hard-liners" produced "purges" in various institutions of higher education throughout Brazil. In general, social and political instability as well as repression have led to fear, emigration of trained and experienced personnel, and a general decline in the quality of education within the universities.[32]

The Quality of Instruction

At the heart of the learning enterprise is the quality of the instruction. In the Latin American universities, the ability of the professors and the instruction they offer has been perhaps the most often criticized aspect of the education system. This is a crucial problem with many dimensions. Until it is adequately dealt with, it will inhibit the development of the universities and the nations of Latin America.

One important part of the overall issue is the problem of recruiting capable persons to the field of university teaching. Inadequate funds for salaries are an obstacle in attracting talented individuals to the profession. Generally, a position as university instructor is not sufficient to support a person desiring to maintain a moderate, middle-class standard of living.[33] Thus, if a professional desires to teach in a university, he must hold more than one job. From the time of their origin, as already pointed out in chapter 1, universities in Latin America have relied on outside personnel. These were clerics, judges, government officials, and professionals who gave a few hours of their time in order to teach and, in return, received little pay but much social prestige. Unfortunately, this pattern is still in existence in Latin America.

Part-time teaching is very much the rule rather than the exception throughout the hemisphere. Chile and Colombia have the highest percentage of full time teaching staffs in Latin America, 37 percent. At the National University of Colombia 28 percent are considered as being full-time. Venezuela, Panama, and Peru follow with roughly one quarter of their teaching personnel working full time. At the University of Buenos Aires only 10 percent of the academic staff carry a complete load. At Mexico's National University, 3 percent of the teaching staff work full-time while 94 percent are hired on an hourly basis. At the National University of Asunción in Paraguay, the comparable percentages are 1 and 96 percent respectively.[34]

The extensive use of these part-time professors, in lieu of a full-time, adequately compensated professorial staff, is generally regarded as a savings mechanism. However, it is costly in terms of educational consequences. These part-time professors, as well as the considerable number of full-time professors forced to hold more than one job, have little time or incentive to engage in research or even to keep abreast of developments within their field. Many are forced to rely on old lecture notes, which are read and reread to classes of bored students year after year. In addition, this system is costly to the education of the students in that it deprives them of meaningful interaction with their professors.

The problem has become more intense in the decades after World War II with the large increase in student enrollments. Governments have found it easier to accede to the demand for more student positions in the universities than for more staff positions. While the number of teachers and teaching positions has increased, it has not kept up with the growth of the student bodies. In some instances, young instructors often teach on a voluntary basis for several years before money is available to compensate them.[35] E. Wight Bakke gives us a profile of the part-time professor:

The symbolic word as to the inadequacy of instructors is "taxi professor." The content of this concept suggests a lecturer who is a professor in name only, carrying on jobs outside the university, who seeks a bit of additional income and the prestige of a university connection by teaching one or more courses. In the midst of his preoccupation with many concerns he suddenly remembers it is time for his lecture, hops into a taxi, rushes to the university, delivers his lecture, and rushes back to his "real" job. Or he may not, and frequently does not, show up at all. Of course he is delighted when the students go on strike, for then he has a good excuse for not coming to class. When he does come, he is poorly prepared.[36]

This part-time and multiple-job-holding system not only debilitates the quality of instruction and research but has negative ramifications for the entire functioning of the universities.

The limited time and energy which professors are able to devote to teaching and research are reduced by other university responsibilities. An inordinate burden of administrative responsibilities, as pointed out above, falls upon their shoulders due to the general absence of a professional administrative staff. The continuing tradition of oral examinations also makes serious inroads into the time of the professors without meaningfully contributing to anyone's educational development. Usually three professors are expected to examine each student orally in each course, a process which can continue for extended periods throughout the academic year.[37]

The poor compensation of professors is not the sole root of the problem in recruiting talented persons. For the most part there continues to be no well-defined path to a career as a university teacher or researcher. Structurally, in terms of quality recruitment, this places the field of university teaching in a poor competitive position vis-à-vis the more established professions.

The idea of establishing institutions specifically geared for the training of professors and the furthering of research, such as the North American graduate schools, has received a growing amount of attention throughout the hemisphere. Such a concept was initially proposed on a hemispheric basis by Bolivia in a graduate College of the Americas. However, virtually all countries and universities concerned with improving the quality of their professoriate generally send their more promising staff or prospective staff to graduate schools abroad, usually in the United States.[38]

This system also has its drawbacks which are increasingly becoming clear to concerned scholars, students, and government officials. First, it still does not solve the problem of institutionalizing visible and available paths to a university career. Secondly, it is costly. It would be much cheaper to train personnel at home or in a regional graduate institution. Thirdly, sending present and future staff abroad for advanced training increases Latin America's dependence on foreign countries such as the United States. The education these scholars receive is largely formed by non-Latin American orientations and values. Finally, some students choose not to return to their native countries upon completion of their studies.

There is another dimension to the problem of the university teachers in Latin America that transcends scarce resources and low salaries. The Latin American professor has been subject to an increasing amount of strain and tension. Prior to World War II, but even more so earlier, the professor had a clearly defined role and was usually well integrated into the social structure. Generally, as a member of the traditional elite or able to at least comfortably identify with this strata, he had secure status. Given the context of an elite student body, the persistence and dominance of traditional values within the society, and the limited demands made upon the university and its staff, the university professor was firmly anchored in his institution and society.

The situation began to change around World War I but especially after World War II. Modernizing and increasingly complex societies and burgeoning middle classes made more and more demands upon the universities. These institutions of higher education were called upon to reorganize and orient themselves to problems of national growth and development. The universities and the professors were disturbed by these changes and demands and tended to hold on to the traditions and procedures of the past for as long as possible.

Professors, particularly in the post World War II era, appeared to be drawn increasingly from the expanding middle class. They also found it more difficult to obtain actual or indirect status from traditional elites. The promised rewards associated with a new and changing situation were not forthcoming, as neither universities nor governments concerned themselves with securing appropriate compensation or facilities for their staff.

The well-ordered world of the university progressively changed during this period into a place of conflict. Students demanded greater competence from their professors and the right to participate in the hiring and firing process. They and their allies outside the university demanded that the university change and expand its functions. Vested interests inside the universities allied with powerful outside forces resisted, and continual battles ensued. The universities became the arenas for the struggles among various social, economic, and political forces.

Bereft of traditional anchors and clear guidelines and confronted by a mal-integrated and in many ways structurally archaic institutional setting, it became ever more difficult for professors to concentrate on teaching or research. Personality conflicts, collegial squabbles, and other petty difficulties mushroomed into crises. Students and nonuniversity groups, particularly political ones, in turn, played on these uncertainties for their own supposed benefit. The scarcity of available university positions meant that these tensions and conflicts grew in intensity, as few could find alternative sources of employment. Professors in such climates and environments were unsure of which paths to pursue. Some, particularly the catedráticos, tenaciously held onto and fought for their traditional powers and prerogatives. Others, especially the younger and better trained professors, risked villification from various quarters to innovate, modernize, and improve their universities.[39] As one social scientist expressed it:

The initiative for placing an emphasis on curriculum and quality in higher education has come largely from exceptionally talented younger men, most of whom received part of their professional training abroad. Perhaps those in medicine, engineering, and the sciences have been most in evidence, but there have been leaders, also, whose own professional interests are in economics, philosophy, sociology, drama, and music. For the most part, they have operated as individuals working within the framework of one university or, even more typically, a particular faculty. They have, in some cases, been reponsible for the organization of completely new universities. They have, in exceptional instances, taken the lead in establishing national organizations for devising and financially supporting higher levels of university instruction.[40]

Student Evaluation of Their Education

While Latin American professors have been criticized for their lack of commitment to students, there is as yet little empirical data revealing how the students actually evaluate their professors. It is difficult, at this stage in the history of the Latin American university, to draw up a picture of the students' conception of the ideal professor. Many students in the 1960s still cherished the notion of their teacher as a philosopher-intellectual. Other students were more prone to talk of the scientist, or dedicated professional, who produces and publishes, and also trains a future generation to compete in the modern world. The existence of these two antithetical ideals manifested itself not only in the power struggles between traditional catedráticos and young full-time professors, but also in the ambivalence and contradictions in the students' attitudes toward

Table 9. Percentages of students indicating a particular quality in university
professors as most important

Quality	Colombia	Mexico	Puerto Rico	Panama	Uruguay	Paraguay
Be good lecturer	52	64	89	51	65	61
Know material well	25	26	8	27	28	31
Be a good researcher	18	4	1	17	6	8
Reject	5	6	2	6	2	0
Total	100	100	100	101	101	100
	(1495)	(830)	(577)	(1027)	(469)	(417)

their professors. On the one hand, students emphasized the significance of upgrading educational opportunities by more varied course offerings and more
abundant facilities. Yet, when asked to identify the quality which they deemed
most important in defining a good professor, the majority seemed interested
not so much in expertise or professionalism, as in the professor's ability to lecture well. The number of students who felt this to be the most important quality
of a university professor ranged from 51 percent in Panama to almost 90 percent in Puerto Rico (see Table 9).

One former student and teacher at a major university in Latin America has
explained the special criterion by which many students seem to be evaluating
their professors. Since students study primarily from their lecture notes, they
are dependent on their professors' speaking at a speed which allows them to
copy their *apuntes* or class notes. In some cases, professors are judged more on
their oratorical capabilities than on their fund of technical knowledge.[41]

The apuntes have been a focal point of the formal learning experience in
Latin America universities. The problematic aspect of this situation as well as
current reactions and remedies have been described by Gino Germani.

Many students and the most advanced educators reject the use of *apuntes*
simply to be memorized and repeated at the exams. They demand instead that
the readings consist of good textbooks and a variety of bibliographic sources.
The new ideal emphasizes the individual and joint effort by students and instructors. It is expected that the student may reach this goal under the guidance of
the professor and through discussion in small groups or by other appropriate
means. But the well known poverty of the libraries, the insufficiency of com-

petent staff at the teaching assistant level, and in many cases the limitations in time of the professor, frustrate to a great extent the possibility of bringing into practice these innovations.[42]

Our own survey findings do not suggest that the students were either indiscriminate or totally accepting in their evaluations of their teachers. Thus, while the majority of students evaluated their professors favorably, those in the later years, when queried as to the excellence of the majority of their professors, were consistently more critical than those just beginning their studies (see Table 10).

Table 10.   Percentages of students who evaluate their professors as excellent by year in the university

Country	1st–2nd year	3rd–4th year	5th–7th year
Colombia	75	56	49
Mexico	57	46	38
Puerto Rico	86	67	59
Panama	87	82	78
Uruguay	58	58	50
Paraguay	45	33	22

It was noted earlier that those in the final years of study were also more likely to emphasize the importance of courses geared toward practical application. It would appear that those students who had survived the high failure rate which characterizes many Latin America universities and who were ready to embark upon a career were most concerned with an opportunity to benefit from the knowledge and skills of professors. They were critical when they felt such interaction to be lacking. In addition, it is quite likely that the added experience of the students in the upper years made them far more demanding of their professors and universities than those with fewer years at the university.

In all of the countries a similar pattern prevailed with respect to students' evaluation of their professors. The longer the student was enrolled, the less satisfactory he thought his professors to be. The Paraguayans gave the least positive evaluations of their professors. This was true for students at all stages of their training. Only in Paraguay were *less* than half (45 percent) of the students in their earliest years willing to rate their professors as excellent. This figure dropped to about one-fifth (22 percent) for those in the last stages of their university careers. Student opinion seems to reflect what occurs when a government systematically purges university personnel and emphasizes political criteria in the selection of professors.

When considering evaluation of professors by students' field of study, science students in our sample tended to be among those who were most positive about their instructors. A similar tendency was found among Chilean university students in 1964 where science students were enthusiastic about the quality of their instruction. In Chile the science professors were exceptionally well-trained and motivated. This seems to indicate that where schools have been able to recruit well-trained and dedicated professionals to their staffs, the students are appreciative and respectful of the quality of their professors.

Similar positive responses were found among medical students in our comparative study. They, too, had enrolled in schools in which the professors had attempted to keep abreast of the rapid changes in their fields. Medical students in Panama, Colombia, and Puerto Rico were all very enthusiastic about their professors. Even in Paraguay, where students were generally most critical, those studying in the Faculty of Medicine were notable for the high percentage of positive evaluations. These results were again corroborated by the Chilean data. Chilean medical students respected the efforts of the prestigious men who were recruited to the medical faculty. The medical catedráticos were the most respected specialists, and students were constantly in contact with them in hospitals, clinics, and other professional work situations. Many of the neophyte physicians aspired to be exactly what their professors were – teachers, specialists in the hospital, and men with large private practices.

On the other hand, in Paraguay, Uruguay, and Puerto Rico, engineering students were generally far less positive in their assessment of their professors. In Chile the engineers had also been more negative towards their teachers than any of their peers in the other careers surveyed. Informants indicated that, unlike the best scientists who tended to gravitate to the university for lack of alternative opportunities, it was difficult to recruit the country's best engineers to the faculty. The extremely challenging material required above average teaching talent. Since the failure and dropout rates were very high, the students were particularly sensitive to any deficiencies among their instructors.[43]

Student Evaluation of the Total University Experience

While many observers have asserted that professors are largely peripheral to the students' experience, our survey results indicate that teachers play a more important role in the students' professional socialization and their total university life than had previously been assumed. Evaluation of professors was a major

Table 11. Percentages of students indicating degree of satisfaction with university life

Evaluation	Colombia	Mexico	Puerto Rico	Panama	Uruguay	Paraguay
Very satisfactory	14	12	11	4	12	9
Satisfactory	61	58	64	51	68	48
Unsatisfactory	21	29	20	39	20	38
Very unsatisfactory	3	0	3	5	0	5
Reject	0	1	1	2	0	0
Total	99	100	99	101	100	100
	(1495)	(830)	(577)	(1027)	(469)	(417)

component of student assessment of their total university experience. As is clear in the data from Mexico, Colombia, Puerto Rico, Uruguay, and Paraguay (Tables 10, 11, 12, and 13), there was close correlation between approval of professors and general satisfaction with the university as a whole. Only from 10 to 15 percent of those who rated their professors' performance highly were dissatisfied with their total school experience.

On the other hand, students who judged their professors negatively tended to view the total university experience in similar terms. In Paraguay, where students were by far the most critical of their professors, more than three-fifths of the students who evaluated their teachers negatively were also critical of their total university experience. While the relationship is complex, it is apparent that professors' actions vitally influenced the students' attitudes.

In all the countries sampled, students in the upper years stressed the need for more practical courses and were more critical of their professors than were other students. Similarly, in every case except Mexico, the highest percentage of general discontent was found among students in their last year. This tendency was most extreme in Paraguay where student satisfaction dropped sharply from 62 percent in the early years to 44 percent in the final years. The criticism expressed by the more advanced students is particularly significant. Because of a high dropout rate, these comprised only a small percentage of the student body in every country. Nevertheless, their impact probably far exceeded their numbers. They were important because of their leadership positions at the schools. They, no doubt, have a significant influence on more recent arrivals to the university.

Table 12. Percentages of students evaluating the teaching ability of their professors

Evaluation	Colombia	Mexico	Puerto Rico	Panama	Uruguay	Paraguay
Majority excellent	67	50	70	6	49	38
Few or none excellent	31	48	28	–[a]	37	62
Majority good	–	–	–	76	–	–
Majority bad	–	–	–	15	–	–
Reject[b]	2	3	2	2	14	0
Total	100	101	100	99	100	100
	(1495)	(830)	(577)	(1027)	(469)	(417)

[a]–indicates less than 0.5 percent.
[b]Respondent did not answer question.

Table 13. Percentages of students satisfied with university by year

Country	1st–2nd year	3rd–4th year	5th–7th year
Colombia	80	68	65
Mexico	76	64	75
Puerto Rico	86	74	68
Panama	56	58	51
Uruguay	82	78	78
Paraguay	62	55	44

Our discussion in chapter 4 will show that students in the later years also tend to be the more radical ones.

Student Activism and Educational Quality

The issue of the relationship of student activism to the quality of higher education in Latin America has been one of much concern for scholars and laymen alike.[44] Despite the general interest in the subject and the numbers who have studied or looked into it, there is at present no significant comparative social scientific study of the relationship of student politics and educational quality. There are, however, a variety of different as well as opposing conclusions and evaluations that have been put forth by those who have given the issue some thought. Often these assessments are based on personal impressions or experiences in one or two universities, in one or several countries, over a limited period of time. This limited knowledge and variety of viewpoints stem from the substantial methodological difficulties inherent in the study of this question and in the way the issue has generally been framed or conceptualized. The methodological problems center around the issues of representative samples and valid measures. Given the length of time and the number of universities and countries in which Latin American students have been active, adequate criteria for the selection of representative time periods, universities, countries, and activist students must be formulated. Also, more valid measures of educational quality need to be constructed. Probably most important is the significant problem of isolating the influence of student activism from the variety of other factors affecting educational quality, as our discussion in this chapter reveals. Unfortunately, no consideration of the issue of the impact of student activism on higher education has been able to incorporate all these above named factors and to that extent each is flawed.

Another major difficulty associated with the methodological ones, but analytically distinct, deals with the way in which the issue has been conceptualized. Too often the observer or essayist limits his area of investigation by focusing almost entirely upon the activities of the students while paying scant attention to the contexts   political, socioeconomic, and university   which shape and affect student political activities and attitudes. The interaction between student activism and educational quality does not occur in a social or political vacuum, as we emphasized in chapter 1.

We have contended that any examination of the relationship between student politics and the university in Latin America necessitates consideration of the national political scene. Universities in Latin America, particularly the older, major, national ones located in the capital cities, are integral parts of their societies as well as sensitive reflectors of societal conditions. As such, we would expect them to be troubled and politicized institutions. There is scarcely a country in Latin America which has enjoyed prolonged periods free from authoritarian rule or significant political and economic instability. Few countries have been able to attain a firmly grounded political consensus or few governments a widely based legitimacy for any length of time.[45] In such situations all institutions become politicized and to varying degrees arenas for partisan conflict. This is especially true of the universities, their staff and student bodies alike, due to their importance and focal position as well as their relative openness to outside forces and differing ideas.

National politics and partisan considerations have been intimately involved in the affairs of Latin American universities in this century. The most direct and continuing nexus between national politics and the university has been the university budget. Financially, universities, both public and private, are highly dependent upon the national government for operating funds. Often political attitudes and noneducational criteria play important roles in the budget allocations for the universities. There is also little doubt that partisan politics is involved in the election or selection of rectors, deans, and catedráticos. This is true not only in the case of authoritarian regimes, such as Stroessner's Paraguay or Perón's Argentina, but also in the relatively more democratic societies of Puerto Rico, Uruguay, and Mexico. In fact, almost every major university in the hemisphere has directly experienced some form of political strife caused by the intervention of the government, national political parties, political personalities, or national issues into the affairs of the university. As a result, educational quality has often suffered.

The basic Reformista demand for university autonomy stemmed from a desire of the students to remove the university from the scope of partisan interests. Although university autonomy has been violated when instituted, most governments are reluctant to openly and constantly repudiate it. This has meant that the university is relatively the safest institution from which oppositional politics can be pursued. Thus, minority parties and oppositional groups have been attracted to the university by its very autonomous status and have looked upon the campus as a haven for the propagation of ideas or for the recruitment of supporters. Again this persistent embroilment in political controversies has detracted from the educational mission of the university.

Outside political forces are not the only factors that have impeded the development of educational quality within the university. Other, generally related, factors more internal to the university have also played a negative role. Latin American universities tend to be beset by severe financial shortages. These financial problems are compounded by the lack of a full-time, professionally trained administrative staff, competent to properly administer the university and efficiently allocate the meager available funds. The inadequate budgets of the universities have meant that most of their professors spend only part of their time teaching, much less doing any research, and work at other jobs in order to earn adequate incomes. Unless more funds are allocated to higher education in Latin America, there will be extremely few quality institutions of higher learning in the hemisphere.

The administrative structure of the universities, in conjunction with the existence of strong vested interests, has also hindered the academic upgrading of these institutions. The division of the university into autonomous faculties or schools, dominated by virtually autonomous catedráticos has made university reform, particularly on a university wide basis, exceedingly difficult to implement. The governing boards of the individual faculties are usually dominated by senior professors whose principle motivation appears to be the protection of established interests and prerogatives. As a result, despite all the time and effort that have been devoted to university reform in Latin America since 1918 and despite the enactment into national law in eighteen countries of various elements of reform programs, contemporary Latin American universities tend to resemble those which the Reformistas originally protested against half a century earlier.

Now that the overall context has been reviewed, let us focus specifically on the role of the students. What effect have they had on the quality of higher education in Latin America? The answer is a complex one since various students have played different roles at different times and places. In order to respond to this query it becomes necessary to simplify and generalize. First, let us examine the negative case.[46] Latin American students have been accused of being academically irresponsible. Their major concerns, it is charged, have been to politicize the university, attack the government in power, and resist needed university reforms which would challenge their prerogatives or force them to concentrate on their studies. Quality education has simply not been a major goal of the students, their critics assert.

There is too much evidence to deny the validity of some of these accusations. Students have, at times, abused positions of responsibility which were often first gained as a result of campaigns to improve the university. Students sitting in official judgment of their professors intimidated these men and thereby contributed to lower academic standards.[47] Unfortunately, Latin American students have subordinated concern for academic quality to political or ideological interests. They have blocked efforts at reform or the depoliticization of the universities. But these charges and facts must be placed in perspective. Which sector of the university community has taught them by example to be responsible or to push for reforms which would be injurious to their power or privileges? Such mentors and exemplars have been conspicuous by their absence.[48] This, however, does not mean that the behavior of the students is therefore justifiable. But, from their perspective, it might be asked why they should be expected to calmly accept the major or perhaps the sole costs of upgrading the quality of their universities.

It is not accurate to assert that the students have been responsible for the politicization of the Latin American university. Historically, the universities were politicized before students became politically involved. And as we earlier pointed out, institutions in unstable political environments or in societies without a dominant political consensus cannot be neutral, apolitical oases. There is no reason to believe that were the students to immediately forego all their political involvements, the universities would become transformed into apolitical academic citadels. In order for this to happen there would have to be dramatic changes in the political structure of their societies, and other groups including politicians and professors would have to abstain from interjecting their political concerns into the universities.

In addition, there is also positive evidence which indicates that Latin American students do care about the quality of their education and that they are desirous of genuine academic reform. Our own survey data clearly reveal that Latin American students are overwhelmingly concerned with the quality of their education. They want very much to see it made more relevant to the pressing problems confronting their societies. In these respects they are the direct heirs of the early Reformistas who were also strongly motivated by the same concerns.

Students have also played prominent roles in the reforming and the upgrading of their universities. In Argentina, student political action, particularly during the period from 1918 until the early 1940s, was credited with making the Argentine university system the best one in the hemisphere.[49] In Chile, a careful study and evaluation of the role of student politics in three time periods, spanning the years from 1918 to 1957, concluded that the major Chilean student political organization had "been a force for progress within the university."[50] In the latter 1960s, Chilean students together with their younger professors were credited with bringing about important and highly constructive reforms at the University of Chile.[51]

Furthermore, research on students in Chile, Brazil, and Venezuela during the 1960s concludes, contrary to popular impression, that political activists are also among the most concerned with the need for educational reform. All of these studies, including our own (see chapter 5), suggest that student political radicalism is directly related to their dissatisfaction with the quality of their educational experience.[52]

Structurally, within the university community, the students are the group most free to innovate and initiate reforms. Their prerogatives and vested interests appear to inhibit them less than do those of their professors and administrators. Often it is the students who are the first to call for upgrading reforms, only to see these demands countered or, if the reforms are instituted, to see them subverted by their elders among the faculty and staff. In many cases the vested interests and the structural constraints of the university are so great that the professors and administrators who do want meaningful reforms feel compelled to rely upon the students to push them through.[53]

Thus, student activism, it appears, has had both positive and negative consequences on higher education in Latin America. This, in large part, seems due to the fact that students are not a homogeneous group. They vary in political attitudes and values as well as behavior. They also differ with respect to their attitudes and values concerning various aspects of university life. There is some indication that different types of students become involved in student political activities, especially when they pertain to university matters, at different periods of time. During the early stages of campaigns to democratize and upgrade the university, the better students become involved for the more positive reasons. As the reforms gain acceptance and become institutionalized, these students then turn their energies to their studies and other matters. As this process occurs, other students, less talented and less altruistic than their predecessors, move to the fore and utilize both the gains made and student politics for selfish or partisan interests. The quality of student politics then declines as does the university itself.[54]

On balance, however, we contend that the students' impact upon their universities has been a positive one. These youth have historically demonstrated their concern with the intellectual and academic upgrading of their universities. Also, the students have been historically committed to the idea that their educational institutions must be transformed into democratic and progressive agencies so as to contribute meaningfully to the development and welfare of their societies.

In conclusion, it seems appropriate to quote the words of a Uruguayan university official to a European visitor in 1956 who was inquiring about the role of students in the governance and working of the university:

You are accustomed to think of the active role of the students in the University only as that of boisterous youth with destructive aggressiveness. I think one pays too much attention to the resounding declarations concerned with political and social subjects, while one forgets that the legitimate expression of the ideas and feeling of youth is coupled with constant work, mature and responsible, in the heart of the various organs of university government. We are aware of the originality of our formula. But it is not a chance occurrence. It is the fruit of a slow evolution which won the respect and admiration of the professors and alumni, who observe around the discussion table the conscientious spirit and devotion of the students.[55]

4 Family Background, University Experience, and Student Politics

During their university years, Latin American students find that politics is an omnipresent factor. In 1970, an extensive review of the litereature on the politics of Latin American students concluded by itemizing a number of questions demanding further study.

Among other things, we need to know more about the relationship between ideology and participation; the effects of family, class, and educational background on student behavior; the importance of the academic environment and extracurricular opportunities in relation to political activism; and the relationship of the unique cultural and historical experience of Latin America to the behavior of students. We need to know more about how students act as a political group; how they organize themselves; what tactics they employ; and whether their overall impact should be characterized as revolutionary, reformist, conservative, or reactionary. Moreover, we need to learn how the university fits into the developmental process in this area of the world.[1]

In the next two chapters we focus directly on many of these issues. Our analysis will reveal why certain universities and disciplines contribute disproportionately to student activism and which background factors are the most important determinants of student political attitudes and behavior. The perennial issue of the relative importance of recruitment and socialization will be given careful attention.

UNIVERSITIES AND THEIR STUDENTS: MAJOR CHARACTERISTICS

The first step is to identify those characteristics of university student bodies most likely to have a bearing on student political attitudes. Such data should provide a rough index of the homogeneity or heterogeneity of these student bodies and suggest the extent to which individual students will be exposed to political norms and values at variance with those of their families. We will then examine the distribution of students' attitudes and indicators of behavior, and the interplay between them and the political climate prevailing on the university campuses.

All of the universities examined in this study are public, with the exception of Javeriana, Los Andes, and Libre (all in Colombia) which are private. Except for Guanajuato, in Mexico, and Cauca, in Popayán, Colombia, all are in the capitals of their respective countries. While there are important variations among the university student bodies, they are all predominantly urban, middle or upper class, and male. Within this framework, the three private universities in Colombia present the most marked contrast in the type of students recruited. Students at Javeriana and Los Andes come mainly from the upper and upper-middle classes, while Libre draws students with a lower socioeconomic status. Attendance by students from the working and lower-middle classes is facilitated by the provision of evening classes, which allows part-time study. Libre also has a larger proportion of students from rural areas than the other Bogotá universities, further evidence that this university is unique in the extent to which it enrolls the geographically (rural to urban) and socially mobile student.

The national universities of Mexico, Colombia, and Uruguay are alike in that they recruit students from a wide range of social origins and in that they provide settings within which student political organization and activity are legitimate. In all of these universities, students have some share in decision-making, both in the *facultad* and in the highest council of the university.[2] This phenomenon is most developed at the University of the Republic in Uruguay, which has a long tradition of student involvement in university government, emphasized, in 1958 by the Organic Law which granted students three members out of twelve on each faculty council and three out of twenty on the Central Directive Council of the university.[3] Further similarities among these three national universities are their secular character, their location in the national capital, and their public image as the major university in the nation (or , in the case of Uruguay, as the only university).

All these factors provide environments conducive to the development and maintenance of active political subcultures. In addition, sufficient student discontent is generated in these universities to provide a basis for political activity. Since university norms permit the formal organization of political groups, institutionalized means are provided for expressing at least some of this discontent through legitimate channels within the university. That these channels are not regarded as adequate is shown by the frequent strikes directed at university authority, especially in Colombia, but also in Uruguay and Mexico. Furthermore, discontent is often fostered by and directed toward conditions in society, so that opposition to university authority becomes linked with opposition to government. Particularly in Colombia, student political activists at public universities perceive the university government as an extension of the national government. This is attested to by the frequent strikes calling for removal of the government-appointed rector and by their success as evidenced in the frequent change in holders of this office.[4]

The universities of Puerto Rico (at the time of our study) and Paraguay differ from the three national universities discussed above by denying student participation in university government and proscribing student political activity on campus. At the University of Puerto Rico, political activity was prohibited in 1948, after violence had erupted over the question of independence. This conflict has recurred periodically since 1965, resulting in clashes between student supporters of statehood and independence.[5] In Paraguay the proscription of student political activity may be regarded as simply an expression of the dictatorial government of General Stroessner. This state of affairs is not new, however, since Paraguay has never had a viable democratic government.[6] Thus, in both of these universities the permissiveness toward student political activity found elsewhere in Latin America has been absent. However, this is decidedly not to equate the two universities or the two societies in other respects, since Puerto Rico has established the civil rights of a free society, including free speech, judicial procedures protecting the rights of the individual and democratically elected government.[7] The only comparative point made here is that the development of active and diverse student political subcultures has been inhibited in Puerto Rico and Paraguay.

Turning next to the regional universities (Guanajuato and Cauca) in our sample, we find that they share the characteristics of the national universities of Mexico, Colombia, and Uruguay in that they recruit from a fairly wide range of at least the middle and upper-middle classes of society and provide for some student involvement in university government. But there are significant differences, especially in environment, these two universities are in more rural, agricultural, and traditional settings. The cities of Guanajuato and Popayán, where Cauca is, retain many physical characteristics of the colonial period. They also lack the differentiated social structure characteristic of the large, industrialized capitals.[8] Thus, there is a less complex class and interest-group structure than exists in the larger, more industrialized cities and a much poorer and less stimulating context for the development of political conflict. In general we might anticipate that students in the small cities would be less exposed to the variety and complexity of mass media, including magazines, newspapers, television, and movies, available to students in large urban centers. In turn, the smaller size of these universities and the greater homogeneity of their student bodies provide a weaker base for the proliferation of student subcultures. This is not to say that there may not be intense and heated political debates in these universities, but rather that there is likely to be less variety of political, social, and economic issues and ideologies in these types of schools than in larger universities located at the political centers of their nations.

The three private universities in our study are located in Bogotá. Two are secular, and one, Javeriana, is Catholic. But the more important differences lie in their organizational structures and their bases of student recruitment. As mentioned above, Los Andes and Javeriana recruit predominantly from the upper-middle and upper classes of their society. While Javeriana students come from more devout homes, the social backgrounds of the students at the two universities are quite similar. Javeriana, founded in 1622 and re-established in 1931 after being closed since 1767, is organized along the more traditional lines of the Latin American university with its autonomous or semiautonomous faculties; Los Andes, founded during World War II, is patterned after the North American, or United States model of a more integrated structure, with somewhat greater stress on general studies and pragmatically designed courses. Neither university provides for student participation in university government. Student protests, strikes, and marches to the Plaza Mayor to express solidarity with workers, fellow students, or revolutionary movements, common at the National University, are practically nonexistent. Students at these private universities come largely from families which provide adequately for creature comforts and assure social contacts which guarantee future occupational security. The two universities offer an education which will provide students with the requisite professional skills to fulfill their aspirations. This is perhaps an idealized version of these students' situation, but our evidence tends to support it.

Libre University, on the other hand, was founded in 1923, to serve as "a center of higher education, popular and rationalist, open to autonomous research, in which the professors would be able to expound all scientific theses without any limitation . . . [It began] with the fervent support of those Colombians who were opposed to confessionalism and who supported the renewal and popularization of culture."[9] Libre is governed solely by representatives from the faculty, students, and former students. It has limited economic resources and offers training in only three fields — education, law, and engineering — while the other universities offer a much wider range of choice. Since Libre offers night courses, allowing working students to continue their education on a part-time basis, the average age of its students is higher than at other Latin American universities. Thus, the lower socioeconomic background and older age of students, together with the "anti-establishment" goals of its founders, have combined to provide an extremely active, leftist student political subculture within the university. Libre and Javeriana stand at opposite poles in terms of social recruitment, views on the church, and political activism and orientation.

The characteristics of universities most relevant to their role as politically socializing institutions are the social characteristics of the students themselves, the political and community environment within which the university is located, and the form of university government. Given a university which recruits students from nonreligious, lower-middle and working-class backgrounds, which is located in a large, urban center of a conflict-ridden society, and which has a tradition of social criticism and political involvement on the part of its students and faculty members, we would obviously expect to find a high degree of politically socializing experiences and of political activity. The opposite would be expected at a Catholic university which is located in a rural or small urban center within a politically stable society, which recruits students largely from upper-middle and upper class backgrounds, and which proscribes student political activity. Libre University fits the ideal type model of a politically radicalizing university. No single university quite corresponds to the extreme conservatizing model. While it is impossible to quantify these structural characteristics to provide a basis for predicting political climate and the impact of political socialization, our data reveal that the universities in our sample fall along an environmental continuum, from the conservative to the radical. At the conservative end we would place Javeriana, Los Andes, and Puerto Rico (at the time of our survey), and at the radical end, Mexico, Colombia, Uruguay, and Libre, with Guanajuato, Cauca, and Paraguay between these extremes. Subsequent analysis will show the relationship between this rough grouping and the political climates and socializing influences of the universities.

UNIVERSITY AND STUDENT ORIENTATIONS: CLIMATES OF OPINION

Student political behavior and orientations toward university, national, and international political issues vary among the several universities. In this analysis we will not differentiate among student attitudes by individual characteristics, but rather utilize attitudes as indicators of the political climate prevailing within the universities. Our concern is to determine the extent to which university political climates correspond to some of the assertions made above concerning the complex of national, regional, university, and individual characteristics that are brought together in these student bodies.

The students' answers to the question — "How satisfied are you with your life as a student, including all aspects — professors, courses, facilities, examina-

Table 14. Student orientations toward the university

Student orientation	Puerto Rico	Mexico		Colombia					Uruguay	Paraguay
		UNAM	Guan.	L.A.	Jav.	U.N.	L.	C.		
Percent satisfied with life as a student	77	68	80	83	82	60	76	72	79	57
Percent who say "the majority of professors are excellent"	71	47	69	81	69	49	73	57	57	38
Percent who agree that "student leaders should express students' views on national, international political matters"	30	35	22	18	21	43	61	24	48	53
Percent who have *not* participated in strikes or demonstrations	79	60	57	85	84	44	24	46	22	47
Percent who have a "lot" or "some" interest in student politics	64	58	73	36	41	60	70	52	71	74
N[b]	(467)	(646)	(141)	(624)	(220)	(385)	(158)	(162)	(410)	(459)

[a]University names are as follows:
Puerto Rico University of Puerto Rico
UNAM Universidad Nacional Autónoma de México
Guan. Universidad de Guanajuato
L.A. Universidad de los Andes
Jav. Universidad Pontificia de Javeriana
U.N. Universidad Nacional de Colombia
L. Universidad Libre de Colombia
C. Universidad del Cauca
Uruguay Universidad de la República
Paraguay Universidad de Asunción
[b]The numbers in parentheses indicate the smallest number of students answering any one of the above questions.

tions, etc.?" – show variations which correspond to some degree to the type of university. Responses at the national universities of Colombia, Mexico, and Paraguay indicated the lowest levels of student satisfaction; the highest levels were found in the three private universities in Colombia and in the public universities of Uruguay and Guanajuato. It is not possible to determine the factors most conducive to dissatisfaction, but answers to the next question – "How would you evaluate your professors?" – indicate that the perceived quality of the faculty is an important ingredient, as discussed earlier in chapter 3. Universities with the lowest level of satisfaction are also those with the lowest level of approval of professors – the national universities of Mexico, Colombia, and Paraguay. These responses may reflect resentment of the part-time professor, whose involvement in other professional activities limits his availability to students and his dedication to lectures and other university responsibilities.[10] This phenomenon is more common in the public than the private universities.

The level of satisfaction, however, is not an accurate predictor of student political activism and radicalism. For example, Libre, where the level of satisfaction and approval of faculty is quite high, has the most radical activist student body of all the universities. Eighty percent of the Libre and Uruguayan students had taken part in strikes or demonstrations, compared to only 20 percent at the universities of Puerto Rico, Los Andes, and Javeriana. These differences mirror the absence of large, active political subcultures at the latter three universities, reflecting the fact that the structural basis for legitimizing student political activism is not present. Students do not formally share in the decision-making process. Other factors also contribute to the reduction of student discontent. Among the more significant are high levels of religiosness (Puerto Rico and Javeriana), and satisfaction with professors (all three). In addition, Puerto Rican students indicate the highest level of optimism with respect to future career opportunities, another factor reducing the level of discontent. (See chapter 2.)

We have so far provided evidence for the rough scale of university political environments suggested above in which Los Andes, Javeriana, and Puerto Rico would be placed at the apolitical pole, while Libre and the national universities of Colombia and Uruguay would be placed at the highly political end, with the remaining universities in intermediate positions. Patterns of response to several questions regarding political orientations toward national and international political issues will further delineate the political climate at each of the universities studied.

First, we can easily place Libre University at the far left of the political spectrum. On every question, two-thirds to three-fourths of the students at Libre

Table 15. Students' nonuniversity political orientations

| | | Mexico | | University[a] | | Colombia | | | | | |
Student orientation	Puerto Rico	UNAM	Guan	L.A.	Jav.	U.N.	L.	C.	Uruguay	Paraguay
Percent who consider the Alliance for Progress "very" or "moderately" beneficial to the country	68	66	77	80	82	57	35	71	–	81
Percent favorable toward the Cuban Revolution	11	52	29	18	17	56	75	42	54	12
Percent who perceive effects of foreign capital as more good than bad, or as wholly beneficial	88	67	68	74	72	51	35	58	37	85
Percent favorable to Fidel Castro's "ideas and actions"	5	46	19	11	8	40	75	37	41	11
N[b]	(562)	(619)	(132)	(589)	(210)	(356)	(140)	(152)	(377)	(333)

– This question was not asked in Uruguay.

[a] See Table 14 this chapter, for names of the universities in each of the countries.

[b] The numbers in parentheses indicate the smallest number of students answering any one of the above questions.

responded with a "leftist" answer, showing, for example, a high level of approval for the Cuban Revolution and Fidel Castro and a low level of approval for the Alliance for Progress and foreign capital. At the other extreme, students at the universities of Puerto Rico, Los Andes, Javeriana, and Paraguay revealed even higher levels of consensus on the "nonleftist" side. Approval of Castro is especially low in these four universities, with 11 percent or fewer indicating that they were "favorable to the ideas and actions" of the Cuban leader.

It should be pointed out that the presence of Paraguayan students among the more conservative student bodies (for further discussion see chapter 5) does not reflect a high level of general satisfaction with student life, or, specifically, with professors (see Table 14). These students do, however, share with the students from Puerto Rico, Guanajuato, and Javeriana, a high level of religiousness, with nearly four out of five indicating that they are "very" or "moderately religious." Perhaps more important is the politically oppressive regime under which the Paraguayan students live, combined with the relative isolation of Paraguay from the rest of the world. On almost every measure of political, social, and economic development, Paraguay ranks close to the bottom among Latin American nations.[11] As noted above, it has never experienced more than the formal trappings of democracy. These factors might appear to be conducive to a high level of radicalism among Paraguayan students. There have been student protests, as in 1959 when Stroessner temporarily lifted the state of siege under which the nation had lived since 1940. This resulted in student riots and other civil disorders, and the siege was reimposed within a month.[12] But the possibility for political organization and opposition to the regime has been limited. Student opposition to the government must remain clandestine, as it is severely punished when discovered.

The regime has tolerated a certain level of political dissent in the 1960s provided it is not aimed directly at the President, his family, and friends. Under such conditions the students have focused their discontent on relatively safe university, as opposed to national, issues. The two issue areas, however, are inextricably interwoven as the national government is directly responsible for the considerable short-comings of the university. The administrators, appointed by the government, have been chosen for their political loyalty and have blocked efforts at university reform or modernization. Professors also have had to pass political tests in order to be hired. The government allocations have not been sufficient to provide even minimally adequate library or laboratory facilities.[13]

In view of the above, a positive attitude toward the Alliance for Progress and foreign capital might be better explained by the special situation in Paraguay than interpreted as support for the regime's foreign policy. The Paraguayan economy has depended to an important degree on American public and private funds, especially on the Alliance for Progress. Students may be favorable to such funds simply because, under any regime, outside economic help appears to be essential for the nation's development. The lack of a positive view of Castro or the Cuban Revolution indicates, however, a rejection of socialist revolution as a model for change, or the students' fear of openly identifying with Fidel.

Thus, there appear to be four universities which are quite conservative in political outlook, three of them being apolitical with respect to participation in demonstrations or strikes. The reasons for conservatism and apoliticism, however, vary considerably. In the case of Puerto Rico, general satisfaction with the university and with chances for a secure economic future, combined in the mid-1960s with stable democratic government on the island, seem to explain this conservatism. Los Andes and Javeriana reflect the conservatism of the upper-middle and upper classes from which their students are largely recruited. Los Andes and Javeriana students are relatively insulated from the subculture of radical student politics. They appear to have better educational facilities than Libre and Nacional students, reflected in their high level of satisfaction with university life. Also, their conservative social and religious family background helps them to resist the call for political involvement coming from other campuses. Conservatism among Paraguayan students, on the other hand, appears to reflect a combination of fear of government repression and limited access to information about radical means to facilitate social change, rather than a high level of satisfaction with the university, future career chances, or the political system.

Students in the smaller provincial universities of Guanajuato (Mexico) and Cauca (Colombia) are less radical than their counterparts at the larger universities located in Mexico City and Bogotá. At Guanajuato, 13 percent of the students are left compared to 32 percent of those at the National Autonomous University of Mexico (UNAM). At Cauca, 30 percent are left while among those attending Nacional the figure is 43 percent. Students at these provincial, smaller universities also appear to be more parochial in their orientation than their peers in the national universities in the capital cities. This is evidenced, in part, by the fact that the proportion of students willing to have student government express student views on national and international politics is much lower than at the national universities. Thus it would seem that geographical isolation in a conservative setting and a relatively small student body combine to work against high levels of radicalism. It can also be safely assumed that radicals and those interested in national politics would not choose to attend such schools, an assumption which would also account for the parochialism and lower level of radicalism found there as opposed to larger public universities in the capital cities.

Our analysis makes us aware of the variety of factors accounting for student attitudes and political behavior. In many respects Uruguay is among the most highly developed nations in Latin America, which might lead one to predict a high degree of political satisfaction among Uruguayan students. But Uruguay is also faced with almost insurmountable economic and political difficulties which inhibit growth and severely restrict the career opportunities of university students.[14] This factor, plus the freedom to organize and communicate politically, the tradition of the university as a center of political agitation, and perhaps also the high degree of exposure to leftist political organizers, combine to make this university one of the most radical in our sample of Latin American universities.

Colombia's Libre University is even more radical than Uruguay's University of the Republic. Libre combines the recruitment of students from lower socioeconomic origins, who are older and less religious than their counterparts in other Colombian universities, with an institutional environment whose traditions and structures encourage the development of radical criticism and opposition to the status quo. In addition Libre has a small student body, which enhances student interaction and the likelihood that radical students will influence those of more conservative backgrounds. In large leftist oriented institutions, there is greater opportunity for the development of a wider variety of peer groups and subcultures, which afford some insulation for like-minded conservative students from their more radical fellow students.[15]

National political and economic development, through their effects on standards of living, future expectations, and assessment of the government as relatively responsive, stable, and effective, do have an impact on student political orientations. Yet the definition of the political situation is in the final analysis largely determined by an interaction between individual and university characteristics. The student's assessment of the political system in which he lives and the conclusions he draws from this for his own attitudes and behavior are heavily influenced by his daily life as a student. The network of student, faculty, and family and political contacts in which he is located, the political norms and role models within the university, and such factors as the amount of time available for informal association with fellow students, all have a bearing on the formation and change of the student's political orientations and behavior.

RECRUITMENT AND SOCIALIZATION: THE DETERMINANTS OF POLIT-
ICAL ORIENTATIONS

The foregoing discussion suggests, then, that there are important variations
in political orientations of Latin American students in different types of universities. We now turn to a major issue in the general field of student politics:
What is the relative significance of recruitment and socialization factors for the
politics of students? In other words, do universities tend to draw like-minded
students from similar backgrounds and does this factor maintain, if not inten-
sify, the students' initial beliefs and orientations? To answer this question, we
will examine the relationship between background variables such as sex, socioeconomic origin, and religion, and measures of the quality and duration of a
student's exposure to the university such as number of years in the university,
degree of involvement in student politics, and others.[16]

Sex and Political Orientation

A number of studies of political behavior suggest that politics is largely a
man's game, especially in those societies in which the woman's roles are ideally
those of wife, mother, and homemaker. Catholic Latin societies are particularly
prone to relegate the female to a secondary status in the occupational, political,
and social worlds outside the family. But even in these societies education
reduces the differences between men and women with respect to interest and
involvement in political affairs.[17] Here, we will be concerned with differences
between men and women in both activity and ideology. Are women students
in Latin American universities consistently less active and more conservative
than men, as other studies would suggest, or does the university situation reduce
these differences between the sexes?

The responses indicate that there are no substantial differences in the politics
of male and female students. First, women are somewhat more likely to prefer
the government party and males are more likely to prefer the left opposition
parties. In Colombia, where the differences were most substantial they only
ranged from 10 percent to 20 percent within the different universities. In the
other countries sex differences in party choice come to 10 percent or less.
Somewhat greater variation is observed with respect to political activity and
ideology, especially in national politics, with male students being more involved.
Males are also more likely to be politically active and leftist in ideology, with
differences ranging from 5 percent to nearly 30 percent. In Uruguay, however,
there is no sex variation in the degree of student political involvement and in
Puerto Rico, no difference in ideology.

No other salient patterns emerge to suggest that in the more traditional, less developed countries women students are significantly more conservative and less active than men. It appears, then, that whatever the effects of socialization on sex roles in the larger population, sex differences play a very small part in determining student political orientations. The university may be the only institution in the more traditional Latin American society in which men and women have equal status. This formal equality may stimulate female students to become politically involved on a par with men, and, thus, to be exposed to the same climates of political opinion. It should also be pointed out that these female students by the very fact of their university enrollment are quite atypical.

Family Social and Economic Status and Political Orientation

In order to measure social status a scale was employed. This is a composite measure utilizing parent's and paternal grandfather's level of education, father's occupation, and the student's estimate of his family's social class.[18] While there are fairly large differences in social status between students at the high and low ends of the scale, the largest concentration of students was found within the middle and upper-middle sectors. Further, students of very high and of very low social origins were more likely to be recruited to different universities, for example, Los Andes and Libre in Colombia.

Although the effect of social status is not great, students of lower social status are more likely to be leftist in ideology, while students of higher status are more likely to be politically active in both student and national politics. The leftist tendency among lower-status students probably reflects the fact that in Latin America leftist parties tend to have their political base among the lower strata and to orient their appeals to these groups. These status differences in ideology and political activity are not great, however, varying between 5 percent and 20 percent. Consistent with these findings is the tendency of lower-status students to prefer leftist political parties and to express "political normlessness" (or as we are employing the term, the belief that elected officials are not honest and do not represent the interests of the voters).

Interesting exceptions to this pattern are found among Libre and University of Paraguay students. At Libre the few higher-status students are 20 percent more to the left than other students on the ideology scale, a figure which perhaps reflects an attempt on their part to compensate for their more favored social origins in the context of a lower-status student body where leftist political norms predominate. In Paraguay, although there is no status difference with respect to political ideology, the high and middle-status students tend to choose one of the token opposition parties, while low-status students opt for the *Colorado*, or government party. Since Paraguay appears to be a "stable dictatorship" with little likelihood of any opposition party coming to power, it is conceivable that lower-status students look to the government party for employment opportunities; political patronage rather than ideology may be the determing factor.[19]

While the major patterns observed here are fairly consistent in direction and strength across universities, it is worth emphasizing that in these relationships, as in others reported here, *interuniversity* differences often loom significantly larger than *intrauniversity* differences. A glance at Table 16 confirms this, since differences between universities as great as 60 percent are reported on such attitudes as favorableness toward Fidel Castro, while the differences within universities rarely exceed 30 percent.

Father's Religion and Student's Political Orientation

In most Latin American societies, as in those of Catholic Europe, conflicts between church and state have played an important part in the development of political parties and institutions. Clerical and anticlerical parties and, in more recent times, Christian Democratic parties and their opponents on the left have expressed major differences regarding official recognition of the Catholic church as the religion of the state and its influence in public education, marriage law, and other matters of central concern to the maintenance and propagation of the faith. Following independence from Spain, liberal and conservative parties were formed in most Latin American societies to express these opposed views.

In Colombia political conflict over the role of the church has continued until recent times and remains a powerful latent political issue. Conflict over religion has become less salient since the Liberals and the Conservatives, the major opposition parties, agreed in 1958 to share power during alternating terms. In Mexico the secularization of political authority and the abrogation of the Concordat with Rome were carried out in 1857. Still, Mexico continues to be a visibly Catholic society, with the church-oriented National Action Party representing the interests of those Catholic voters who seek greater state recognition of their religious interests in such matters as education. In terms of the relation of the church to the state and in the general lack of deference to religious interests in political matters, Uruguay is the most secular of all Latin American societies.

Paraguay and Puerto Rico are Latin American societies in which religious conflict has not been a major factor. In Paraguay, this is perhaps due to a weakly developed church which became very dependent on the national government. Puerto Rico did not experience the postindependence, church-state conflict characteristic of other Latin American societies.[20] In Puerto Rico, the question of church influence was not an issue in the formation of political parties until 1960. The church-sponsored Christian Action Party which did raise the church-state issue received only 7 percent of the vote in 1960 and 3 percent in 1964. It disbanded shortly thereafter.[21]

In this analysis of the influence of religion on political attitudes and behavior, the father's religious practice was chosen as an indicator of family religious influence because of its considerable variation; nearly all students reported that their mothers were "practicing Catholics." If students adopted their fathers' religious and political orientations to some degree, and if religion was, as suggested above, linked to political party and ideology, then political cleavage along the line of religious commitment should have been greatest in Colombia and Mexico and least in Puerto Rico, Paraguay, and Uruguay. The measure most indicative of this cleavage is the political ideology scale, which measures basic values concerning the desired political models of society and the preferred means for instituting political change. Table 16 shows the relationship, in each university, between the father's religious identity (as indicated by the student's assessment), and the student's position on the political ideology scale. To simplify presentation, only the proportions in each subgroup which scored in the upper (leftist) third of the scale are presented.

As the table reveals, the greatest ideological differences between students from practicing Catholic and "other" religious backgrounds were found in Mexico and Colombia, with Paraguay intermediate. In Colombia the secular universities exhibited the greatest ideological differences between students from conformist Catholic and nonreligious families. Apparently, the religious and political values within the Catholic university were so homogeneous that the few students from less religious backgrounds shifted to a more conservative orientation as a result of the prevailing ideological climate. An alternative explanation may be that nonreligious fathers who send their sons and daughters to a Catholic university are themselves politically conservative, despite their religious orientation.

In political party choice, however, we found that religious background had more effect in Uruguay, Paraguay, and Mexico than in Puerto Rico. Uruguay, Paraguay, and Mexico all have Catholic or Christian Democratic parties, and students from practicing Catholic families are more likely, by an average difference of about 20 percent, to vote for these parties. In Puerto Rico, however, few students preferred the church-supported party, regardless of religious background. This was perhaps a function of the newness of the party and the fact that such a party represented a radical departure from tradition.

In Colombia a student from a practicing Catholic background was found

Table 16. Percentages of students who have high scores on leftist ideology, by father's religion and university

University		Father's religion		
		Practicing Catholic	Nonpracticing Catholic	Non-Catholic, atheist, agnostic
Puerto Rico		4	4	7
	N	(142)	(231)	(180)
Mexico				
UNAM		21	36	47
	N	(301)	(225)	(116)
Guanajuato		11	7	62
	N	(89)	(44)	(8)
Colombia				
Los Andes		9	21	13
	N	(384)	(144)	(54)
Javeriana		7	15	0
	N	(197)	(40)	(7)
Nacional		31	55	56
	N	(233)	(108)	(36)
Libre		73	85	93
	N	(44)	(59)	(14)
Cauca		27	36	60
	N	(106)	(42)	(10)
Uruguay		38	33	46
	N	(147)	(162)	(123)
Paraguay		6	9	20
	N	(218)	(176)	(54)

more likely to choose the Conservative party at Los Andes and Javeriana, where there was almost no support for leftist parties. Again, larger differences were found in the secular universities. At Libre the student from a less- or non-religious background was 30 percent more likely to prefer one of the leftist parties than was the practicing Catholic student, and at Nacional, 17 percent more likely. The pattern at Cauca was similar to that for Los Andes.

The effect of religious socialization upon the degree of student involvement followed a pattern somewhat similar to that for political ideology. In Uruguay and Paraguay, religion had almost no effect, while in Puerto Rico, Colombia, and Mexico, students from more religious backgrounds were generally politically less active. The case of Libre, however, provided a noteworthy exception because there *more* students from practicing Catholic backgrounds were active in student politics. The similarity of this pattern to that of students from a higher socioeconomic status in this university provided support for the hypothesis that, within a highly political university, students whose family backgrounds are atypical will seek to compensate by close involvement with the political subculture.

Generally, the relation of religion to "political normlessness" is similar to its relation to ideology and activism – students from more religious backgrounds are somewhat more likely to believe that politicians are honest and that elections do matter. There are interesting reversals of this relationship. In Uruguay and at the University of Guanajuato a practicing Catholic background *increased* the tendency to express low confidence in the government. This orientation may reflect the fact that in both these societies the government had taken an anticlerical stance, especially in Mexico, where the church has since the Revolution been deprived of many of its prerogatives. This relationship between degree of religiousness and confidence in the government is very strong in Guanajuato and very weak at the UNAM. This suggests that the more traditional Catholic in smaller population centers is more sensitive than his counterpart in the larger urban centers to the status of the church. The "modern" Catholic accepts the separation of church and state to a greater extent and is thus less likely to withdraw support from the government on this account.

Father's Political Party and Student Political Orientation

The father's political party preference is an indicator of a very explicit factor in political socialization. If the father's political party identity is clearcut, it is likely to be expressed in a number of ways observable by his children – through an expression of admiration for party leaders, contempt for the leaders of other parties, expression of pleasure at party electoral victory, and so forth. A number of studies show high correlation between party preferences of fathers and offspring, suggesting that party choice is to an important degree an expression of family tradition.[22] However, university students, regardless of social class, might be expected to break away from these traditions to a greater degree than other young people. University experience, at least in some universities, provides an exposure to a wide range of political alternatives, which is not usually the case in other Latin American institutions. The universities are often recruiting stations for leftist parties who look to idealistic, energetic student bodies as a valuable source of political cadres. In fact, studies in several other areas of the developing world suggest that university students are disproportionately supporters of left opposition parties. This is in part because the left parties appear to be the only ones unambiguously demanding wholesale "modernization" of society, a goal which the experience of higher education itself tends to inculcate, perhaps especially in an underdeveloped society.[23]

The most general finding in Table 17 is that a majority of students, regardless of their political ideology, support their father's party or one of similar ideological orientation. This is perhaps not surprising, but it is worth emphasizing to counteract the general belief in a sharp generational break between Latin American students and their parents.[24] The persistence of the effect of family political socialization is well supported by this table. A closer examination of the table reveals, however, that there are two rather distinct patterns within this general tendency. In six universities, including Puerto Rico, the national universities of Colombia and Mexico, Libre, Cauca, and Uruguay, the "holding power" of family socialization appears to decline from left to right across the ideological spectrum. For example, at the National Autonomous University of Mexico, 95 percent of sons of leftist party fathers supported leftist parties. The corresponding percentages for center and right party father-student agreement were 79 percent and 67 percent. A more marked falling off of intergenerational consensus was found at Libre university, from 89 percent to 34 percent due to the pervasive leftist ideological climate of that university.

A different pattern was found in the more conservative universities of Guanajuato, Los Andes, Javeriana, and Paraguay. In these universities, center or rightist-party fathers shared the greatest agreement with their student offspring. In these, shifts of party support tended to be between center and right parties or from left to center and conservative parties. The supporting influence of the university was clearly evident. Conversely, in the more politically active leftist universities, students tended to shift from the right to the center or left or to stay with their fathers' political orientation if that orientation was to the left.[25]

The University of Puerto Rico was somewhat anomalous according to this explanation, however. Here in 1964 a conservative, politically inactive university, revealed a considerable number of shifts to the "left," or independence party. Apparently the idea of independence had considerable appeal for students, regardless of party background. Perhaps this arose from a sensitivity for the preservation of national cultural and political identity, a concern with typically greater appeal to intellectuals than to other groups in the population.[26]

The influence of fathers' political party upon other political orientations is also highly significant. Students whose fathers supported leftist parties were

Table 17. Percentages of students preferring certain political parties by fathers' party preference[a]

Student's party		Father's party			
		Left	Center	Christian Democrat	Right
Puerto Rico					
Left		70	20	20	20
Center		19	64	30	25
Christian Democrat		0	2	40	1
Right		12	14	10	54
	N	(43)	(313)	(10)	(173)
Mexico					
UNAM					
Left		95	13	–	8
Center		5	79	–	25
Right		0	8	–	67
	N	(19)	(305)		(61)
Guanajuato					
Left		(1)	3	–	0
Center		0	84	–	15
Right		0	13	–	85
	N	(1)	(61)		(13)
Colombia					
Los Andes					
Left		55	7	–	8
Center		32	88	–	35
Right		14	5	–	57
	N	(22)	(333)	–	(120)
Javeriana					
Left		(1)	6	–	3
Center		(4)	83	–	25
Right		0	11	–	72
	N	(5)	(112)		(67)
Nacional					
Left		85	20	–	25
Center		15	75	–	26
Right		0	5	–	48
	N	(20)	(173)		(72)
Libre					
Left		89	52	–	46
Center		11	41	–	20
Right		0	7	–	34
	N	(18)	(54)		(41)

Table 17. (continued)

| | | Father's party | | |
| | | | Christian | |
Student's party		Left	Center	Democrat	Right
Cauca					
Left		44	28	–	22
Center		33	69	–	22
Right		11	3	–	56
	N	(9)	(67)		(73)
Uruguay					
Left		77	18	6	16
Center		4	60	6	8
Christian Democrat		19	17	75	19
Right		0	5	12	56
	N	(26)	(169)	(16)	(101)
Paraguay					
Left		53	6	0	4
Center		18	66	12	10
Christian Democrat		24	14	77	16
Right		4	14	12	71
	N	(49)	(131)	(17)	(140)

[a]Parties are grouped into four categories for each country, as follows:
Puerto Rico:
   Left: Party for Puerto Rican Independence (PIP)
   Center: Popular Democratic Party (PPD)
   Christian Democrat: Christian Action Party (PAC)
   Right: Statehood Republican Party (PER)
Mexico:
   Left: Popular Socialist Party (PPS), Communist Party of Mexico (PCM),
   People's Electoral Front (FEP), Authentic Party of the Mexican Revolution
   (PARM)
   Center: Institutional Revolutionary Party (PRI)
   Right: National Action Party (PAN)
Colombia:
   Left: Movement of Liberal Recovery (MRL), Communist Party of Colombia
   (PCC), National Popular Gaitanist Movement (MNPG)
   Center: Liberal Party (PL), National Front (FN)
   Right: Conservative Party (PC), supporters of Alzate Avendaño, Laureano
   Gómez, Rojas Pinilla
Uruguay:
   Left: Communists, Fidelistas (FIDEL), Socialists
   Center: Colorado Party (Battlistas)

considerably more likely than those from rightist-party backgrounds to be leftist in political ideology, to be active in student and national politics, and to have little confidence in government. These differences were greater in universities where the student body was larger and more heterogeneous and where politics at the national level represented a wider range of ideological positions. In Uruguay, those who scored at the left end of the ideological scale were 63 percent more likely to come from left rather than right party backgrounds. At the National Autonomous University of Mexico, this difference was 59 percent; at the National University in Colombia, it was 46 percent. In those universities which were either smaller, more homogeneous, or located in societies with a narrow ideological range, father's party preference had less influence on ideology, as in Puerto Rico (18 percent), Paraguay (17 percent), Libre (30 percent), Cauca (26 percent), Guanajuato (15 percent), and almost no influence at Javeriana University.

Thus, returning to the initial question of the determinants of student political orientations, the data clearly indicate the influence of family background. Our results support the findings of other scholars that there is a strong continuity between the politics of the parents and those of the children. However, our analysis goes beyond this point to reveal that political orientations acquired prior to becoming a university student are modified within the university setting under certain circumstances. Generally in universities with a strong leftist political climate, leftist parents exhibited the greatest "holding" power, and when shifts did occur they tended to be from the right to the center or left. The converse tended to be true in the more conservative universities.

Year in University and Political Orientation

We now focus upon influences more directly attributable to exposure to the university environment — social, intellectual, and cultural. While it is not easy to separate the diverse aspects of university socialization, we can differentiate

---

Christian Democrat: Christian Democratic Party
Right: Blanco Party, Union Blanca Democratica (UBD), supporters of Herrera, Federal League for Rural Action
Paraguay:
  Left: Febrerista Party
  Center: Liberal Party
  Christian Democrat: Christian Social Democratic Movement
  Right: Colorado Party

between the effect of varying degrees of involvement in student political activity and the presumably countervailing influence of family involvement.

We will first examine the most general measure, that of the number of years of exposure to the university. By comparing students at different stages of their university careers, we can estimate the extent to which the university appears to change political orientation.[27] However, since the rate of attrition in most Latin American universities is high, the socioeconomic and perhaps religious backgrounds of students in different university years may vary considerably. Thus, religion and social class were controlled in the analysis of differences across years of university.

In nearly all the universities the most consistent pattern shows a gradual increase in political radicalism to the left, political normlessness, and political involvement. In some universities this pattern is curvilinear, with an initial increase in leftist ideology and activism, followed by a decline in later years, but with a net increase in these behaviors and orientations over time. The percentage increase in leftist orientation reaches a maximum of 20 percent between the first and later years only in the Colombian universities of Libre, Cauca, and the National University. Even the University of the Andes shows an increase in leftism of 14 percent during the university career. In Puerto Rico and Paraguay, this change involves more of a shift from right to center on the political ideology scale, than a general shift to the left.

While the largest ideological shift occurs in three Colombian universities, our findings suggest that university exposure tends to enhance political involvement and to shift political orientations from right to center or left, regardless of the university or the nation. There is , however, one notable "deviant case" which challenges this generalization – the National Autonomous University of Mexico. At UNAM there are consistent *declines* in the levels of student and national political involvement, leftist political ideology, and support for parties of the left. For example, the decrease in national political involvement between the first and later years is 34 percent, in leftist ideology it is 20 percent, and in student political involvement, 10 percent.

These differences cannot be attributed to social background characteristics of the students, such as socioeconomic class and religiosity. UNAM students, over time, showed a consistent decline in political radicalism and activism, regardless of father's religion or familial socioeconomic status. What, then, does explain these findings?

The answer appears to be found largely in the interrelationship between the students and their national political environment. An important clue which points in this direction is that the longer the students attend the university, the more likely they are to shift their allegiances to the governing party, the Institutional Revolutionary Party (PRI), and away from the various Mexican leftist parties. Mexico is a de facto one-party state, and the influence of that party permeates all the major sectors of the society. There is virtually no organized opposition to the PRI, and it is widely believed that the various leftist parties and their leaders cooperate closely with the PRI. Most of the occupational and other interest-aggregating associations in the society, such as labor unions, civil service associations, and cooperatives, are affiliated with the PRI.[28] The real politics in Mexico occurs within the PRI, among its various sectors and factions, and not between PRI and other parties. Given the apparent stability, diffuseness, legitimacy, and power of the PRI, the Mexican students, as they came closer to graduation, tended to become more pragmatic in their politics. Arthur Liebman's interviews, conducted with Mexican student leaders in 1967, also lent support to this contention.[29]

Place of Residence and Political Orientation

Students are differentially involved in the life of the university. The degree and nature of this involvement is affected by a variety of factors, including the availability of extracurricular activities, the location of the students' residences, and the amount of time students spend on the campus. Are students who live at home any less likely to engage in political activity, thus inhibiting their exposure to experiences which might change their political ideology?

The evidence is somewhat mixed with respect to the effect of residence on level of student political involvement. The greatest differences between students living with families and those living elsewhere were evident in the Nacional and Libre universities in Bogotá. The differences at other universities were less pronounced, nonexistent, or reversed, but none of these differences exceeded 10 percent. Thus, place of residence, as such, appears to have little to do with the degree to which students become involved in political activities.

Analysis of the effect of residence on political ideology, again reveals few differences. The largest differences were found at the universities of Mexico, Colombia (Nacional), and Cauca, with differences between students living at home or elsewhere of 18 percent, 25 percent, and 14 percent respectively. While these differences are not great, they are suggestive of a wider discrepancy between the typical family and university political environments in these university situations. Since religion is an important determinant of political orientation in Mexico and Colombia, it would seem likely that students from Catholic families were most likely to be politically conservative if they continued to live at home. An examination of all the universities, controlling for both place of residence and father's religion, revealed little difference between students living at home and students living elsewhere, regardless of father's religion. But in Colombia among National University students, those who lived away from home were consistently more to the left. This was especially true among students from nonpracticing Catholic backgrounds. The differences in left political ideology between "home" and "other" residence students is 32 percent among the nonpracticing Catholics and 17 percent among those from more and less devout backgrounds. Smaller differences in the same direction were observed for nonpracticing Catholic students at Javeriana and Los Andes, and for practicing-Catholic background students at Cauca. No differences were observed for Libre students.

In Mexico at the UNAM a pattern almost identical to that for students at the Nacional University in Colombia was observed — students from nonpracticing Catholic families who lived away from home were much more leftist than those who lived at home, by a difference of 35 percent, with smaller differences among students with other religious backgrounds. The University of Guanajuato, however, revealed no ideological differences between students living with the family or in other settings.

These findings suggest that in the large, national university with large and active political subcultures, located in societies where religious socialization is an important influence on student political orientations, the question of student residence has a significant bearing on political orientation. Further, the influence of residence is greatest among students from the less devout Catholic families. Among students from practicing Catholic families, religious socialization may have a more persistent influence which provides a shield against the impact of student radicalism. The student from a nonreligious home has probably already been exposed to radical, or at least to anticlerical, ideas at home and finds that university radicals tend to be similar to himself. It is the student from the less devout Catholic background who is most subject to change. His family environment is more conservative than that of the university, but its influence is also less intense than in those instances where both parents are practicing Catholics. Thus, living away from home removes the student from the presence of those who are likely to sustain a conservative orientation and makes him available for radicalization through closer involvement with student political activists. This interpretation is supported by the finding that, at the National University of Colombia, students from nonpracticing Catholic backgrounds were 20 percent more likely to be politically active if they lived away from home than if they resided with their families.

Involvement in Student Politics and Political Orientations

Students with radical predispositions are most likely to take part in some form of student political activity, simply because such activity is the most available means for expressing their predispositions. In many Latin American universities student representatives sit on the highest decision-making bodies in the university, taking part in significant debate on major aspects of university life.[30] Further, student political organizations do not confine themselves to representing their constituents' interests in university affairs, but take it upon themselves to represent the student body in the area of national and international politics as well. Their action often takes the form of strikes, demonstrations, marches, and manifestoes expressing radical opposition to the national government or to foreign powers deemed inimical to the national welfare. The tradition which links the university with national and international political concerns is an old and well-established one. The University Reform Movement expressed student concern regarding the structure, functions, and goals of university education and combined these with reformist zeal at the national and international level. The growth of the movement was rapid and influential and, as discussed earlier, helped to create the model of the ideal student as one taking an active interest in the affairs of his university, community, and society.[31]

The visibility of this model and tradition is quite high in Latin American societies. Many students have either chosen or rejected the model before entering the university. Anticipatory socialization toward this model takes place in many secondary schools, in which students organize for their own local interest or join forces with university and other groups in broader causes.[32]

Nevertheless, student political involvement in the university does have an effect on political orientations and, rather than merely confirming orientations, involvement may change both their direction and intensity. Our data support the contention that the greater the number and kinds of political activity engaged in, the more likely the participant is to have a leftist political orientation. As it stands, this assertion simply supports the assumption that radical students, or those who wish to become radical, seek out political activities as a means of finding like-minded students and of publicly validating their ideal political self-images. But the variations in the strength of this relationship suggest that student political subcultures vary considerably in their political intensity and radicalism, and that, whatever the base from which students are recruited, political participation may increase radical orientations in some universities and have little effect in others. Comparing students with "low" and "high" levels of political involvement, Colombian National University students show the greatest difference in the proportions in each category who have a "left" score on the political ideology scale. Of those highly involved, 60 percent were left compared to only 18 percent for those who had low involvement. Differences in the degree of left orientation were nearly as marked among students at the University of Cauca and the national universities of Mexico and Uruguay. In each of these universities there was a difference of close to 30 percent between high and low activists (see Table 18). These are all universities with active political subcultures which recruit students from rather diverse socioeconomic and religious backgrounds and which to an important degree maintain the traditions of university reform and the model of the university student as a politically conscious activist. While self-recruitment of radicals to activist subcultures may explain part of this relationship, it is also likely that membership in such a subculture has an independent socializing effect. That is, some activists were probably radical *before* becoming active in university politics, but, for others, political involvement shifted their ideology to the left.

The size of this difference in leftist ideology between low and high activists is reduced in the remaining universities. It constitutes about 20 percent in Javeriana and Puerto Rico, 15 percent in Libre, and only 11 percent in Los Andes and Paraguay. There is no difference at the University of Guanajuato. These smaller percentages reflect the greater homogeneity of social origin at Libre and Los Andes, the more pervasive political environment at Libre, and the absence of such influences at Los Andes. The relatively large influence of activism on ideology at Javeriana is surprising and suggests political activism at this university may include participation in activities organized by the more radical universities in Bogotá since Javeriana itself permits few of these kinds of political activities. As Table 18 reveals, however, only a few students are highly active.

A test of the independent effect of activism on political ideology can be made by comparing students with differing degrees of political involvement whose fathers support the same party. This comparison should reveal whether the difference in ideology between low and high activists is due primarily to self-selection by radical students of political activism or whether active involvement is the major factor in changing political ideology. We will assume that students come to the university with a political ideology expressive of their fathers' party. "Change" will be inferred from the *difference* in political ideology among students from a common political party background, between those who become active in student politics and those who do not.

Looking first at Colombian students, the greatest differences in ideology between those low and high on the political activism scale, among those whose fathers have the same party preferences, was found for Nacional stu-

Table 18. Percentages of students high on Leftist Ideology Scale by level of student political participation

University		Student political participation		
		High	Medium	Low
Puerto Rico		21	3	1
	N	(81)	(217)	(279)
Mexico				
UNAM		54ʳ	37	21
	N	(114)	(240)	(236)
Guanajuato		15	11	14
	N	(40)	(71)	(37)
Colombia				
Los Andes		21	21	10
	N	(19)	(130)	(491)
Javeriana		25	8	6
	N	(16)	(65)	(171)
Nacional		60	40	18
	N	(142)	(139)	(110)
Libre		88	72	73
	N	(82)	(50)	(11)
Cauca		46	32	21
	N	(48)	(59)	(58)
Uruguay		49	32	18
	N	(234)	(159)	(79)
Paraguay		12	7	1
	N	(243)	(166)	(70)

dents. Those who are high on the political activism scale are about 45 percent more likely to be leftist than are those who are low on the scale. This held for students from all political party backgrounds except the Liberals and the Conservatives; for these students the difference was only 13 percent. At the other universities these differences ranged from 0 to 31 percent. (Comparisons were not possible in every case, due to the small size of subgroups in the smaller university samples.) At Libre students from conservative party backgrounds appeared to change most (25 percent), while at Los Andes students from leftist party backgrounds revealed the most change (31 percent). In every case, however, activism either produces no change, or else a change in the leftist direction — there is no change among students in any of the universities in a rightist direction.

When we compare low and high activists, controlling for father's party, the differences in political ideology for Mexico range from 11 percent to 20 percent, for Uruguay from 13 percent to 32 percent, for Puerto Rico from 13 percent to 35 percent, and for Paraguay from 2 percent to 16 percent. Although part of this apparent change is probably still an effect of self-selection, the evidence supports the argument that some of this change is due to the effect of involvement itself, that taking part in demonstrations, strikes, and political campaigns tends to push students in a leftward direction. This effect is, however, modified by other factors. When political activity is highly ideological and when it probably involves frequent acts of a dramatic and oppositionist character, it is likely to have a stronger ideological effect. This is borne out by the findings for the National University in Colombia and the University of the Republic in Uruguay. The content of "high" political activism at the universities of Los Andes and Javeriana in Colombia is undoubtedly different from that at Libre or Nacional. Students are rarely if ever involved in political opposition to university or national authority figures or institutions at Los Andes and Javeriana. At Libre, on the other hand, it is clear that students tend to be leftist whatever their party background and whether or not they are politically active. As noted above, it is the pervasive political atmosphere, as well as the selection of students for this university, which accounts for the high level of leftist ideology among students. Further, the lack of a large difference in ideology between activists and nonactivists among students from families preferring the Liberal and Conservative parties at the Nacional University in Colombia suggests that these students are less likely than those from other party backgrounds to be involved in the frequent strikes, demonstrations, and other oppositionist tactics of the student movement. The activism of the Liberal or Conservative party supporters is more likely to be made up of the more conventional activities of discussion, voting, and attending meetings. Similarly, the nature of political activism at the University of Puerto Rico differs considerably between students from *independentista* and other political backgrounds. There is a 35 percent difference in left political ideology between the low and high activists among the former group and much lower differences among the latter. The political sentiments and involvement of independentistas are similar to those of leftists on the typical Latin American campus in their opposition to United States domination and capitalism and their support for political autonomy and socialism.[33]

Student's Field of Study and Political Orientation

Perhaps the major differentiating factor among students is the field of study in which they are enrolled. In the Latin American university this differentiation is especially distinct, since students typically take all their courses within a single discipline or faculty and lack the options available to most students in North American universities. In such a program students are likely to develop a strong identification with their peers and to have little personal contact across careers. Similar social integration among students is found in North American professional schools such as medicine, engineering, and law.[34] In Latin America the higher rate of social interaction of students with their colleagues within the same career field suggests that there is a strong likelihood that common occupational and political ideological perspectives will develop.

This is especially true in fields in which the concepts and skills taught are directly relevant to analyzing and planning for the distribution of power, wealth, and other social goods. Such fields as sociology, economics, political science, and law have in common a desire to understand the social order. The field of architecture in Latin America also tends to be similarly oriented. While study in these fields is not focused on learning specific political ideologies, it is likely to sensitize students to problems inherent in the existing social order and to suggest means by which these problems may be dealt with. In contrast, study in such fields as medicine, agronomy, engineering, business, and education is confined to more limited aspects of the social structure and involves skills which are applicable to a more limited range of social institutions. Clearly the problems of health and agriculture are related to the distribution of wealth and land, but the training of physicians and agronomists is more likely to focus on the specific problems of their future clientele as individuals, rather than on problems such as the availability of medical services to the population as a whole or the distribution and concentration of land ownership. If this analysis is correct, then we might anticipate that students in the social sciences, especially in less developed societies, are more likely than students in other fields to be receptive to political ideologies which assert the need for a radical restructuring of the social order.[35] This statement can be most directly tested by the distribution of student attitudes on the political ideology scale.

Table 19 reveals, in fact, that in eight out of the ten universities, the fields of law or social sciences, including economics and architecture are the most likely to have the highest proportions of students with leftist responses on the political ideology scale. At Los Andes and Javeriana, on the other hand, medical students are highest on the scale, but in each of these universities a social science field ranks second. Although there are some variations in the general pattern, the data reveal that fields oriented to the analysis of the social structure of society most often have the highest proportion of leftists within each university.

Another point to be made about the relationship between field of study and political ideology is that this relationship is a strong one in some universities

Table 19. Percentages (and numbers) of students scoring high on Leftist Ideology Scale, by university and field of academic specialization

Puerto Rico			UNAM (Mexico)		
Social science	13	(73)	Economics	76	(99)
Law	7	(96)	Science	47	(55)
Humanities	6	(49)	Law	34	(169)
Education	3	(95)	Engineering	18	(236)
Engineering	3	(71)	Medicine	18	(62)
Natural science	2	(50)	Philosophy	10	(59)
Business	1	(70)	Total	32	(682)
General education					
(1st year course)	0	(60)	Guanajuato (Mexico)		
Medicine	0	(13)	Law	25	(48)
Total	5	(577)	Science	18	(17)
			Engineering	5	(83)
			Total	13	(148)
Uruguay			Paraguay		
Architecture	57	(46)	Law	22	(41)
Economics	50	(50)	Architecture	17	(46)
Vet. medicine	44	(23)	Engineering	13	(45)
Dentistry	41	(49)	Humanities	10	(39)
Chemistry	38	(48)	Social service	10	(30)
Agronomy	36	(50)	Economics	8	(59)
Medicine	36	(36)	Total	9	(417)
Law	29	(49)			
Engineering	29	(49)			
Humanities	26	(50)			
Total	38	(469)			
		(Colombia)			
Los Andes			Javeriana		
Medicine	26	(61)	Medicine	16	(45)
Architecture	16	(62)	Social science	8	(51)
Economics	14	(70)	Law-economics	8	(26)
Engineering	12	(319)	Engineering	7	(45)
Social science	11	(9)	Humanities	2	(42)
Humanities	6	(78)	Total	8	(209)
Exact science	6	(32)			
Total	13	(631)	Libre		
			Law-economics	90	(79)
Nacional			Engineering	83	(12)
Social science	74	(38)	Education	47	(68)
Law	52	(89)	Total	71	(159)
Economics	46	(24)			
Medicine	44	(45)	Cauca		
Humanities	39	(13)	Law-economics	47	(17)
Exact science	31	(45)	Engineering	30	(78)
Engineering	31	(65)	Medicine	26	(54)
Education	15	(27)	Total	30	(149)
Total	43	(347)			

and a relatively weak one in others. If the percentage difference in the proportion of leftists between those fields at the top and bottom of the list in Table 19 is taken for each university, we obtain the following results:

National Autonomous University of Mexico	66 percent
National University of Colombia	59
Libre University	43
University of the Republic (Uruguay)	31
University of Cauca	21
University of Guanajuato	20
University of Los Andes	20
Javeriana University	14
University of Paraguay	14
University of Puerto Rico	13

As we can see, the greatest percentage differences among fields are found in universities with the most active and ideologically left political subcultures. Within these universities, then, it would appear that political subcultures are formed to an important degree within careers. In universities containing a smaller proportion of leftists there is greater similarity across fields of study. In the more conservative universities, the prevailing political climate seems to prevent the emergence of highly differentiated political orientations linked to careers.

Differences in Political Orientations Among Faculties by Year in University

So far, we have discussed fields of specialization without respect to the student's year of enrollment. But the specific year may conceal important variations due to trends in political orientations over time within different faculties or to variations produced by differences in the social composition within faculties due to differential recruitment and retention rates. There is evidence that fields of specialization vary considerably in the drop-out rate, whether because of academic failure, economic difficulties, or other causes. It may be that the more "radical" careers are those which retain more of their entering students, while the more "conservative" careers suffer a higher selective drop-out rate, with students from lower socioeconomic origins withdrawing at a higher rate than those from higher social status origins.

Table 20 shows the proportion of students enrolling in 1963 in the second year in several faculties in Colombia, as a percentage of the first year enrollment during the previous year, 1962. This is an indirect index, since students enrolling in the second year may include those who had withdrawn before

Table 20. Retention rates for selected fields of study, Colombia, all universities, 1962–1963; second year enrollment (1963) as percentage of first year enrollment (1962)

Field	Percent
Law	91
Natural science	85
Economics	83
Medicine	77
Humanities	74
Civil engineering	65
Engineering	58
Agronomy	39

Source: Jorge I. Domínguez, "Universities and Development" (Harvard University, unpublished paper, 1967), Table IV.1A, p. 50, derived from Republica de Colombia, Departamento Administrativo Nacional de Estadística, *Estadísticas Culturales, 1962*, pp. 364–366; *Ibid., 1963*, pp. 356–358.

1962, and are re-enrolling, and those who did not enroll in the second year, 1963, but who may enroll in some subsequent year. Nevertheless, the differences are sufficiently large to indicate significant variation in the retention rates among the various fields.[36]

Engineering and especially agronomy show particularly low rentention rates, perhaps because of the high prerequisites in mathematics. Law, on the other hand, has a very high rate of retention and is probably the least demanding field in terms of special preuniversity preparation. These findings suggest, then, that what appear in Table 19 to be marked differences among fields of study in student political orientations, may be due in part to differences in the difficulty of entering and remaining in the fields. Such difficulties could affect the social and political composition of the student cohort in different years of each course. If this were the case, it would argue for recruitment rather than socialization as the factor which explains the variations among the different fields. We have already discussed differential recruitment to the various faculties and found that this was relevant for explaining ideology.

To examine year of enrollment and social origins by field of study simultaneously would be difficult because of the small sample sizes. Therefore, we utilized another approach. Table 21 shows difference in political orientations (Left/Right scale) for three of the four universities which were found to have the greatest interfaculty variation in student ideology — the national universities of Uruguay, Mexico, and Colombia (Libre is omitted because it has only three faculties, thus restricting comparison).

The faculties have been ordered from left to right, in order of decreasing proportions of leftist ideology for the faculty as a whole. Reading across the rows, for each university, it is evident that for the Universities of Colombia and Mexico, and to a lesser degree for Uruguay, the original rank order is preserved when year of enrollment is controlled. For the first two universities, then, the original finding that showed social science and law students highest on the left ideology scale and engineering and education students lowest, obtains for each year of enrollment. This suggests that whatever the effects of selective recruitment and "dropping out" within different fields of study, these factors do not appear to influence significantly the overall pattern of ideological orientations among the various fields.

But this finding tends to raise some difficulty with our original explanation of the variations among the fields – that the content of ideas and problems focused upon in various fields explains the extent of student radicalism in each. Differences in the percentages of leftist students within fields over time were compared with percentage differences between fields (far right column).

This analysis reveals that the variations *among* fields of study are much greater, by and large, than is the difference between entering and later years of study *within* fields of study. Thus, socialization within fields does not appear to contribute as much to the variation among fields as does the initial recruitment of students to each field. For instance, our findings for Colombia would suggest that entering social science students are overwhelmingly more radical, as a group, than are the entering education students and that this difference in ideology is maintained over time.

This table also affords us the opportunity to compare the influence of socialization within fields as opposed to socialization within the general university setting. The bottom row of figures, showing change over time within university field of study indicates that in two-thirds of the fields for which there are adequate data in Table 21, there is a sizable increase in the proportion of leftist students. This suggests that universities do have a generally radicalizing influence upon students, whatever the field of study. But it must be reemphasized that the table suggests that initial career choice is closely related to ideological orientation. As measured by our scale, those who have come to take leftist positions on a wide range of political figures and issues appear to choose those fields of study which they perceive as compatible with their ideological perspectives – the social sciences, and to some extent, law – in Colombia and Mexico. But once enrolled in a field, the student tends to change his initial

Table 21. Percentages of students scoring high on Leftist Ideology (left/right) Scale by university, academic course, and year of enrollment

National University of Colombia

Year	Social science	Law	Medicine	Exact science	Engineering	Education	Diff. hi-lo[a]
First	80 (10)	39 (23)	25 (8)	20 (20)	20 (25)	0 (10)	80
Second	81 (16)	65 (20)	40 (10)	36 (11)	33 (24)	17 (6)	48[b]
Third or higher	70 (10)	53 (45)	52 (27)	43 (14)	44 (16)	27 (11)	43
Diff. 3rd–1st	-10	14	12[b]	31	24	27[b]	—

National Autonomous University of Mexico

Year	Econ.	Law	Engineering	Medicine	Philos.	Science	Diff. hi-lo
First	65 (17)	36 (22)	0 (1)	0 (0)	29 (7)	75 (4)	29[b]
Second	75 (47)	37 (101)	20 (123)	0 (0)	0 (0)	100 (3)	55
Third or higher	82 (34)	29 (38)	18 (99)	18 (62)	8 (52)	40 (45)	74
Diff. 3rd–1st	17	-7	-2[b]	b	b	b	

University of the Republic (Uruguay)

	Arch.	Econ.	Dent.	Chem.	Vet. – Agron.	Med.	Law	Engin.	Hum.	Diff. hi-lo
First	50	38	29	27	19	0	29	36	17	21[b]
	(6)	(16)	(7)	(11)	(16)	(6)	(17)	(11)	(12)	
Second	69	58	38	42	36	29	33	30	23	46
	(13)	(12)	(16)	(19)	(22)	(14)	(12)	(10)	(13)	
Third or higher	52	57	46	39	48	47	25	26	29	32
	(27)	(21)	(26)	(18)	(33)	(30)	(20)	(27)	(24)	
Diff. 3rd–1st	−17[b]	19	8[b]	12	29	18[b]	−4	−10	12	

[a] Difference between highest and lowest percentages among academic courses, by year.
[b] Percentages representing numbers less than 10 have not been used in calculating either difference.

Table 22.   Percentages of students scoring high on Leftist Ideology (left/right) Scale by university, academic course, social status[a], and year of enrollment

Year	Social science[b]			Natural science		
	Low SS	High SS	Diff.	Low SS	High SS	Diff.
National University of Colombia						
1-2	53	45	+8	34	20	+14
	(57)	(42)		(53)	(45)	
3-4	57	50	+7	65	33	+32
	(30)	(34)		(23)	(18)	
Diff.	+4	+5		+31	+13	
National Autonomous University of Mexico						
1-2	53	37	+16	26	20	+6
	(133)	(60)		(57)	(74)	
3-4	45	21	+24	18	26	-8
	(64)	(57)		(84)	(103)	
Diff.	-8	-16		-8	+6	

[a]The Social Status Scale was arbitrarily divided as close as possible to the median, to provide roughly equal categories of "low" and "high" for each university.
[b]"Social science" includes education, law, sociology, psychology, economics, and humanities.

orientations in a leftward direction, regardless of the field of study, a change which suggests the pervasive influence of university experience rather than the specific ideological impact of the field of study.

By combining academic courses into two major categories, "natural" and "social science," and by dichotomizing socioeconomic status, we can obtain sufficient numbers to analyze the simultaneous effect of year in university, social class, and academic courses in two major universities — UNAM and Nacional (Colombia). (Table 22.) Within field of study and year of enrollment, students from lower SES (socioeconomic status) origins are consistently more leftist than are their higher SES counterparts. This difference is especially large for third-to-fourth year natural science students at the Nacional — two-thirds of the low SES students are leftist, compared to one-third of the high SES students. Finally, when we control for SES and year of enrollment, we find that the social sciences have consistently higher proportions of students with leftist ideology.

Thus, the effects of social class origin and field of study upon political ideology appear to be stronger than the effects of time in university.

This finding for these university students provides further support for our major argument that political predispositions are shaped to an important extent *prior* to university entrance by family socialization and intellectual-vocational interests. When these interests are "ratified" by choice of career within the university, the student is, in effect, choosing a like-minded peer group within the university. We therefore contend that faculties or fields of study do exert an ideological influence, precisely because they provide a social and physical environment within which students with similar backgrounds and interests group together.

There also appears to be another factor intervening in and accentuating the relationship between field of study and student politics particularly in the early university years and in the more activist or leftist schools. Evidence from studies of Paraguayan and Chilean students indicates that political activists in the more politicized faculties or schools make a determined effort to contact, socialize, and politicize newly arrived students. This effort does not seem to be made in the less active or more conservative schools. In fact, in both Paraguay and Chile, student activists obtain the names of incoming freshmen and begin to politicize them before they are even officially enrolled.[37]

One would expect that these political tactics bring some degree of positive results thereby reinforcing the relationship between field of study and ideology. Newly arrived students are politically socialized by student activists before they enter their chosen field. Conversely, those pre-enrollees who hold strong political views which are contrary to those which predominate at a school might be expected to chose another field rather than subject themselves to significant political tensions during their freshman year. In either case, such personal efforts apparently contribute to strengthening the association between school or field of study and student politics, particularly in the earlier years and in the more politicized schools.

Our results indicate the relative importance of recruitment and socialization as significant factors in accounting for variations in political ideology among the different fields. *Recruitment* or the political orientations that the student carries with him into the university rather than the political socialization which occurs within different fields during his tenure as a student, appears to explain most of the differences between students in different fields. This finding contributes to the closing of a major gap within the field of student politics. Unfortunately, there is virtually no other available evidence bearing on this essential point to which we can relate our findings.

There is, however, at least one piece of research which does support our conclusion that preuniversity political orientations are more significant than those learned while in an academic field while attending a university. In a study of 944 Cornell University students who were questioned in 1952 and then again in 1954, the investigators were interested in assessing the relative effects of values and field of study. In the entire sample, they found that the values the students brought with them into the university were more salient than the socialization impact of an academic discipline. After two years students were more likely to change their field of study to bring it into accord with their values than they were to change their values to bring them into line with their academic field. Further investigation utilizing a subsample, business majors, reached the same conclusion with respect to the interplay between socioeconomic values and the choice of business as a career, a field presumed to be inherently a conservative one. Among those who were business majors in 1952 holding a weak socioeconomic orientation, two-thirds had changed their field by 1954. Conversely among those who were strongly conservative initially, about three quarters remained in the business field two years later.[38]

We would argue that there is a need to push back the study of political socialization of students to the level of the secondary school, if not further, in order to determine the points at which student ideology is most heavily influenced. While students enhance the basis of their political beliefs as a result of their university experience it should not be assumed that students are "ideologically underdeveloped" on entrance to the university and that the university provides the environment within which most ideological socialization takes place. Thus, although there is a tendency for students to modify their initial political orientations in a leftward direction during their university years, it would appear that students come to the university with fairly well-developed political beliefs.

5 Conservative Students

Until quite recently, the political attitudes and behavior of the nonradicals, particularly those of the conservatives, among the Latin American students have been neglected by social scientists and the mass media. Attention has been focused almost entirely upon the student radicals. Actually, the Latin American student radicals represent only a minority of the students.[1] The majority, indeed the vast majority, are either moderates or conservatives who eschew active participation in politics. The primary function of this chapter will be to delineate the social profile of this major body of students.

THE NONRADICALS

The first task is to determine the distribution of radicals and nonradicals in the Latin American student population.[2] Let us, initially, use two key political indicators to differentiate the students: (1) attitude toward Fidel Castro and (2) the number of strikes or demonstrations in which the student has actively participated.

Looking at Table 23 we observe that in *none* of the five societies does a majority of the students express favorable attitudes toward Fidel Castro. In fact, even in the countries in which the students are most favorable to Castro, Uruguay and Mexico, six out of every ten claim to be anti-Castro. The proportion of anti-Castro students increases until in Puerto Rico, ninety-five out of every one hundred evaluate the Cuban prime minister negatively. A further indication of anti-Castro sentiment was revealed when the students from the two countries with the highest proportion of pro-Castro sentiment, Mexico and Uruguay, were subjected to additional analysis. The students in each country were divided into those who gave the most extreme pro- and anti-Castro responses. When the extreme "pro" category was compared with the extreme "anti" category, in both cases the percentage of students in the most unfavorable category was

Table 23. Percentages of students indicating pro or con attitudes toward Castro by country

Attitude toward Castro	Country				
	Uruguay	Mexico	Colombia	Paraguay	Puerto Rico
Pro	41	41	26	11	5
Con	59	59	74	89	95
N	(414)	(751)	(1447)	(332)	(562)

twice as large as the percentage in the most favorable category – among the Mexicans it was 17 percent versus 38 percent, and for the Uruguayans it was 19 percent versus 41 percent. Thus, in no country is there intense support of Castro by any significant percentage of students.

How active are the students in strikes and demonstrations? With the exception of the Uruguayans, approximately half or more than half of the students in each country, ranging from 47 percent of the Paraguayans to 79 percent of the Puerto Ricans, asserted that they had not participated actively in any demonstrations or strikes. It is interesting to note that the comparable percentage of nondemonstrators in the United States, in 1969 at the height of American student activism, was approximately the same as that in Puerto Rico, roughly about 70 to 80 percent of the student population.[3] Turning back to the Latin American students, an examination of those who stated that they had actively participated in two or more demonstrations reveals that only among the Uruguayans did the percentage exceed one-third, and among this group the percentage rose to an impressive 70 percent. Thirty-two percent of the Paraguayan students claimed to have actively participated in two or more strikes or demonstrations. No doubt, given the nature of the dictatorial regime and its toleration of token dissent these were directed toward university issues.[4] Of the three remaining groups of students, the percentage of participants did not exceed 19 percent, with the Puerto Ricans having the lowest percentage, 8 percent. Thus, considering all five national groups, Latin American students, with the notable exception of the Uruguayans, tend not to participate actively in strikes and demonstrations, and those who do participate in two or more represent small percentages of their fellow students, again with the exception of the Uruguayans.

In order to obtain a more general measure of political ideology with which to compare students from the various countries, a political ideology scale, the same one as in chapter 4, was utilized.[5] The scale was trisected, again as in chapter 4, with the upper third designated left, the middle third, center, and

Table 24. Percentages of students actively participating in strikes or demonstrations by country

Number of strikes or demonstrations	Country				
	Uruguay	Mexico	Colombia	Paraguay	Puerto Rico
0	22	60	64	47	79
2 or more	70	17	19	32	8
N	429	822	1577	469	569

the bottom third, right. On the basis of these cutting points, in every country with the exception of Uruguay, the proportion of rightist students was larger than the proportion of leftists. In Uruguay the left and right were fairly balanced; among the Mexicans and the Colombians the right was almost twice as large as the left, and among the Paraguayans, the right was thirty-five times as large. In Puerto Rico the left with 2 percent, was virtually nonexistent, while the right comprised about three-quarters of the students. Thus, on the basis of this distribution, the left in the mid-1960s comprised a small minority of Latin American students. In every country the right, combined with the center, represented the large majority of the students, from 74 percent among the Uruguayans to 98 percent of the Puerto Ricans (see Table 25).

Table 25. Position of students (by percent) on left/right scale and percent activists among those students (by country)

Position	Country				
	Uruguay	Mexico	Colombia	Paraguay	Puerto Rico
Position of students on scale					
Left	26	17	18	5	2
Center	50	50	48	49	26
Right	24	33	34	46	72
N	(475)	(830)	(1594)	(482)	(577)
Activists					
Left	35	31	45	7	9
Center	44	49	46	51	40
Right	21	20	9	42	51
N	(277)	(221)	(380)	(293)	(124)

Therefore, on the basis of the above data, the typical student in Latin America cannot be portrayed as a radical activist. The majority of the students do not actively engage in strikes or demonstrations. The majority of the students are anti-Castro. And the vast majority of the students in each country can be categorized as conservatives or moderates. The radical activist is part of a small minority in Latin America. In fact, there are probably few student bodies in any of the countries surveyed in which the majority of the students profess to be radicals and to be constantly engaged in strikes and demonstrations. In the United States, during the current era of the "activist student," it has been estimated that the total membership of all student leftist groups totals about 12,000 to 50,000 in a student population of 7,000,000.[6] In 1968 a Harris Poll estimated that 100,000, or about 1 to 2 percent of the student population, were radical activists.[7] If there is such a thing as a *typical Latin American student*, he is much more likely to be politically conservative or apathetic than he is to be radical.

Rightists and centrists constitute a majority among Latin American students, but they have been unable to translate their majority status into commensurate political influence. Throughout Latin America leftist students are a minority, yet leftists and their parties tend to win in student elections.[8] Ironically, during the late nineteenth and early twentieth centuries, working-class parties in Europe and North America found themselves in the reverse of this situation. Conservative parties, the spokesmen for the interests of the upper strata, were able to best the working-class parties in elections despite the fact that the latter ostensibly represented the interests of the majority of the electorate.[9] The question raised by the political situation of the Latin American students is, how has a minority been able to exercise a political influence on their campuses far beyond that which their numbers would indicate?

Various factors and lines of argument have been employed to explain this phenomenon. One is that the left is more interested in and works harder at politics than the right or the moderates.[10] In each of the five countries in our study, conservatives and radicals were divided according to the extent of their involvement in student political activity as measured by a scale of political involvement.[11] In every country, among those students who were highly involved in student activity (as measured by those in the top half of the scale), the proportion of rightists was smaller than their proportion in the general student population (see Table 25). Conversely, the percentage of leftists in the activist population was higher than in the overall student body. Similar findings were obtained in a study of Argentine and Brazilian students.[12] Indeed, among the Mexican and Colombian activists, the left outnumbered the right (69 to 45 and 170 to 42) even though among the general student population their numbers were half those of the rightists. However, among the Puerto Ricans and the Paraguayans, even in the activist subgroup, the right was larger than the left although the percentage differences were smaller in this group than in the general sample. Thus, overall, the right is larger than the left in each country except Uruguay where the two are almost equal. Among the activist students, however, the left is larger than the right in three of the five countries, and in the other two the left has grown while the right has declined. These figures reveal that, relatively speaking, the right does not contribute the same number to the ranks of the activists as does the left. This fact helps to explain why, despite its overall numerical superiority vis-à-vis the left, the right does so poorly politically. Rightists are unwilling to become involved in or work as hard at politics as the leftists. In any political situation, the size and the character of the activists or cadres tend to be important factors in the shaping of politics. They are often more meaningful than the political attitudes and behavior of the vast majority who tend not to be involved.

It has also been suggested that the electoral success of the student left is not a good indicator of support for the left *qua* left on Latin American campuses. Student leftists tend to be concerned with a number of areas and policies. Among their varied concerns, from the time of the Córdoba Manifesto, are the campus and the extension of the rights and powers of the students. Alistair Hennessy suggests that the pursuit of student interests is the root of the electoral success of student leftists. Leftists, he contends, are regarded as more forceful and more effective in the promotion of basic student interests than are conservatives or moderates. Thus, the majority on campus may oppose or be indifferent to the informing ideology and the off-campus positions of the leftist candidates and support them strictly on the basis of their stands on issues pertaining to the campus.[13]

It is also precisely in the area of practical student concerns that the right forfeits potential supporters to the left. The concerns of the right do not span as wide an area as those of the left. In fact, the primary focus of the right appears to be the existence and activities of the left on campus. Among the countries in our study, Puerto Rico and Mexico have, in recent years, given birth to right-wing student organizations whose sole *raison d'être* is the fight against communism in the universities.[14] On another level, both the University Federation of Anti-Communists (FAU) in Puerto Rico and the University Movement for a Renewed Orientation (MURO) in Mexico, the former implicitly and the latter explicitly, were in favor of the removal of politics from the campus so that the university, as one MURO leader expressed it, can become a house of studies or a temple of knowledge.[15]

Furthermore, the right offers the mass of the students very little in terms of self-interest. The appeals of the right are limited to those students who are militantly anti-Communist and those who favor a campus without student organizations making demands upon faculty and administration. Why, given this situation, should the mass of students cast their votes for the right? Until the right choses truly to enter the political marketplace and to fight for supporters and voters on issues that have immediate relevance to student lives, it will continue to be in a weak political position on campus.

Seymour M. Lipset views the problem in a similar vein. He contends that the ideology of conservatism has much to do with the political inactivity of the conservatives on campus. From the perspective of conservatism, the university is seen as an apolitical institution which should be concerned solely with studies and education. Moderates and centrists are likely to share this perspective of the university. Thus, in effect, Lipset contends that the political field is open to the minority, primarily the liberals and the left, who conceive of the university as an instrument for social and political change. In the case of the left then, ideology helps thrust its student adherents into political activism while in the case of the right, the ideology of conservatism inhibits such activity.[16] As pointed out above, when the conservatives do enter into political activity, their policies tend to be limited in scope, defensive in nature, and primarily intended to correct a campus situation which, in their view, has gotten out of hand.

Another factor or mechanism accounting for the lack of political influence by conservative students among their peers in Latin America is the popular feeling that casts the university student, particularly in less developed nations, in the role of a progressive force. Therefore, implicit in the status of "student" is the expectation that he will be an idealist concerned with equality, freedom, and social justice and that he will, during the course of his life as a student, eschew personal and materialistic concerns.[17] The framers of the Córdoba Manifesto were aware of this popular definition of the student when they wrote, "Youth is always surrounded by heroism. It is disinterested. It is pure. It has not yet had time to contaminate itself."[18] This perspective is not limited to the developing nations. The "silent generation" label placed on the American student generation of the 1950s was a shorthand criticism of the fact that that generation seemed not to care about the inequities in American society.

Leftist students in Latin America appear to have been able to create an identification between themselves and the ideal student. Various Marxist and social ideologies have become interwoven with the concept of youthful idealism and indeed tend to be regarded as the political expression of that idealism. In such a situation, it becomes difficult for the right to mobilize and to attack the left.

In a similar fashion, the conservatives are denied an ideological platform from which to attack the left. Student advocates of the right or the status quo are in a poor strategic position, especially in societies marked by extremes in living standards, racism, colonial exploitation or the like, to oppose, or rally support for an attack on, students who wrap themselves in the mantle of social concern and propose to do something about societal inequities.

Lacking an ideological platform, the conservatives and centrists have focused on tactics, thus clearly demonstrating the ideological dominance of the left. Without the expression of a counter ideology or the setting forth of counter goals, the right does not have political ideological leverage. The middle mass, lacking an ideological position to compete with that of the left, either moves to the left or becomes politically neutralized. In any case, it is the left which sets the political tone of the campus. In sum, the ideology of the left functions both as a shield for its adherents and as an impetus for action, while the ideology of the right inhibits its adherents from acting on the basis of their beliefs or from building a mass base on the Latin American campus.

Finally, it should be noted that the defeat of the conservative student in Latin America is limited to the campus. After graduation, he enters institutions and bureaucracies in the world of business or of government which are sympathetic with his ideological outlook. It is the victorious student leftist who, upon leaving the university, confronts a hostile environment. At that point he must decide whether to continue his political activity, in the context of a political party which can guarantee him few opportunities for status or victory, or move into business and government agencies in which he must modify or moderate his political views. The pressure is on the student leftist to be active while he is a student. The conservative can afford to lose on campus because his defeat is usually limited and temporary. If the leftist does not win while at the university, his opportunity for victory in any other institutional arena is virtually nil.

DETERMINANTS OF CONSERVATISM

National Politics

If we examine the distribution of students on the political ideology scale by country (as in Table 25), we note that Uruguay has the lowest proportion of rightists or conservatives, while Puerto Rico has the largest. Paraguay, with 46 percent, is second to Puerto Rico in the percentage of conservatives while only about a third of the Mexicans and Colombians can be so classified. Is there any relationship between the size of the conservative proportion and the politics or development stage of the country? In terms of socioeconomic development, as measured by per capita income, percent of school-age children in schools, physicians per 1,000 population, and other such indicators, the rank ordering of the five countries is: (1) Puerto Rico, (2) Uruguay, (3) Mexico, (4) Colombia, and (5) Paraguay. If we look at the countries with the highest and lowest percentage of student conservatives, we find Uruguay with 24 percent and Puerto Rico with 72 percent, the two societies of the five under consideration that are most similar according to indicators of development.[19] (See Table 25.) Paraguay, given its relative position on the same indicators, would be considered the least developed or least advanced of all five. Unlike what could be predicted Paraguay has a comparatively high percentage of conservative students, 46 percent, second in this regard to Puerto Rico. A look beyond the gross socioeconomic indicators into the national context of each of these countries provides important insights into the relative distributions of conservative students.

Puerto Rico, with the highest percentage of conservative students is not an independent Latin American country; it is a Commonwealth of the United States and has been in the possession of the United States since the turn of the century. Economically, it has benefited from this relationship, and if it were to be considered an independent country vis-à-vis the rest of Latin America, it would be the most advanced economically. During its years of association with the United States, Puerto Rico has had its educational system molded by Americans. As a result, Puerto Rico today ranks next to the United States in the world in the percentage of the college-age cohort attending college. Puerto Rico has also been influenced by the values, norms, and mores of the United States in other areas, particularly the political. To a large extent, Puerto Rico can be described as "more royalist than the king." Most Puerto Ricans in 1964 [the date of the student survey] seemed fearful of jeopardizing, in any way, the relationship with the United States which has proven so beneficial to them. In fact, in 1960, 1964, and 1968 elections the sentiment for statehood has grown while the number of proindependence votes has rapidly diminished. In addition, the same political party, the Popular Democratic Party (PPD), governed the island from 1940 to 1968, and this meant political stability for almost three decades. It is therefore not surprising that one would find so many Puerto Rican students in 1964 committed to the status quo and to conservatism.[20]

Uruguay, on the other hand, has the lowest percentage of conservative students. It has had since early in the century a quasi-socialist, welfare oriented government. Public employees constitute about one-quarter of the labor force. The nation's liberal pension plan encourages early retirement and has resulted in a situation where 30 percent of the total population are completely reliant on government pension payments. In addition, Uruguay has a family allowance, liberal unemployment benefits, and has even written the provisions of Christmas benefits into the law. From the mid-1950s to the present, however, the economic situation has rapidly deteriorated. Rampant inflation, industrial and agricultural stagnation, and growing unemployment and trade deficits have plagued Uruguay during this period.

Politically, Uruguay has gained an international reputation for its political stability and its democratic practices. Two parties have dominated politics in this century, the *Colorado* and the *Blanco* or Nationalist Party. Between them they account for approximately 90 percent of the total vote. Despite this competition, the Colorados have been the governing party since 1865 with the recent exception of the years from 1958 to 1966 when the Blancos held office. Other parties also run in the elections, including Communists, Socialists, various Marxist organizations, and the Christian Democrats. These elections are free and all points of view tend to be represented either by factions of the major parties which run as semiautonomous units or by small independent parties.

Comparing the two major parties, the Colorados have been considered to be the more liberal. Based in the urban middle and working classes, the Colorado party during the long period of its governing instituted numerous reforms and created the welfare oriented system referred to above. The Blanco party has had its major base of support in the countryside particularly among the major landowners. In actuality, the two parties have shared power. The Colorados limited their reform measures to the major urban areas and allowed the Blancos to have a free hand in the countryside. As a result, while Montivedeo developed democratic and progressive institutions, the countryside scarcely changed, remaining in the hands of a virtually feudal landed oligopoly. By the 1950s the reforming impulse of the Colorados seemed gone. Increasingly, whatever historic differences once existed between the two major parties narrowed to the point in the 1960s where it became very difficult to distinguish politically between them. Both appear to have grown more cynical and corrupt and both have proved unable to satisfactorily deal with Uruguay's persistent economic problems.[21]

The political developments which occurred within the university community and at the national level in Uruguay during the 1950s and 1960s elucidates the interrelationship between student and national politics. The continuing deteriorating political and economic conditions can be viewed as an important and everpresent context during this period. In 1950 the Uruguayan Federation of University Students (FEUU) established a committee to draft a new Organic Law for the governing of the University of the Republic. It was prompted to do so by the actions of the national government and the university administration. The Parliament had passed an antireformist bill and the University's Central Council had mismanaged, in the students' view, a dispute within the School of Agronomy. By the end of the year, the FEUU committee had completed its work and the leaders of FEUU secured the agreement of the Central Council of the University to convene the General Cloister for the purpose of writing a new Organic Law for the University.

At the same time at the national level, political leaders had decided to revise the constitution of the country. The debate over the revision as well as the fact that the constitution was to be revised prompted the students to launch a major campaign for the inclusion of a provision granting autonomy to the university and the entire public school system. The inclusion of Article 205 in the 1951 Constitution granting autonomy to the University was regarded by the students as a great victory and spurred their efforts on behalf of University reforms.

During the next seven years there was incessant bargaining between the students and other sectors of the university community over provisions in the proposed Organic Law, particularly those pertaining to the students' role in the selection of professors and in the governance of the university. Finally in the Spring of 1958, the Central Council of the University approved the final draft and the rector dispatched it to the government. The students, fearing for the fate of the legislation in hostile parliamentary hands, mounted a major campaign including mass meetings and heated street demonstrations, to pressure the legislature. By the end of October, 1958, the University of the Republic had a new Organic Law.

The FEUU had won a new and greater victory that it had in 1951. The new law gave the students direct and significant representation in all of the governing bodies of the university. In addition, professors, who now were limited to five year appointments, were faced with student representatives who evaluated them for purposes of selection and re-election. Inspired by their political victories in 1951 and especially in 1958, the FEUU, utilizing the positions and leverage gained, steered the university students on a more militant and a more radical course over the next decade. The victory of Castro in 1959 gave additional impetus to this tendency.[22]

This turn toward increased militancy also coincided with important political and economic developments within Uruguay, which again had the effect of reinforcing the students' movement and commitment to the left. From 1958 until 1966, the national government came into the hands of the conservative Blanco party and the already deteriorating economic situation became even worse. Corruption increased and the political ineptitude of the Blancos grew increasingly evident.

In 1964 another study of the Uruguayan university students corroborated our findings about the depth of student alienation and disillusionment with their government and the economic and political systems of their nation. Over 80 percent felt that their government was corrupt. A like percentage also believed capitalism to be incompatible with economic growth. And, less than 50 percent thought that "the representative democratic system was giving 'satisfactory results'."[23]

In the 1960s the students led by FEUU became progressively oriented toward the national and international scene. They saw the country's economic situation go from bad to worse. Neither the Blancos nor the Colorados, who returned to power in 1966, offered meaningful approaches to the handling of the mounting problem. The long standing means of coping with the economic crisis through deficit financing and increased government hiring lost even their short term effectiveness. Inflation increased while agricultural and industrial productivity failed to expand. Rising unemployment, numerous business failures, and waves of often violent strikes were testaments to the gravity of the situation.

The government almost desperately began to impose increasingly severe anti-inflation measures culminating in 1968 with the imposition of wage and price controls. These and other stringent measures engendered an increasing level of popular opposition, even among the middle class. Protests grew in number and intensity and, of course, the students were active in them. In fact, several students were killed in clashes with the police. The most visible political outcome which flowed from these events and developments was the formation and then rise of the *Tupumaros*, the most successful urban guerilla unit currently fighting in Latin America.

The Tupumaros originated within the militant wing of Uruguay's Socialist party in 1962 and 1963. The leader of this faction and a prime organizer of the Tupumaros was Raúl Sendic, an advanced student of law at the university. Frustrated by unsuccessful nonviolent efforts to organize and improve the conditions of the sugar cane workers, Sendic and his left socialists moved toward armed conflict and political terrorism. Throughout the 1960s, the Tupumaros have continually embarassed the government and weakened its legitimacy through robbing banks, exposing government corruption, seizing arms, and kidnapping prominent Uruguayans and foreign diplomats. Their long range objective is to coalesce the left and create a revolutionary situation in Ururguay. The Tupumaro membership appears to consist mainly of students, former students, and professionals. Various schools of the University of the Republic including Arts, Architecture, and Medicine have been especially active in the provision of recruits and sympathizers as well as serving as sites for secret Tupumaro meetings. The success and daring of the guerillas' operations, coupled with the government's relatively ineffective but repressive measures taken to deal with them, all the while against a backdrop of a worsening economic situation have served to increase support for the Tupumaros among the students in particular and the Uruguayan population in general.[24]

Student support of political terrorism can be seen as almost the logical culmination of events beginning in the early 1950s. Years of political activity and organizing on the campus crowned by major university related victories coupled with the inability of the established parties to deal with serious political and economic problems produced a militant student body while inhibiting the growth and development of a more conservative student force.

The second largest proportion of conservatives is found among the Paraguayan students. Paraguay is a traditional Latin American dictatorship with power concentrated in the hands of General Alfredo Stroessner, president of the country since 1954. Paraguay is also one of Latin America's poorest states ranking ahead of only Haiti with respect to per capita income. Although the Stroessner regime has permitted the existence of a token opposition, in reality a genuine political opposition has not been allowed to function. The regime has used terror and repressive techniques against its opponents, both real and suspected. As a consequence of these measures as well as a poor economic situation it is estimated that about one third of the Paraguayan population is in exile, mostly in Argentina.

The government has paid close attention to the students in order to prevent the university from becoming a base of opposition. There was some justification for this concern for in the mid-1950s the university students did indeed constitute one of the most active oppositional elements in the country. In 1955 the students launched a strike, the first one in thirty years, in order to press for basic civil liberties such as the right to speak, freedom to associate, and freedom for the press as well as for university autonomy. In response to this perceived threat the regime systematically purged the university of actual and potential faculty and student dissidents. It invoked political critera in the selection of both professors and students. Administrators selected by and responsible to the regime run the university. Close attention is paid to the students and student affairs in order to detect any signs of political dissidence. In the 1960s, however, the regime adopted a more liberal attitude toward dissent, provided it was limited in scope. The students have utilized this leeway to protest against university related grievances, particularly the policies of the elderly rector of the National University, Dr. Crispin Insaurralde, who also happened to be a long time leader of Stroessner's ruling party. The Stroessner regime, nonetheless, has not been hesitant in its use of repressive measures including expulsion, arrest, or exile against students whose activities transcend the government established political boundaries.

The government's threats and repressive measures restrain the expression of radical impulses among the students, but the normal functioning of the Paraguayan political, social, and economic structure also operates to inhibit student radicalism while at the same time promoting conservatism or at least its overt display among the students. Paraguay, unlike other Latin American countries with a low per capita income and small gross national product, has a surprisingly open and fluid class structure. There is no well established long-term aristocracy, due to the peculiarities of Paraguayan history. The government, however, plays a key role in determining mobility. Both directly and indirectly the regime is the major distributor of occupational and monetary rewards. It affects the mobility chances of individuals through the dispensation of contracts, favors, and especially jobs. The government is the country's biggest and most significant source of employment. Naturally, under prevailing circumstances the government's rewards and positions are distributed on the basis of political loyalty and reliability.[25] As reported in a detailed study of the Paraguayan economy completed in 1968:

The prime criterion for employment in government positions is political affiliation, past and present; members of opposition parties or their friends and relatives have little chance of being employed in the governmental organization, particularly in supervisory or professional posts. The almost universal method followed for securing government jobs is through family members or friends already in government positions.[26]

Although these various "carrots" and "sticks" have limited the number of radical students while increasing the amount of those professing conservatism, university students throughout the Stroessner years of power have been disproportionately represented among the few who have dared to actively oppose the dictator.[27]

It is more difficult to isolate the particular elements in the political-economic scene of Mexico and Colombia, as of 1964 and 1965, which would contribute to an understanding of the relative proportion of the conservative students in these two countries, 33 and 34 percent respectively. Mexico, which will be discussed in greater detail in chapter 6, has made steady social and economic advances in the 1950s and 1960s. Although its economy is acknowledged to be in the "take-off" phase of development, the income distribution is highly skewed and large numbers exist below the poverty line. As briefly outlined in chapter 4, the government has been under the control of the Institutional Revolutionary Party (PRI) or its predecessor for over forty years. The PRI regularly obtains between 80 and 90 percent of the vote in elections for president and the national legislature. Opposition parties usually do not have much difficulty in gaining access to the ballot, but the real political battles are fought within the context of the PRI. The most significant opposition to the PRI is offered by the National Action Party, which is a conservative, church-oriented party. Outside of the PRI, the left is weak and fragmented; within the party, the left has declined as the PRI has become more concerned with business and foreign investments than with the conditions of the peasants and of the blue collar workers who have not shared proportionately in Mexico's economic advances. Along with the drift to the right, the PRI has increasingly been charged with corruption and political ossification. However, the PRI still claims to be the institutional embodiment of the revolution. Once this claim had political meaning. Lately, it has come to be regarded by more and more segments of the population, particularly the disadvantaged and the students, as hypocritical political rhetoric.[28]

From 1946 through 1971, Colombia has experienced guerrilla warfare, banditry, and civil war. The worst period was from 1948 through 1953 during which a savage fratricidal struggle, primarily between the followers of the Liberal and Conservative parties, claimed between 100,000 to 200,000 lives. *La violencia*, as the Colombians called it, subsided in 1953 with the military's seizure of power under the leadership of General Gustavo Rojas Pinilla. He was overthrown four years later by a broad front spearheaded by students and led by the leaders of the two major parties, the Liberals and the Conservatives.

Since 1958, these two parties, on the basis of a private agreement ratified into law, have shared power alternating the presidency at four year intervals and distributing elective and appointive offices equally between them. Under the presidency of the first National Front executive, Alberto Lleras Camargo (1958-1962), Colombia experienced its first significant period of economic and political stability in decades. However, this period proved to be only a brief interlude, since from 1963 until 1971 economic and political crises as well as increased guerrilla activity returned to plague Colombia. After the Lleras government, it became increasingly clear that the National Front would not and perhaps could not bring about the sorely needed economic and political reforms.[29] The Conservative and Liberal parties "prevented by their elite dominated party structures from generating dramatic new programs . . . have lost much of the reason for their existence."[30] Although the National Front has tried to bring about some economic and social progress and to begin to modernize Colombia, its primary commitment has been to the preservation of the basic social and political structure.[31]

Our survey of Colombian students in 1964, it would appear, occurred approximately during the time of this transition from economic and political stability to instability and crises. One would expect that the students in this period were in a state of flux. This interpretation is supported by the changes and the lack of direction of student political organizations from 1958 until 1964. In fact, in the early 1960s due to internal squabbling no active national student federation existed in Colombia.

From 1964 through 1970, conservativism among the Colombia students seems to have declined as the students have become increasingly more radical and militant. In November 1963, Communist and other leftist students re-created the National Federation of University Students (FUN). The FUN has agitated and led or supported an increasing number of strikes.[32] Another radicalizing influence has been the small but increasingly militant group of Colombian clergy. Specifically, the writings and activities of Camilo Torres, a priest, and prior to his death in 1966, chaplain and member of the Sociology Faculty at the National University. He made a significant impact upon students as he moved from liberal reformer to revolutionary. His death at the hands of a military patrol while fighting as a guerrilla transformed him into a virtual martyr in the eyes of the students.[33] Also, the students have become quite concerned over the growth of private universities. From 1962 to 1970, seventeen private universities were founded compared to five public universities. They fear that the private universities will cater to the more wealthy and lead to a bifurcated stratification system within Colombia. They were also concerned that these institutions would fall under the influence of North Americans and Colombian private business interests.[34]

The university disturbances that swept across Colombia in 1970 are further indications of how militant and political the students have become. Emanating from a strike of medical students at the National University over demands for participation in faculty appointments, demonstrations spread throughout the country's universities. Three universities including the National University were closed by the government. These events occurred during a period when the students' political consciousness was being raised by a heated national election in the midst of a continued deteriorating economic situation and the continued failure of the coalition National Front government to enact significant and needed reforms. Ironically, one of the major defenders of the student demonstrators and strikers and the one candidate who seemed to attract the most student support was Rojas Pinilla, the former dictator whom students had helped overthrow in 1957, and in 1970, a populist candidate for president.[35]

In essence, what our findings indicate is that student politics, whether of the right or the left, cannot be understood without knowledge of the political and socioeconomic contexts in which the students are located. In Latin America, the universities are not divorced from politics, but are, on the contrary, generally intimately involved in the political processes and struggles of the society. Political parties look to the university student bodies for supporters and party activists. National political struggles are often foreshadowed by developments within university student politics, often influenced in turn by off-campus political events and parties. The governing parties usually control university budgets, recruit government and party personnel from the universities, and in other ways, such as through the appointment of rectors, deans and professors, make their influence felt. Politicians and government officials in Latin America whether they be in dictatorships or parliamentary governments pay careful attention to the political activities of students. It is only natural, then, that the political, ideological distribution of the various student bodies would to an important extent reflect the political tensions and power balances of their societies.

The Family

Conservatives tend to evaluate order, tradition, and stability positively. Since Aristotle, social theorists have looked upon the family as an important source of conservative values. A strong and viable family structure is regarded as an important contributor to a well-ordered society. Families tend to orient their members toward the past and are important carriers of parochial traditions. Societies which are heavily influenced by leftist ideologies, such as Russia, China, and the kibbutzim of Israel, have at times adopted policies designed to weaken the authority of family members over the young and to attempt to some extent to supersede family allegiance through allegiance to broader social units like the state or the kibbutz. The value orientations associated with the family, such as ascription, particularism, affectivity, and diffuseness, are thought to be somewhat incompatible with leftist ideologies which emphasize achievement, universalism, and egalitarianism. Conservative regimes and religions such as Roman Catholicism, on the other hand, look upon the traditional family and the maintenance of familial obligations and duties as a positive force.[36]

If this is the case, then individual attitudes toward family and family responsibility form an element in the social profile of the conservative student to which attention should be directed. The importance of the family to the student in Latin America can be inferred from the fact that Latin American university students tend to live at home or with relatives while attending school. This is primarily because (1) Latin American universities tend not to build dormitories, and (2) it is costly to establish a separate residence. The proportion of the students in our study who lived with their parents or relatives varied from 63 percent among the Puerto Ricans to 77 percent among the Paraguayans. That is to say that from about two-thirds to three-quarters of the Latin American students shared the same residence with their parents or relatives while attending the university.

To carry this point further, the residence of the student was related to his political ideology, according to the political ideology scale. The data (not shown here) did indicate that in each country the conservative student was more likely to reside with his parents or relatives than to live by himself or with other students. The differences in the percentages of conservative students who lived at home compared to those who lived elsewhere, however, were not substantial. This can be attributed in part to the fact that "residence of student" is a rather crude indicator of familial attitude or influence, since it tells us nothing about the pattern of interaction and attitudes between family members. As student radicals expressed it during the course of interviews, home was a place where they slept and occasionally ate their meals. They reported that they rarely spoke with their parents – particularly about politics. Therefore, despite the fact that they lived with their parents, who for the most part strongly disagreed with what they were doing, these student militants continued their radical activities. The mere physical act of residing in the same house does not necessarily mean that the student and his parents reside in the same social world.

As a more meaningful indicator, a scale of family traditionalism, consisting of responses to four items, was used as a measure of the respondents' attitude toward traditional family values and relationships.[37] The students were divided into familial traditionalists and familial nontraditionalists on the basis of their responses to the scale items. After this division, the two groups' distribution on the political ideology scale was ascertained.

The results are shown in Table 26. In each of the five countries, the political conservatives were more likely to be among the family traditionalists than among the family nontraditionalists. In Mexico and Colombia, the family traditionalist was twice as likely as the nontraditionalist to be on the right. The general import of the findings in this table is that students who believed in marital faithfulness and opposed having women work outside the home, two component items of the traditional scale, were also likely to evaluate Castro negatively and to be procapitalist. Although there is no extrinsic relationship between attitudes toward the family and attitudes toward politics and politico-economic matters, the data revealed that a conservative orientation in one

Table 26. Percentages (and numbers) of rightist students holding traditional or nontraditional attitude toward family (by country)

| Country | Attitude toward family | |
	Nontraditional	Traditional
Uruguay	20 (335)	33 (128)
Mexico	20 (402)	44 (370)
Colombia	21 (583)	42 (888)
Paraguay	16 (185)	27 (266)
Puerto Rico	42 (132)	56 (275)

sphere was supportive of a conservative orientation in the other. In many aspects of life, Latin America remains a conservative region. Even in Mexico, the one country in our sample which had had a great political and social revolution, traditional family relationships appeared to prevail.[38] The Catholic and Hispanic heritage that informs the culture of Latin America has tended to reinforce traditional family patterns and values.

Data from American studies of students suggest that conservative and nonactivist students also tend to be conservative or traditional in their attitudes toward the family. These studies also indicate that the parents of the conservative students, more so than the parents of the more liberal or leftist students, are likely to have conservative familial attitudes.[39]

It would thus appear that traditional familial attitudes in some way support conservative political attitudes. This finding might have been expected. Most men strive for consistency in their values and norms. To hold a radical political position while maintaining conservative family attitudes is to be in an actual or potential conflict situation. In the United States today, a youthful radical is more likely than his conservative counterpart to be nonconformist about his personal appearance, clothes, attitude toward the opposite sex, and the use of drugs. In Latin America the student left does not appear to have made such a public break with convention. Student radicals whom Liebman interviewed in Mexico and in Puerto Rico or whom Glazer studied in Chile were for the most part neatly dressed and "properly" groomed. It is probably easier at this point in Latin America to be a political leftist than it is to be a nontraditionalist in matters and attitudes pertaining to the family. There is much more cultural support for the former than for the latter. However, even in traditionalist societies, it would appear that a deviation in the political sphere is in some way associated with a break in traditional family attitudes. The basic point still remains that a conservative in the family sphere is also likely to be a conservative in the political arena.

Political Inheritance

Another indicator of the relevance of the family to student political orientations, conservative as well as nonconservative, is the extent of political leaning inherited by Latin American students from their fathers. It is virtually a truism in United States political science that the best predictor of the politics of an individual is the politics of his family. Political inheritance, it appears, is also a powerful predictor among the Latin American students as we stressed earlier in chapter 4. For those students in the Latin American countries with which we are concerned, the percentages of students whose party preference was the same as their father's were high. They ranged from 79 percent of the Mexicans to 67 percent of the Paraguayans to 61 percent of the Puerto Ricans to 60 percent of the Uruguayans to 58 percent of the Colombians. Samuel Lubell reports that among students in the United States during the mid-1960s "more than three-fourths would vote for the same political party as their parents."[40] Other studies also indicate the potency of political inheritance among students and young people.[41]

For every country, the student's political party preference and his ideological position were also related to the party preference of his father in order to determine whether the high rate of political inheritance was uniform or varied with the political leanings of father or son. Both factors were used because in some countries, such as Mexico and Puerto Rico, where the governing party is so dominant, it may include, within itself, both conservatives and leftists. Thus, if party affiliation was the sole political indicator used, it would fail to differentiate the conservatives from the others. In every country, the data revealed that the children of fathers with conservative party preferences tended to be conservative in their own party preference and in their ideology. This was also true, as we stated in chapter 4, for the nonconservatives. Students of all political persuasions tended to follow in their father's footsteps. In general, however, the rate of inheritance among conservatives tended to be slightly less in each country than for the left, with the exception of Paraguay, where the reverse was true. The basic point, though, is that there is a great deal of political continuity between the two generations, regardless of the political affiliation of the father or the student.[42] It is also true that Latin American students tend to be less conservative than their parents, a finding which, as noted previously,

may be attributed to the youth of the student or to the liberalizing environment of the university.[43]

These phenomena are not always true of youth vis-à-vis their parents. Karl
Mannheim has stated, "Nothing is more false than the usual assumption uncri-
tically shared by most students of generations, that the younger generation is
'progressive' and the older generation *eo ipso* conservative. Recent experiences
have shown well enough that the old liberal generation tends to be more politically progressive than certain sections of the youth."[44]

Seymour M. Lipset in *Political Man* has also pointed out that the characteristics of the period when a generation comes of political age are an important
determinant of that generation's politics. He raises the hypothetical point that
"if a society should move from prolonged instability to stability, it may well
be that older people would retain the leftist ideas of their youth, and the
younger generations would adopt conservative philosophies."[45]

Klemens Von Klemperer, among others, has called attention to the fact that
during the Nazis' rise to power in Germany during the late 1920s and early
1930s, the university youth became more conservative than their parents.[46]
In the United States, in a study of eleven universities during the 1950s, it was
found that when the student did rebel against his father's affiliation, "it was
more likely to be in the conservative direction."[47] There appears to be no guarantee then that university students will be more leftist than their parents. A
great deal seems to depend on the era in which the student is attending college.
In one study, Vassar alumnae of different decades were compared as to their
mean score on the F scale and the E scale, scales measuring authoritarianism
and ethnocentricity respectively. On both the F scale and the E scale, the
Depression and the World War II classes had the lowest mean scores.[48]

The data in this section have shown that family and attitudes about the
family have an influence on or are related to the conservative political orientation of the Latin American student. Conservative parents generally produce
conservative students just as leftist parents usually produce leftist students.
However, when students do shift in their political preferences, it is generally
in a direction that is to the left of their parents. Conservative students in Latin
America also tend to be traditionalists in their attitudes relating to the family.

Religion

In Latin America, Roman Catholicism is the dominant religion. Although a
religious organization, the Catholic church has been intimately involved in
politics throughout Latin American history. From its earliest days in the New

World, the church relied and was dependent on secular governments and societal elites to protect and further its interests. Historically, this has meant that the church has been closely allied with the right and tied to the status quo. In many Latin American nations, the classic conservative triumvirate was the church, the landed oligarchy, and the army. In the nineteenth and twentieth centuries, its political involvements and orientations as well as its economic and political interests and privileges have caused the church to become embroiled in the major political controversies of the hemisphere. In many of the republics populations were politically divided into warring camps based on the position that they took toward the church. Generally, the divisions have been along liberal-conservative lines, with the religious cleavage reinforcing and exacerbating cleavages in other political, social, and economic areas.

The Roman Catholic church in Latin America, however, is neither a monolithic nor a static institution. Various elements within it have become aware of the need of the church to adapt to the significant changes that have taken place in the hemisphere during the last fifty years and especially in the post-World War II era. As a result, at different levels in varying countries, the socio-ethical or prophetic orientation of the church has been reinforced. Organizationally, this has meant some degree of support for Catholic reformist parties such as the Christian Democratic parties. This change in orientation was spurred by the papacy of John XXIII (1958-1963) and the ideas and themes emanating from the Second Vatican Council (1962-1965). These internal Church developments coupled with long-term, ongoing secular trends have given rise in the mid- and latter 1960s to growing numbers of politically liberal, reformist, and radical priests. Generally they have been the younger clerics, but in some countries even the members of the hierarchy have adopted a more liberal and reformist stance. In fact, even the Latin American bishops, traditionally highly conservative, have moved towards a more radical or prophetic position. In the latter 1960s important sectors of the Latin American church have been promoting a "theology of revolution" as well as actively opposing conservative and dictatorial governments. However, despite these changes and increased flexibility, the dominant elements within the Latin American churches generally remain opposed to basic reforms and linked to conservative interests. This was particularly true at the time of our student survey in 1964 and 1965.[49]

The conservative influence of Roman Catholicism is not only evident in the manifest political role of the organized church. Traditional religious orientations emanating from Catholicism as practiced in Latin America have encouraged its adherents to accept their situation, no matter how miserable it may be. Ivan Vallier has described some of the consequences and secular orientattions that emanate from basic beliefs of Latin American Catholics in the following manner:

This [basic belief system] breeds ritualism, multiplies prayers, stimulates devotionalism, and fosters alienation from the world. Ritual rather than problem-solving action results. Religious inclinations are tied to sacramental formalism instead of being channeled into ethical behavior. Moreover it rewards and encourages a privatistic or individualistic value framework, since each person is first and always concerned with fulfilling the requirements for eternal salvation. This religious view predisposes the believer to place supernatural objectives and concerns above the things of this world. It does not generate a positive basis of action for the world; the chief concern is to refrain from sins against God.[50]

Given both the conservative political and religious nature of the Roman Catholic church in Latin America, again particularly at the time of our study, one would expect that its more devout adherents would be conservative in their political orientations, especially university students if there is little in their life circumstances which would cause them to resist such a political stance. The data in Table 27 reveal that in every case the most religiously involved, as measured by a scale of religiousness, are the ones most likely to be conservative in their political ideology. In each of the countries there is a progression: as religiousness increases from low to middle to high, the percentage of rightist students also increases. In Mexico the percentage of conservatives rises from 10 percent to 54 percent as one moves from low to high religiousness. In Colombia only one out of every four of the least religious students is a conservative, while almost half of the most religious students may be classified as such. In Uruguay the corresponding increase is from 14 percent to 35 percent, while among the Puerto Ricans it is from 39 percent to 58 percent, and for the Paraguayans there is a 17 percent increase in the percentage of conservatives, from 14 percent of the least religious to 31 percent of the most religious. A study of Brazilian university students done in 1966 and 1967 using different measures of religiousness and conservatism also obtained results similar to ours. Nine percent of the practicing Catholics were left whereas 25 percent of the same group were highly conservative. Among those Brazilian students who did not practice any religion, 6 percent were highly conservative and 41 percent were left.[51] This indicates that in the mid-1960s despite the reformist stirrings in the Latin American churches religion as practiced and defined by students was still a force which pushed them to the right or at least was a formidable barrier enabling the more devout to withstand entreaties from the left.

It is interesting to observe how the percentage differences between the least religious and the most religious students reflect the political experiences of the

Table 27. Percentages (and numbers) of conservative students by degree of religiousness

Country	Religiousness		
	Low	Middle	High
Puerto Rico	39 (124)	56 (113)	58 (171)
Paraguay	14 (165)	23 (126)	31 (147)
Colombia	25 (427)	38 (553)	47 (495)
Mexico	10 (245)	34 (265)	54 (231)
Uruguay	14 (146)	22 (174)	35 (141)

Roman Catholic church in the various countries. Mexico, the country in which the percentage of conservatives increased from 10 percent among the least religious to 44 percent among the most religious students, was the one country in our sample which had experienced violent religious and political conflict. During the course of the Mexican Revolution, churches were destroyed and priests were killed. The wealth of the church was seized and its power in politics and education severely curtailed. Today, the church in Mexico has been once again accepted as legitimate by the government, and its wealth and power are on the increase. The association between the political right and the church has continued to the present. The most conservative political parties in Mexico, the National Action Party or PAN and the *Sinarquistas*, are very religiously oriented and promote the interests of the church. Although the church officially sanctions no political party, many Mexicans feel that it looks kindly upon the efforts of those who work politically on its behalf. Despite the government's accomodation of sorts with the Mexican church, the religious issue is still alive in Mexico and continues to divide the left and the right.[52]

This cleavage which has yet to be closed is seen more closely among the Mexican students when the percentage of leftists as well as rightists among the various groupings is considered. Among the least religious 70 percent are left and, as mentioned above, 10 percent are right, while among the most religious 16 percent are left and 54 percent are right. In no other country is the split as great.

This religio-ideological cleavage is also evident in the student political organizations. There are Catholic student associations whose major function is to oppose Communists and other groups they consider to be Communist-dominated. There is also the semisecret organization on the campus of the National University in Mexico City called *MURO*, which devotes itself to opposing leftists and Jews. It is widely believed that this organization receives financial support from elements in the PAN and the church. The diverse leftist organizations are, almost as a matter of course, opposed to the church.

Colombia is second to Mexico in the impact of religiousness upon the political ideology of the students. The Colombian church is the richest, strongest, and most conservative in Latin America. The church hierarchy is closely allied with the conservative forces and the government.[53] According to Ivan Vallier,

> The Colombian Church is deeply grounded in the whole institutional life of the society and thus holds higher degrees of ritual, educational, and territorial monopoly than do the Churches in Argentina, Brazil, Chile, and Mexico. Priests are visible, as well as influential, in every sphere of society and correspondingly play key roles as religious authorities, ritual agents, diffuse communal leaders, and members of important secular decision making groups. Structural interdependencies between the Church and the major role systems in the society are typical: in education, welfare work, rural development, and social elite circles . . . the basic trends that have marked the Colombia Church for many years — clerical influence, expansive educational programs, loyal and passive laymen, and close ties between Church and State — continue.[54]

Due to the Church's political policies and its diffuse and deep commitments throughout the Colombian political and socioeconomic structure, it has historically become embroiled in the political and civil strife that has continued to beset Colombia, always as an ally of the right.

The identification of the Church with conservative forces has reaffirmed the conservative orientation of the more religious students. Also, as in other strata, it has served as a source of division. Attitudes toward the Church divide the students into mutually hostile camps reinforcing already existing political divisions. This is particularly so in Colombia because of the Church's involvement in university affairs. In accordance with a concordat between Colombia and the Vatican, clergymen sit on the executive councils of the public universities. This has incensed the students, further increasing the division between the more religious-conservative ones and those who are less religious and more liberal.[55]

Unlike Colombia and Mexico, the churches of Paraguay, Uruguay, and Puerto Rico have not been major political forces, and though conservative in political orientation, they do not appear to have been significant sources of political socialization. Religious influence in these societies seems to be less important in the formation of student political ideologies than in Colombia and Mexico. In Paraguay the church is poor and historically has been subservient to the government, which throughout most of Paraguayan history has been under the control of dictators. The church has not been identified as the partisan of any particular party or ideology. However, beginning in the early 1960s the leaders of the church have progressively attacked the policies of General Alfredo Stroessner even to the point of encouraging student demonstrations. By 1970 the hierarchy of the Paraguayan church evolved into ardent opponents of the regime, openly declaring themselves to be revolutionaries.[56] In Uruguay, church and state have been officially separated since 1919. The church has rarely been a divisive political issue in Uruguay, for although the liberally oriented, long-governing Colorados were hostile to it, none of the other major parties or factions was an ardent supporter of the church. Twentieth-century Uruguayans, influenced by radical, Marxist, and anarchist ideologies since the turn of the century, are noted for being the least religious people in Latin America.[57] The Puerto Rican church historically has been weak, poor, and sorely lacking in clerical manpower. The church was controlled by Spaniards while the island was part of the Spanish empire, and when the United States took possession in 1899 these Spanish clergy, particularly in the hierarchy, were replaced by North Americans, generally of Irish-American backgrounds. Its scant resources in addition to its foreign taint and personnel have meant that the Puerto Rican church never became a strong indigenous institutional force capable of deeply influencing a native Puerto Rican population in the political realm. During the many years the Popular Democratic Party held executive power, the church opposed the reformist measures of the PPD without weakening PPD popularity at the ballot box. The Christian Action Party launched in 1960 with the support of the hierarchy proved electorally insignificant and short-lived. In addition, since the church has not taken a firm stand on the status of the island, the basic issue of Puerto Rican politics, religion has not contributed to the existing political cleavages. It should be noted, however, that changes are also occuring in the Puerto Rican church. Native Puerto Ricans are moving into the church establishment and have begun to voice proindependence sentiments.[58] Thus, in general, unlike the situation in Mexico and Colombia, religion in Puerto Rico, Uruguay, and Paraguay traditionally has not strongly reinforced conservative political orientations or divided the respective populaces into hostile pro and anti clerical camps. Societal cleavages based on religion are less likely to occur in societies where the power of the church is limited.

Socioeconomic Status

What are the socioeconomic class backgrounds of student conservatives in Latin America? Are the conservatives disproportionately drawn from the ranks of the upwardly mobile lower and lower-middle strata or are they representatives of the upper strata? To respond to this question, social status was related to political ideology, with social status being measured by the social status scale (used in chapt. 4).

The results obtained were consistent in each country. The higher-status student is disproportionately the most likely to be a conservative. Also, except for Paraguay, the lowest-status student is least likely to be a conservative. The difference in percentage of conservatives between high- and low-status students ranged from thirty-one points among the Colombians to two points among the Paraguayans. The differences for the Mexicans, Uruguayans, and Puerto Ricans were seventeen, fourteen, and thirteen percentage points respectively.

These results indicate that although social class is not a major factor differentiating the students politically, higher-status students do tend to be more oriented toward conservatism. Similar results were obtained with our own data when radical students were studied in chapter 4 as well as for Brazilian and Chilean university students in the 1960s.[59] Thus, it appears that in Latin America, irrespective of the nature of the government or the condition of the economy in a country, those students who are by ascription already members of the higher strata are pulled to the right.

Given the fact, previously cited, that Paraguay has so fluid a class structure, it is not unexpected that social class is so unimportant a differentiating factor among Paraguayan students. As one social scientist observed: "many Paraguayans hold almost as a dogma that social class differences do not exist in their country. . . Wealth of course brings advantages, but it is primarily wealth, not ascribed status or cultural background, that brings them."[60] Students are cognizant, particularly those from lower-status backgrounds, that their chances for upward mobility are highly dependent upon the army or other sectors of the national regime. Thus, where his higher-status peer may have somewhat of a natural inclination to the right, the lower-status student is pulled in the same direction by a process of anticipatory socialization, a process based on reality.

Furthermore, the structure and tradition of Paraguayan politics does not support a significant identification between class and political ideology. From the time of its independence early in the nineteenth century, Paraguay's dictatorial governments and major political parties, the Colorados and the Liberals, have cut across class lines. The major social distinction differentiating major and minor party supporters appears to be an urban-rural or a cosmopolitan-provincial orientation. Leaders and activists of the newer and smaller parties such as the Communist, Christian Democratic, or *Febrerista* appear to be disproportionately drawn from the urban-cosmopolitan grouping. Although these latter parties are more ideological than the two traditional ones and appeal more to the working class and peasantry than the Colorados and the Liberals, the fact that the government does allow for social mobility benefitting in particular university students from the lower strata vitiates the class appeal of the Communists, Christian Democrats, and Febreristas.[61]

In Colombia, the country where the percentage spread between lower and higher-status students is greatest, the situation is somewhat different. Colombia is a society with a tradition of political instability and political cleavages. There are important parties and movements which advocate both reform and revolution on behalf of the lower strata. The government is not strong and is beset by threats from the right and the left as well as the withdrawal of confidence by the populace, as reflected by the fact that almost two-thirds of the voters failed to vote in the elections of 1964.

The Colombian students were the only students in this study confronted by major ideological and political splits within their society. In the mid-1960s when the survey was conducted, only in Colombia was the left a meaningful and revolutionary force, as evidenced by widespread guerrilla activity in various sectors of the country. Where there are deep divisions within the society and where intellectuals and student activists are exacerbating and emphasizing these divisions, it is only natural that they should be mirrored among the university students.

Looking at the students in all five countries, we find that the students from the higher strata are more likely than those from the lower and middle strata to be conservative. While individual members of the higher strata may deviate ideologically or politically from the right, as a group they tend to support the status quo and the interests of their higher-status families who are, throughout the five countries, the dominant economic and social elements of their societies.

Religion and Socioeconomic Status

What is the relationship, if any, between religion and socioeconomic status as they affect the tendency to be a conservative? To answer this question, three variables were interrelated as shown in Table 28. In order to highlight the effects and to simplify the reading, only those students who were previously placed "low" and "high" on the scales of religion and socioeconomic status were selected for presentation in this table.

The data in Table 28 reveal how religion and socioeconomic status reinforce each other. In every case but Paraguay, the students who were both the least religious and in the lower strata were also the least likely to be conservative. Conversely, in every case the high-status, highly religious student was the most conservative.

Among Mexican and Colombian students, the addition of low status to low

Table 28. Percentages (and numbers) of conservative students by degree of religiousness, socioeconomic status (SES), and country

Country	Religiousness: Low		Religiousness: High	
	SES: Low	SES: High	SES: Low	SES: High
Mexico	9 (98)	12 (77)	40 (78)	67 (91)
Paraguay	17 (81)	14 (43)	31 (67)	36 (44)
Puerto Rico	34 (44)	53 (32)	48 (56)	64 (36)
Uruguay	11 (46)	15 (41)	32 (44)	37 (60)
Colombia	3 (176)	25 (131)	34 (95)	55 (21)

religiousness formed such a barrier to the development of a rightist orientation that the percentage of conservatives among students with these characteristics was less than 10 percent for the Mexicans and as low as 3 percent for the Colombians. The reinforcing effect of these two variables upon the percentage of conservatives among Colombian and Mexican students was indicated by an increase in the percentage of conservatives from the low-low group to the high-high group by a factor of seventeen for the Colombians and by a factor of seven for the Mexicans. It should be recalled that of the five socieites in the study, these two countries have experienced the most political and social violence. These conflicts tended to divide the societies into warring camps, as the more religious tended also to be the higher-status members of the societies, while the less religious tended to be the lower-status members.[62] This has not been the experience of Puerto Rico, Uruguay, or Paraguay. In these three countries, the percentage point spread between the low status–nonreligious and the high status–high religious students is not as great as the differences found in Colombia and Mexico. However, the important point remains: in all cases the combination of religiousness and high status produced the most conservative students.

Satisfaction with Life as a Student

All universities are faced with the fact that the role of student is replete with tensions and anxieties. Newspapers and popular magazines often given accounts of student demonstrations in the United States and Latin America which were allegedly sparked by difficult examinations or unpopular regulations. The degree to which a student is satisfied with his life as a student should be considered when dealing with variables which influence his politics. There is no guarantee, however, that student frustrations must necessarily find political expression.

E. Wight Bakke argues that in Latin America the students lack outlets for their surplus energies and tensions since they do not have the various extracurricular activities and organizations that are available to American students, and that therefore, almost by default, the Latin Americans turn to political outlets.[63] Analysis of data from the students in our five-nation sample shows that, on the contrary, Latin American students do participate in extracurricular activities. The average Latin American university student in our study belongs to between one and two formal voluntary organizations. Only a small minority of the total memberships are in any kind of political organization. Our analysis (not shown here) of the relationship between political activism and organizational membership revealed, on the whole, weak and inconsistent relationships.

Bakke, as well as other scholars, also attributes to the Latin temperament and to tradition the propensity of Latin American students to respond to problems with political action.[64] Again, we find little support for this hypothesis, as our data show that the relationship between political activity and a self-defined state of happiness or mental health is generally weak and inconsistent. This is not to deny the possibility that in political crisis situations students with problems may disproportionately participate, seeking an outlet for their personal difficulties. But we have little evidence to substantiate this, if indeed, there were such a relationship, it is difficult to comprehend why it would uniquely apply to Latin Americans.

It does not seem necessary, however, to invoke the Latin American temperament or tradition in order to explain the seeming propensity of Latin American students to involve themselves in politics and political activity. In Latin America, to a greater degree than in the United States for example, the government and national politics, as we have discussed earlier, are deeply involved in university affairs and in the lives and careers of the students.

The national government is the prime source of funds for the operation of all Latin American universities, private and public but especially the latter. Therefore, national legislatures or presidents, through the power of the purse, ultimately decide on the number of students to be admitted, the size of the professorial staff, professors' salaries, incidental student fees and tuition, and the quality and availability of libraries and other facilities. Students in many countries in the hemisphere are also aware that governments and major national political parties are not only influential in determining the number who can enroll in institutions of higher education but are also very important in deciding their occupational fate when they complete their university education. Even in such a seemingly trivial and non-university-related matter as bus fares, there is a close connection between the life of the student and the national government. In view of the fact that governments do not allocate money for dormitories, the quality and cost of bus transportation takes on significant meaning to the many students who live far from their campuses. The buses they ride and the fares which they pay are generally regulated by the government. In recent years, announcements of fare increases have precipitated student protest demonstrations and riots, whose target ultimately is the national government or one of its agencies.

Furthermore, students desirous of virtually any measure of university reform soon find themselves in the political arena, many times directly at the national level. In virtually all public universities in Latin America, only the president and or the national legislature can amend the universities' charters. Thus reform efforts by necessity must transcend the university community.

National politics has traditionally entered the life of Latin American universities through the selection and appointment of professors, deans, and rectors. This is most evident in the case of dictatorships such as that of Perón in Argentina and Stroessner in Paraguay. Under both of these rulers, little effort was made to conceal the fact that academic and administrative appointments were primarily made on the basis of political loyalty and reliability. However, even in more democratic and progressive societies such as Puerto Rico and Mexico, the universities, including the University of Puerto Rico and the National Autonomous University of Mexico, have experienced political intervention and influence in the selection of important administrative officials up to and including the 1960s.[65] In Chile the rector of the University of Chile is elected by the students, alumni, professors, and nonacademic university employees. His election, especially the most recent one in 1971, has turned into a contest of strength between national political parties and ideologies.[66] In Venezuela, the government's amendments to the University Law in 1970 giving it a greater role in internal university matters have stirred nationwide student and professorial protests, particularly after the enforced resignation of the Rector of the Central University of Venezuela, Jesus Maria Bianco in 1970.[67] It is not only the national governments, however, which intervene in university affairs. As noted in previous chapters, various political parties and ideologies have focused on the university as a major institutional arena for their operations, including student elections, professorial selection, and administrative appointments. Thus, the historic and present intimate relationship between politics and the university in large part explains the students' proclivity for political action in response to problems associated with the university and with the status of student.[68]

In what political direction has the student's dissatisfaction pushed him? In considering this question, the item dealing with the student's assessment of the extent to which he was satisfied or dissatisfied was correlated with political ideology. In every country, the data revealed that the satisfied student was more likely to be on the right than the dissatisfied one. The relationship between satisfaction/dissatisfaction and conservative political orientation was most pronounced among the Colombians and the Puerto Ricans and weakest among the Uruguayans and the Mexicans.

In order to tap another dimension of satisfaction/dissatisfaction, the relationship between the respondent's perception of the probability of working within his chosen field of study after graduation and his political ideology was observed.

The inability of students to find work in fields for which they had been trained is regarded by social scientists as a major contributant to student politics and demonstrations.[69] This variable proved to have little relationship to the political ideology of the student. In general, the group composed of those who felt that there were many opportunities to work within their field of study after graduation was likely to have almost the same proportion of conservatives and leftists as the group containing those who perceived few or no opportunities. Similar results were also found in a study of Brazilian students,[70] further attesting to the fact that the perception of employment opportunities by itself at least for Latin American students is not significantly related to their political attitudes and values.

We proceeded to take our analysis a step further. Responses to the occupational outlook items were combined with the answers to the question of satisfaction as a student to form a "scale of contentment." Those who answered the occupational item with "many opportunities" and who were also "satisfied" were categorized as "contented" while those who said "few opportunities" and were "dissatisfied" were grouped together as "discontented." The remaining respondents who gave other substantive responses to both questions were labeled as "mixed." As can be seen in Table 29, the "contented" students were the ones most likely to be conservatives and the "discontented" were the least likely to hold such an orientation in each country except Uruguay (which might be a function of the small number of cases in the "discontent" category). Thus, students' evaluations of their future professional opportunities are not, alone, a potent factor affecting their politics. Yet when coupled with their estimation of their total university experience, the combination clearly reveals a strong

Table 29. Percentages (and numbers) of conservative students by satisfaction with university experience and views of employment prospects (by country)

Country	Contentment		
	Content	Mixed	Discontent
Puerto Rico	55 (226)	46 (143)	38 (26)
Paraguay	30 (142)	21 (204)	14 (95)
Colombia	42 (652)	33 (668)	13 (187)
Mexico	34 (224)	33 (364)	27 (134)
Uruguay	25 (311)	15 (101)	47 (15)

relationship between "contentment" and student conservatism. Students "contented" both with their university experience and their employment prospects can be expected to be supporters of the status quo.

Intellectual, Scientific, and Professional Identifications of Students

When compared to scientists and professionals, intellectuals generally have been found to be leftists.[71] They have a broader perspective, are subject to more frustration, suffer greater anxiety, and have the role of societal critic built into their identity. Although Latin American intellectuals have in the past been associated with the right, the tendency, especially since the defeat of fascism in World War II, has been toward a more radical orientation.[72]

Those who identify themselves as scientists and professionals are thought to be more likely than the intellectuals to be conservative. Their identities tie them into narrow, relatively fixed roles within the ongoing political and socioeconomic structure. These roles carry no mandate to criticize or to speak out on behalf of the lower and deprived strata. Their orientation might be described as particular and specific as opposed to that of the intellectuals, which is univeral and diffuse.[73] To a large extent, they are members of what John Johnson has called the "middle sectors" who eschew radicalism and desire ordered progress.[74]

What is the relationship between these three stated intellectual, scientific, and professional identities and the propensity to hold a conservative political position? Unfortunately, there is little empirical data which focuses upon the relationship between the right and being an intellectual, scientist, or professional.[75] The students in our study were divided into these three categories on

Table 30. Percentages (and numbers) of conservative students by category and by country

Country	Category[a]		
	Intellectual	Scientist	Professional
Puerto Rico	42 (101)	59 (61)	54 (230)
Paraguay	15 (147)	17 (23)	29 (266)
Uruguay	19 (118)	30 (66)	22 (213)
Colombia	30 (637)	37 (191)	38 (641)
Mexico	28 (176)	29 (58)	34 (497)

[a]Categories were determined on the basis of response to question: "How does respondent classify himself?"

the basis of their own subjective evaluation. As might be expected, self-defined intellectuals were the least likely in each country to be conservative. This was especially true among the Paraguayan intellectuals, of whom only 15 percent were conservative (see Table 30).

The category containing the highest percentage of conservatives varied by country. In Uruguay and Puerto Rico, the scientists were the most conservative of the three groups. The situation was different with students from the other countries. In Paraguay, Mexico, and Colombia the professional was the most conservative, although the difference between professional and scientist was slight among the Colombians.

A comparison between the two countries where the scientists were the most conservative and the three in which the professionals were the most conservative revealed that those countries in which the scientists were the most to the right were the more advanced and developed. Uruguay and Puerto Rico have the most advanced economies and the smallest percentage of work force engaged in agriculture. They present the most opportunities for scientists. They are also modern societies in which tradition has been weakened by outside forces — the United States influence in Puerto Rico and the effect of considerable European immigration in Uruguay. Thus, one would expect that in these societies the scientist would be more accepted than in the more traditional Paraguayan, Colombian, and Mexican societies. Having been spared a *Kulturkampf* between traditional society and science, Uruguayan and Puerto Rican scientists have not been forced to the left. The relative availability of opportunity to engage in scientific work also tends to create a commitment of sorts to the status quo.

Politically, one would expect the scientists of Uruguay and Puerto Rico to be most at odds with the left. In Uruguay the economic crisis can be attributed to the policies of the left. It is the parties on the left which appear to foster continual economic chaos through strikes, demands, demonstrations and policy statements calling for programs which some have felt were the original cause of the chaos. It is the right that calls for order, financial reform, and a rational reorganization of the government and the economy.[76] In Puerto Rico, the left as of the mid-1960s tended to be either idealistic or demagogic, with little other than freedom for Puerto Rico included in their programs and policy statements. Most Puerto Ricans felt that the victory of the left would mean social and economic chaos for the island. It is the right which has called for statehood and for increasing ties with the United States as a means of sustaining and promoting Puerto Rico's stability and relative prosperity.

In the latter 1960s and in the early 1970s, changes have taken place in the tactics and policies of the left. The extreme ideologues and demagogues no longer monopolize and control the direction of the left as it has grown in size and become more differentiated. More detailed and more pragmatic programs and policy statements have been drafted in order to demonstrate both the responsible nature of the left and the fact that independence will not bring economic and social chaos in its wake.[77] However, in the mid-1960s, at the time of our surveys, it was the right in both Puerto Rico and Uruguay that identified itself with order, responsibility, and economic growth, while the left appeared to be threatening to progress and stability.

To repeat, it is the intellectuals in each case who are the least likely to be conservative. Among the Puerto Ricans and the Uruguayans, scientists are the most conservative, while among Colombians, Paraguayans, and Mexicans it is the professionals who are the most conservative.

Faculty or Field of Study

The faculty or school of a university attended by a Latin American student, as indicated previously, is more akin to a professional training school in the United States than it is to a liberal arts college. Students within the Latin American faculties are trained to be practitioners of a craft. This means that during their university career their classroom exposure is limited to the students, professors, and subject matter of that one school. Thus, one would expect that students in such a homogeneous environment would be deeply imbued with the norms, values, and ideology emanating from the school and from the field in which they are studying.

Table 31. Faculties with the Highest percentage of conservative students, by university and country

Country	Faculty	Percent	N
Paraguay	Science	63	(51)
	Engineering	53	(45)
	Dentistry	52	(29)
Puerto Rico	Medicine	100	(13)
	Business	90	(70)
	Natural science	80	(50)
Uruguay	Humanities	34	(50)
	Chemistry	29	(48)
	Engineering	29	(49)
Mexico			
UNAM	Engineering	45	(106)
	Philosophy	47	(59)
	Medicine	39	(62)
Guanajuato	Science	47	(17)
	Engineering	42	(83)
Colombia			
Popayán	Medicine	28	(54)
Los Andes	Science	63	(32)
	Humanities	59	(78)
	Engineering	51	(313)
Javeriana	Humanities	64	(42)
	Engineering	53	(45)
Nacional	Education	30	(27)
	Exact sciences	27	(45)
	Engineering	25	(65)
Libre	Education	16	(68)

We emphasized in chapter 4 that the student's field of study is significantly related to his politics. Here we focus on the field of study and a conservative political stance. The students were divided according to country, university, and faculty. Table 31 lists the two or three schools within each university having the highest percentage of conservatives. With the apparent exception of students in four schools of humanities and philosophy, students in schools concerned with science or its application or with business and education were the most conservative. A closer examination of the exceptions, those in the schools of humanities, reveals that they do not necessarily represent a deviation from the pattern. At the National Autonomous University of Mexico, 87 percent of the students in the sample in the school of philosophy were actually studying for degrees in psychology. Among the Colombians in the schools of humanities, a large proportion were also studying psychology. In Uruguay, 42 percent of the sample in the faculty of humanities were studying science-oriented subjects and as this faculty trains its students to be secondary school teachers, many in the sample were undoubtedly training for this field. When we take into account the science and education orientation of many of the students in the schools of humanities, it is possible to reiterate that conservatives were disproportionately more likely to emanate from fields oriented toward science, business, and education.

It is interesting to note that the rank ordering of conservative fields holds true despite the character of the country or the university. Conservative students were most likely to come from the same schools, whether these schools were parts of leftist and secular universities such as the University of the Republic in Uruguay and Libre in Colombia, or whether they were attached to more conservative and religious universities such as the University of Asuncion in Paraguay or Javeriana in Colombia.[78]

Various explanations have been advanced to account for a given relationship between field of study and conservative political position among university students. Seymour Martin Lipset's assertion that "students engaged in courses of study which entail some apprenticeship for a definite profession, e.g. engineering, medicine and preparation for secondary school teaching . . . are less likely to be rebellious than students in courses without determinate destinations,"[79] appears to be quite appropriate as far as these Latin American students are concerned.

The students in these areas are preprofessionals who have acquired technical skills in a context having little to do with the political and social problems of the society. They have limited or in many cases no exposure to social science, history, and other liberal arts books and courses which provide the student with a broader perspective or a critical frame of reference with which to assess his nation. The training of science, medical, engineering, business, and to some extent education students, relative to their liberal arts peers, is oriented toward the acceptance of the status quo as well as the learning of technical skills.

Also, students in these more applied or technical fields are rarely made the objects of concerted efforts by leftists, students or nonstudents, to educate, propagandize or recruit. Leftists tend to alternate between disregarding or being antagonistic to them, thus leaving these students open and available to conservative political forces and ideologies. There has, however, been some recognition of this problem and some attempts to deal with it. At the University of Puerto Rico, leftist or proindependence student groups have attempted to link their political position to the professional or technical role identity of the students in the non-liberal-arts schools. Thus as part of their overall political communication with these students, the left stresses the need to upgrade and improve the level of technical and scientific training because of the importance of trained and skilled manpower in an independent Puerto Rico. As of 1971, this new political position and effort vis-à-vis the students in the applied fields has born some fruit.[80]

Our overall findings based on our five nation sample indicate that the student's school does seem to make some difference as far as his propensity to be a conservative is concerned. In ten universities located in five different countries, students in fields pertaining to science and its application, business, and education were the most likely to be conservative.

In many ways conservative students are more representative of their fellow students and their societies than are radicals. A majority of the Latin American students are opposed to the ideas and actions of Fidel Castro. Few continually engage in strikes or demonstrations. A plurality of the students are located in the center of the political-ideological spectrum, but the majority of the remainder can be found on the right. Radicals are a small minority of the Latin American student population, and statistically there are more conservatives than radicals among the students in the Latin American universities. However, conservatives are less likely than radicals to act out their politics and consequently tend to leave the political field open to their leftist opponents.

Any attempt to understand the politics and the political distribution of the university students must take into account their societal context. With the exception of Cuba and Chile in 1970 there is no socialist or Communist government in the Western Hemisphere. In none of the five societies included in this chapter (Puerto Rico, Colombia, Uruguay, Paraguay, and Mexico) is the political left a dominant factor in government. The governing parties of the five can be described as moderate or rightist. In each of the five countries in our study during the mid-1960s, the leftist parties were either small, weak, fragmented, disorganized, or co-opted by the government.

Despite the political complexion of the governments, all five have highly stratified societies in which the upper strata hold the most political, social, and economic influence. In Uruguay, Puerto Rico, and Mexico governments which once nationalized industries and emphasized welfare programs have turned their energies to encouraging and subsidizing private industry and to promoting foreign, primarily U.S., investments. Paraguay is ruled by one of the last traditional military dictators on the continent. Colombia is governed by a two-party coalition committed almost solely to stability.

In every case the students are drawn predominantly from the upper and middle strata. On the basis of this ascribed status alone, one would predict that they should be conservative. As university students they occupy a status which places them among their nation's elite. On this basis too, they should lean to the right. They are also well aware that economic success depends largely on obtaining government positions, government favors, or family contacts which are in turn linked to government officials. In such circumstances, it is difficult to comprehend why the already large proportion of conservatives is not even greater and why the proportion of leftists is not even smaller.

However, when we look at the students in the individual countries, national differences are discernible. In those countries where the left is a meaningful force and where there is a tradition of egalitarianism and anticlericalism, as in Mexico and Uruguay, the proportion of conservatives is the smallest. Where the political left is small or nonexistent and the government is strong and stable, as in Puerto Rico and Paraguay, the proportion of conservatives is the largest. It would seem that the students to some extent reflect the divisions which exist in their societies.

Conservative students are directly linked to and nourished by the conservative elements of their society. In family matters, they are traditional. They inherit political preferences from their fathers as do most other students. They are faithful to their church and religion, which in Latin America is Roman Catholicism. There is a tendency for conservative students to be disproportionately drawn from the higher strata, generally the most conservative strata.

There appear to be few things, at least in economics or campus matters, that disturb the conservative student. He tends to be satisfied with his status as student and optimistic about future job opportunities. When the Latin American student is not satisfied with student life and with future employment possibilities, his propensity for conservatism declines.

Conservatives are disproportionately found in the faculties or fields of study where the occupational "payoff" is highly visible. These are also fields in which the students are not likely to acquire a critical framework with which to judge their societies nor do they focus substantial attention on the problems of societal power and poverty.

It would appear, then, that the proportion of conservatives among the students of a country varies with the conditions and traditions that exist within that society. In general, the numerical advantage of the conservative and nonradical students in Latin America reflects the still considerable power of conservative and traditional forces within the region. The apparent rise in the level of student radicalism and activism in Latin America in the latter 1960s and early 1970s may be an indicator of a general turn from conservatism and apathy by Latin American students. They increasingly realize that traditional institutions and parties either have not adequately dealt with important and pressing national problems or, indeed, have been among the causal factors producing these various crises.

6 Student Politics and National Context: The Cases of Mexico and Puerto Rico

In the preceding two chapters we have focused on the variety of factors influencing student political orientations and behavior. Here we would like to examine in depth the dynamics as well as the more specific forces involved in the development of student activism in Mexico and Puerto Rico. In both of these societies, student political activity has become dramatically prominent in the latter 1960s. An analysis of these two situations enables us to understand the interplay of university and national factors in the growth of student activism. Such a comparison is particularly enlightening given the different historical and political contexts in which Mexican and Puerto Rican students are located.

A NOT SO COMMON HISTORY

Both Puerto Rico and Mexico were colonies of Spain, and therefore both were influenced by Spanish institutions and the Catholic church. Today, nearly five centuries after Spain's initial colonizing efforts, the impact of Spain upon the culture of Mexico and Puerto Rico is quite evident. The fact that Spanish is the national tongue in both places is an obvious testimony to the influence of Spain. Catholicism, carried along with the *conquistadores*, is the de facto national religion. In both Mexico and Puerto Rico the Spanish monopolized all offices of power in the government, the church, and the economy.

In their history, however, the two countries were quite different, a major differentiating factor was their reaction to Spanish rule. Mexico was the first of Spain's colonies to rebel. Its rebellion began in 1810 and was successfully culminated in 1821. Puerto Rico, by contrast, experienced only one minor armed rebellion against Spain. This was primarily limited to the town of Lares in 1868 and lasted less than a week.

Having achieved independence and liberty, the Mexicans protected these achievements with fervor. In 1867 they fought to unseat the Emperor Maximillian, who had been imposed and supported by Napoleon III. In 1910 after thirty-four years of dictatorship under Porifio Díaz, the Mexicans revolted, thus commencing the first great social and political revolution of the twentieth century. The Puerto Ricans, however, with minor exceptions never fought for either independence or a change in government. No major or grand historic events have occurred in Puerto Rico which the present generation can recall with pride. By contrast, the Mexican revolution is still prominent in the national consciousness of Mexico and Mexicans regard it with pride. Mexicans are more aware of their history and have a greater sense of identification with it than do Puerto Ricans.[1] Oscar Lewis, who studied various groups of Puerto Ricans and Mexicans closely, has commented upon the differences: "It would be difficult to find two Latin American countries with greater contrast . . . perhaps the crucial difference in the history of the two countries was the development of a great revolutionary tradition in Mexico and its absence in Puerto Rico . . . In Mexico, even the poorest slum dwellers have a much richer sense of the past and a deeper identification with the Mexican tradition than do Puerto Ricans with their tradition.[2]

THE ECONOMY

Puerto Rico and Mexico have economies that are stable and expanding and which compare favorably with the economy of any other Latin American country. In both cases the government or, more precisely, the governing party has played a major role in the development of a relatively stable economy. No matter which indicator of economic progress is chosen, both economies show relatively steady growth in the era after World War II. The standard of living of the two peoples, as a result of progressive legislation, has also improved, and various medical and social benefits are available to large sectors of the lower strata in each country.

In Puerto Rico, during the years in which the Popular Democratic Party held a parliamentary majority (1940 to 1968), per capita income increased from $118 to over $1,000. Life expectancy increased from forty-six to over seventy years while the rate of infant mortality declined by about two-thirds. Illiteracy dropped from over 32 percent in 1940 to less than 17 percent in 1960. Puerto Rico increased its educational, health and welfare expenditures until it had, by 1968, budgeted half of the governmental expenditures for these purposes. There has been a steady increase in the gross national product, and in the period from 1964 to 1967 this growth rate was one of the world's highest, averaging 10 percent in current prices.[3]

In Mexico, during roughly the same period of time, 1940 to the mid-1960s, there was a 312 percent increase in the gross national product. Infant mortality declined from 130 deaths per thousand live births in 1934 to 80 in 1958. The illiterate population, ages six and over, constituted two-thirds of the population in 1930 and slightly over one-third in 1960.[4] From the time of the Mexican Revolution until 1963, "108 million acres of all types of land — more than 50 percent of all the productive land of the country — have been distributed among two million peasants."[5] As one prominent economist put it, in terms of overall economic development Mexico is "one of the handful of so-called underdeveloped nations to effect the transition to sustained, more or less self-generating economic expansion."[6]

In view of these facts, the Mexican and Puerto Rican governments can justifiably identify themselves as agents of social change and economic improvement. Both have been active in expanding the economy, improving living standards and introducing social welfare measures. Thus, it would seem that opposition to the governing parties, whether on or off campus, must be beset by formidable obstacles in trying to make headway against parties with such records of accomplishment.

However, despite the progress under the aegis of the PPD of Puerto Rico and the PRI of Mexico, the economic and social situation in both countries is not entirely positive. Official unemployment rates in Puerto Rico have continued to remain in the vicinity of 13 percent.[7] Other sources place the true level of unemployment closer to 30 percent.[8] In addition, unemployment, regardless of how it is calculated, is most heavily concentrated in the 14–24 age group.[9] Despite the rise in per capita income, the income distribution is considerably skewed. According to Commonwealth calculations, in 1963 the poorest fifth of Puerto Rican families earned 4 percent of the income while the richest fifth earned 52 percent.[10]

Puerto Ricans have had to pay a heavy social price for their economic progress. They have become a heavily acquisitive people as evidenced by their large consumer debt, larger at each income level than in comparable groups in the United States.[11] As the economy and the gross national product increased, consumer debt was not the only item to rise. During the 1960s thefts increased by nearly 50 percent while drug addiction quintupled. One researcher estimates that the rate of alcoholism in Puerto Rico may be the highest in the world. The homicide rate has increased as have the rates of suicide and mental disturbance. Oscar Lewis reports that despite the fact of societal progress and even economic improvement within the generations of the Puerto Rican slum families that he studied, "most of the characters . . . feel that progress has passed them by, that they were better off before, 'when food cost less.' They are generally hostile to government and find the idea of Commonwealth difficult to understand."[12]

The Mexican picture also has its dark aspects. Most Mexicans, by any economic indicator, can still be classified as poor.[13] Income distribution is skewed even more markedly than in Puerto Rico. It is estimated that 65 percent of the population receive approximately 25 percent of the income while 5 percent, those at the top of the income ladder, receive 37 percent.[14] This skewing or maldistribution of income has worsened in recent years.[15] Unemployment is a problem, as is underemployment. Mexico, like Puerto Rico, has attempted to alleviate its problem by, in effect, exporting its surplus population to the United States. Although the *bracero* (seasonal migrant labor) program is no longer operative, many Mexicans continue to work in the United States while others leave Mexico to take up permanent residence because of the poor employment prospects in their native land.[16] There is a housing shortage as well as a spread of slums, particularly around Mexico City.[17]

Despite the land reform measures taken in earlier decades, conditions in the countryside have deteriorated. There are about three and a half million agricultural laborers, representing over half the population active in agriculture, who do not own their own land and who are not the beneficiaries of any government programs. Their numbers increased by over 50 percent between 1950 and 1960. Conversely, there has been an increase in the number of large landowners, many of whom are members of prominent political families.[18]

Pablo González Casanova, a noted Mexican economist who in 1970 was appointed rector of the National Autonomous University of Mexico, has observed that "Mexico's economic growth is a fact; Mexico's development is only partly so."[19] Economic and social inequities still persist and on a large scale. "If we accept the premise that 1000 pesos per family per month is a minimum for a modest standard of living, then during 1961–62 only one out of every five Mexican families had a modest or better standard of living . . . the marginal population still represents between 50 and 70 percent of the total; in absolute figures the marginal population has increased."[20]

Like the Puerto Rican economy, the Mexican economy is also tied heavily to that of the United States. In 1965 the United States accounted for 64 percent of Mexico's imports and 72 percent of its exports. In 1957, 78 percent of all foreign investments came from the United States.[21] American-owned or controlled firms represent a large proportion of the bigger industries within Mexico. In 1953 "of 31 businesses with a gross annual income of over 100 million pesos, 19 were North American owned or controlled, 5 were Mexican government projects . . . and only 7 were private Mexican firms."[22] In 1962 of the 400 largest enterprises in Mexico, 232 or 54 percent were foreign owned or controlled, primarily by Americans, 25 percent were government enterprises, and

21 percent were private businesses. One of the major economic consequences of having so large a proportion of the economy in foreign hands is the severe revenue drain which occurs when these enterprises return their profits to the "home" country. In 1965 the total annual foreign investment in Mexico was $155.7 million but the returned profits or "de-investment" totalled $225.9 million resulting in a direct foreign investment deficit of $70.2 million. This situation is further compounded by Mexico's large annual trade deficits resulting mainly from the fact that the foreign price of raw materials, the bulk of her exports, has declined while the price of her imports, primarily capital or finished goods, has increased. From 1957 to 1961 as a result of de-investments and trade deficits, Mexico's foreign accounts deficit was $20 billion. In order to counterbalance these factors Mexico has had to borrow heavily and depend on revenues from tourists and from citizens working abroad. This has meant increased financial dependence on the United States for it is the prime source of loans, tourists, and work for "overseas" Mexicans.[23] Though not formally part of the United States like Puerto Rico, Mexico's economy and economic well-being are largely dependent upon decisions made in the United States.

It is clear that Mexicans and Puerto Ricans have in recent decades witnessed economic progress and experienced higher standards of living. However, poverty and other traditional problems remain and other more recent problems flow from rapid urbanization and industrialization, the very processes that have contributed to economic and social improvements. The existence of these economic and social problems means that student and adult opposition in each society has economic issues to use as political weapons. Also, the very fact of economic progress may in itself create political dissatisfaction as it can whet appetites beyond the capacity of the government to satisfy them, as well as highlight the problems remaining to be solved.

The principal economic problems in both societies are unemployment, inequitable income distribution, and foreign or United States control of the economy. To date the Mexican and Puerto Rican governments have through their economic and social welfare programs been relatively successful in muting political attacks emanating from the economic situation in their respective societies. However, the existence of these problems and others stemming from the economy means that, should major political issues arise in other sectors of the society, the opposition could easily add economic issues to supplement the others and thus exacerbate antigovernment feelings. Also, as the fate of both the Puerto Rican and Mexican economies is strongly affected by the United States, continued economic growth and stability are in large measure dependent on the state of the United States economy and the nature of decisions made outside of the scope of the influence of the Puerto Rican and Mexican governments or businesses. Adverse economic conditions in the United States or adverse economic decisions made by North Americans would have serious negative implications for Puerto Rico and Mexico. Although both governments have been fairly successful in covering their economic flank against serious political attack, recent trends call into question their ability to be as successful at present and in the near future as they were in the past.

THE POLITICAL CONTEXT

During the postwar era and into the latter 1960s, the political situation confronting students opposed to the governments of Mexico and Puerto Rico did not seem very promising. Both the PRI in Mexico and the PPD in Puerto Rico, appeared firmly in control of the legislative and executive branches of their respective governments, a condition of political life that had been true for over two decades in Puerto Rico and more than four in Mexico. In the five presidential elections in Mexico since 1940, the candidate of the PRI, on the average, obtained about 90 percent of the votes cast. In Puerto Rico, in the gubernatorial elections starting with the 1940s and up until the 1968 election, the PPD candidate garnered about 60 percent of the ballots. While there have from time to time been charges of electoral fraud and coercion in both countries, there is little doubt that both parties won their elections through popular support. Prior to 1968 the size of their victories in the elections for the executive and legislative was so embarassing that both the PRI and PPD sponsored legislation to ensure that other parties would have representation in the national legislatures.[24]

The position of the student left in both societies is weak, in large part because the nonstudent left in Mexico and Puerto Rico is small and fragmented. In the 1964 presidential election in Mexico, only one leftist obtained the 75,000 signatures necessary to place his name on the ballot. In 1970 no leftist ran for president. In the 1964 and 1968 gubernatorial elections in Puerto Rico, the leftist party on the ballot, the Puerto Rican Independence Party (PIP), obtained approximately 3 percent of the votes. In both countries leftists have begun to despair of using the electoral route as the avenue to power. The major left party in Mexico, the Popular Socialist Party (PPS), is considered suspect in that it has at times, including the 1970 election, supported PRI presidential candidates and accepted positions and concessions from the government.[25] In Puerto Rico, until quite recently, the PIP has been an extremely mild leftist party which the government has encouraged to stay alive in order to maintain the image of a legitimate left opposition. The Pro-Independence Movement (MPI) is militant but has few members or supporters. Its leadership appears to be devoid of knowledge or interest about basic structures or institutions of Puerto Rican life. It is totally committed if not fixated on the objective of independence for Puerto Rico. The MPI has contributed to its own weakness through its failure to calm the fears or reassure the large numbers of Puerto Ricans who think that independence would bring economic and social chaos in its wake.[26] There are legal Communist parties in both Puerto Rico and Mexico. The former is so small as to be practically nonexistent, and the latter is ineffectual. The Mexican Communist Party is widely regarded as a self-serving bureaucracy whose leaders have some sort of working relationship with the PRI.[27] The weakness of the left in Puerto Rico and Mexico can further be gauged by the fact that in both, the major opposition parties are parties of the right.

Given these political facts of life, which existed as of 1968, student oppositionists in Mexico and Puerto Rico were quite aware that their chances of moving from the campus to seats of power or of profoundly influencing government policy on important issues through the vehicle of student politics or demonstrations were virtually nil. This was a dominant theme in Arthur Liebman's interviews with Mexican and Puerto Rican student activists in 1967 and in 1965.

Despite the overt similarities in the political positions and prospects of student leftists in the two countries, there are differences in the two political landscapes that could potentially stimulate different political reactions from the students and the national governments. In Puerto Rico the dominant political issue is the status of the island. The left, student and nonstudent alike, has identified itself with independence, while the right has vigorously pushed for statehood. The PPD has taken a middle position, the promotion of the Commonwealth status. From the time it came to power in 1940 until the mid-1960s, the PPD has attempted to subordinate the status issue to that of social reform and economic development — and with considerable success. For the almost two and a half decades it was in power, the PPD was able to mute concern and discussion of the island's status.[28] However, as developments in the latter 1960s (which will be discussed below), have shown, it is not possible long to ignore the most potent political issue in a society.

It is the status issue that gives the left students in Puerto Rico political leverage. As long as the government is in the hands of parties unfavorable to independence, the left or proindependence students have a cause. Until a proindependence party attains power, no amount of public housing, schools, or social welfare programs can undercut the fundamental position of the Puerto Rican left or thoroughly diminish its appeal. Despite the decline in the percentage of independence voters, there are a considerable number of Puerto Ricans, particularly among academics and intellectuals, with whom a proindependence appeal strikes a responsive chord. This also implies that should the economy falter or serious social problems develop, there will always be some form of left opposition which will be in a position to capitalize on the problems and to which the discontented Puerto Ricans can turn.

The Mexican student oppositionists, of whom the great majority are leftists, have not been as "fortunate" as their Puerto Rican counterparts. There are no great issues that divide the Mexican nation, nothing that even comes close to resembling the political status issue in Puerto Rico. The religious cleavage that split the Mexicans at the time of the Mexican Revolution and into the 1930s has been absorbed and little is made of that subject. No class or stratum is excluded from political participation or any government programs open to the general populace. Political issues and social problems do, however, exist. There is extensive poverty, a maldistribution of income, widespread corruption, electoral manipulation, and a single party that has dominated political life for almost half a century. However, none of these factors has been significant enough to mobilize mass opposition either on or off campus.

What has been the source of the power of the PRI? How has it been so successful that there has been no external legitimate or nonlegitimate threat to its rule in more than four decades? One of the more important obstacles to the success of any opposition, student or nonstudent, has been the mystique of the Mexican Revolution and the use to which the PRI has put it. In the view of Robert Scott, probably the most prominent American observer of Mexican politics, the Mexican Revolution has almost religious or mystical qualities: "Everything and everyone Mexican . . . exists in an atmosphere permeated with its spirit. Every major topic is approached, considered, accepted or rejected in terms of what the Revolution is supposed to stand for, and no serious proponent of just about anything would dream of forgetting to claim legitimacy for his particular point of view by labeling it the authentic voice, perhaps the only voice of the Revolution."[29] In Mexico, the revolutionary mystique is considered a leftist one. Seymour M. Lipset has asserted that Mexico, of all the Latin American countries, "is the one country which has identified its national ethos with that of equality and an open society."[30] The revolution and its tradition have become so institutionalized that even reactionary or conservative groups use it to legitimize their positions and thus gain support.[31]

The PRI has had the most success in identifying itself as the rightful standard bearer of the revolutionary tradition. As the ruling party, it has attempted to monopolize all claims of revolutionary legitimacy, and party leaders continually assert that the PRI is the only rightful heir of the revolution. Rarely is there a party gathering or a meeting of a significant secondary association that is not replete with impassioned oratory that equates the incumbent president and the official party with the Revolution.[32]

This does not necessarily mean that all sectors of the Mexican populace believe what they hear from the PRI and most of the mass media. They are well aware that they are governed by men and not revolutionary idealists. In fact, Mexicans do tend to be quite cynical about the PRI and the other Mexican political parties as well. Joseph Kahl recently claimed that Mexicans are able to and do make distinctions between the Revolution and its institutions and the people who occupy positions of importance within the governmental bureaucracy and the political parties.[33] Mexicans are also quite aware that government officials are not really motivated by the Revolution in their dealings with the people. In a five nation study by Gabriel Almond and Sidney Verba it was revealed that Mexicans, more so than Americans, British, Germans and Italians, expect the *least* consideration for their views from bureaucrats and the police. In Mexico Almond and Verba infer, graft and official corruption are notable features of life.[34]

Yet despite the cynicism of the populace and the widespread graft of officialdom, Mexicans have continued to point to their governmental and political institutions as the aspects of their nation of which they are the proudest.[35] Mexican respondents in Joseph Kahl's study were asked to choose one of two statements concerning the Revolution closest to their preference:

"Mexico is much better off today because we had the Revolution."

"The Revolution has not solved our problems."

Seventy-eight percent voiced their preference for the first statement.[36]

The position of the PRI with reference to the Revolution and the left has been questioned, especially after the 1968 Mexican student disturbances. A leading Mexican historian, Daniel Cosio Villegas, has been among the more serious challengers to the argument that the PRI has successfully identified itself with the Revolution. He has contended that the moral authority of the PRI and its leadership has been on the decline.[37] Despite the PRI's own claim to be "leftist," there have been a variety of indications to the contrary. The Communist Party of Mexico has been denied access to the ballot, and during any major disturbance, regardless of the evidence available, its leaders tend to be imprisoned. The Mexican penal code contains the crime of *social dissolution*, a law which makes it a crime to diffuse the ideas or programs of any foreign government that disturb the public order or affect Mexico's sovereignty. This law has been invoked against dissident labor leaders, such as Demetrio Vallejo and Valentín Campa of the railway workers who led an unauthorized strike in 1958, and against Communists and other leftists. The government has sanctioned the use of violence against political opponents, especially in the countryside.[38] And the government has been an adept practitioner of co-optation by providing political opponents with money and or prestigious positions, a political technique for which Mexico has acquired an international reputation.[39]

These deviations from a leftist orientation are rarely brought to the attention of the populace by the mass media in any meaningful fashion. Although there is no official censorship, the fact that the government is the sole source of newsprint has helped it to obtain a sympathetic press. At the same time that it takes authoritarian measures against leftists and suspected leftists, the PRI government can cite its leftist credentials. Mexico was the only Latin American country to recognize Cuba until 1971 when the Allende government in Chile extended recognition and only one of seven countries in the world still to maintain diplomatic relations with the Spanish Republic. The Communist party, although in effect barred from the ballot, can exist legally in Mexico, one of the few countries in Latin America where this is possible. In 1969 and 1970 during a wave of political kidnappings by leftist organizations in various Latin American countries, the human ransom, generally jailed leftists, was invariably flown to Mexico at the kidnappers' request. Also, there are still anticlerical articles in the Mexican Constitution, albeit unenforced. Critics point to these examples as relatively inexpensive gestures to the left, gestures which have little impact upon the social structure and the distribution of power and wealth.

Whatever the nature or the number of the PRI's inconsistencies, the fact remains that it publicly and continually identifies itself with the left and with the Revolution. Few individuals or organizations publicly and consistently arise to challenge the PRI on this issue. There is a dearth of alternative ideologies or challengers to the mantle of the Revolution. Student leftists have had difficulty grasping the leverage available to their counterparts in other developing societies. In such societies students could politically use the sentiment held by their compatriots, particularly the disadvantaged, that they were the only selfless or idealist segment of the society. In Mexico the students are forced to contend with the fact that their claim to idealism is challenged by the government's more publicized claims.[40]

How do leftists mobilize opposition to a government that heralds itself as the embodiment of a popular and momentous revolution? How do leftist students politically utilize moral leverage against a government whose president boasts that his government is one of "the extreme left within the law."[41] Ironically, despite the contrasting historical traditions of their two societies,

Puerto Rican and Mexican students find themselves in a somewhat similar position. Leftist Puerto Rican students have had difficulty in appealing to and identifying with Puerto Rican history in their struggle for independence. There is no glorious past to commemorate, no great deeds of Puerto Ricans committed to independence to be recalled. In fact, strident appeals for independence place one *outside* the mainstream of Puerto Rican tradition and history. The Mexican students, on the contrary, have a great historic, in fact a revolutionary, tradition to which they might appeal. However, they have found that much of the heroic past has been co-opted by the governing party in order to maintain the status quo. Thus, in both cases, students have been denied the platform of history and tradition on which to stand and appeal to their respective populations for support.

Prospective Mexican student oppositionists are confronted with another disadvantage that is not shared to the same degree by their Puerto Rican counterparts. In Puerto Rico there are meaningful opposition parties which seriously contest with the PPD in elections. In 1964, at the time the survey data on the Puerto Rican students were collected, the Republican Statehood party (PER) received 35 percent of the vote in the gubernatorial election. In 1968, as the result of a split within the PPD, the New Progressive party, a successor to the PER and like the PER a prostatehood party, won the governorship with 43 percent of the votes. There is no such phenomenon in Mexico. Despite some local victories and challenges by the conservative National Action party (PAN), Mexico is a de facto one-party state. There are few if any independent bases of opposition to the PRI government as the PRI has effectively eliminated such bases through co-optation or repression. It has broken the back of the landed aristocracy, reduced the prerevolutionary power position of the foreign capitalists, made the small farmers dependent upon the central government, obtained major influence over the labor unions and gained substantial leverage vis-à-vis the industrialists.[42] In addition, the ruling party has greatly reduced the size and importance of the military and effectively removed it from the political scene as an independent force.[43] As William Glade, an American economist expressed it, "the federal government established its control over competing power structures and created a relationship of direct dependence on the machinery of government among the major interest groups of national life . . . for in so linking the central government with the people, it reduced the independent role of other potential focus points of popular loyalties."[44] An analysis in *Le Monde* indicated that Mexico's economic growth is strongly associated with the strength of the PRI government, an assessment with which others also concur. The government has been able to resist the demands of various groups and sectors, primarily the most disadvantaged, and ensure a favorable economic and political climate for foreign investments and enterprises as well as for prominent native businessmen through strong measures. *Le Monde* bluntly summarized the situation: "the secret of the Mexican 'economic miracle' lies in the use of the iron fist in imposing law and order, a policy which has been applied since 1910."[45]

An additional consideration in the PRI's power and influence, particularly over university students and graduates is the fact that it and the government are the more important channels for social mobility in Mexico. As the governing party, the PRI is able to offer positions in the government and the governmental bureaucracy and even to obtain positions for its favorites in various sectors of private enterprise. The government itself, William Glade has pointed out, hires "a rather large proportion of the available national leadership talent."[46] Similar to the old style United States political organizations or "machines" that dominated U.S. cities like Chicago, the PRI rewards those who serve its interests but on a national and not a local basis. The PRI, which has a very small permanent organization, relies a great deal upon volunteers who are aware that the PRI does not have to share patronage or other political spoils with any other party.[47]

University students are quite knowledgeable about the power of the PRI and the rewards it can offer. This is especially true of law students whose professional success is directly and immediately linked to the PRI-dominated government.[48] The influence of the PRI is strengthened by the fact that in Mexico as in many other developing countries, family-owned firms stress familial ties rather than educational qualifications in hiring their personnel.[49] The importance of contacts is not lost among the Mexican students. In our survey, when asked to name the most important factor for professional success, 57 percent of the Mexicans replied "competence" compared to 76 percent of the Puerto Rican students. The increased support for the PRI as the students move from freshman to senior year, as reported in this volume in chapter 4 is another indication that the Mexican students, particularly as they prepare to enter the job market, begin to accomodate to political reality. In interviews conducted with student activists and leftists at the UNAM by Arthur Liebman in 1967, not one expressed any intention of joining the government opposition after graduation. Student activists opposed to the PRI contended that they could bring about desired changes and reforms more effectively by working within the government. Whether this sentiment represented a response to reality or a rationalization, the point remains that even student oppositionists seek employment within the government. E. Wight Bakke found in his interviews with

Mexican students that they realized that a reputation as a student politician was a major factor in achieving success after leaving the university.[50] In other words, the power of the PRI, for good or for evil, is not lost upon the students of Mexico.

This situation is qualitatively different in Puerto Rico. There is an organized opposition that participates in elections and, as the election of 1968 revealed, can even win. Unlike Mexico, where prior to 1968 public criticism of the chief executive was almost nonexistent, the Puerto Rican mass media have freely attacked the governor and the PPD when it was in power as well as the current New Progressive Party governor. In Puerto Rico, there are United States constitutional limitations and federal courts which somewhat restrict the governor's powers. In Mexico the president is the focal point of power and can run the country almost in whatever manner he chooses without worry of formal challenge from the courts or the legislature. Virtually the only constitutional or political restraint upon him is that he cannot be re-elected. In Puerto Rico there are important sectors of society such as the church and industrialists which are not appendages of the ruling party and which have frequently demonstrated their opposition to the governing party through political acts as well as public statements. On the whole, the PPD when it was in power, was more restrained and less authoritarian than the PRI. In addition there are more elements and sectors independent of governmental control in Puerto Rico than in Mexico. Finally, the fact that Puerto Ricans are United States citizens means that the United States is open to them as a political safety valve, similar to the way emigration has already been used as an economic safety valve, should the situation ever arise where emigration might be called for. Mexicans don't have this option available to them on the same scale.

Thus, in both societies there are formidable obstacles to students either gaining power or exerting a serious influence upon government personnel or their policies. Because of the dominance of the long-ruling Institutional Revolutionary Party, this is particularly so in the case of Mexico.

THE STUDENTS

The University of Puerto Rico and the National Autonomous University of Mexico

The University of Puerto Rico (UPR) and the National Autonomous University of Mexico (UNAM) are the largest and most prestigious universities in their respective societies. Both serve as the major sources of administrators, engineers, scientists, social scientists, teachers, and future political leaders for their countries. Each is an urban university located in the capital. Neither university has sizeable dormitory facilities, which means that virtually all students at each are commuters. Given the distance of the UNAM from appropriate student housing, most students commute on busses daily, a ride that averages about three-quarters of an hour each way.

Both the UPR and the UNAM have come under criticism for their academic standards. Neither university is regarded as intellectually demanding. Both professorial and student informants have complained about the widespread cheating and plagiarism, some of which appears to take place with the overt as well as tacit consent of the instructors. Academic standards have been so deficient that various schools at the UPR have started special honors programs for students planning to pursue postgraduate education in the United States. Without such programs, it was felt that their chances in mainland educational institutions would be slim. The UNAM professor resembles the "taxi" professor who commutes from his job to read his old lecture notes to a class of bored students. Indicative of the students' attitude toward their professors at the UNAM is the fact that 48 percent of the students in our survey stated that few, or none, of their professors were excellent. This compares with 28 percent of the Puerto Rican students who gave similar responses about their instructors, reflecting the fact that more of the UPR than UNAM academic staff are full-time and hold advanced degrees. Another indicator of the academic standards at UNAM was that the credits earned there could not be transferred to colleges in the United States. One study of students at the UPR summed up its conclusions by stating that "there was general agreement that students lack motivation, have little intellectual enthusiasm, and tend to be apathetic toward scholarship."[51] These findings seem to apply to the Mexican students as well. Both student bodies have been charged with being apathetic and overly concerned with the status-conferring function of their degrees.[52]

Mexican Student Politics

One of the important features differentiating the two student bodies is that, until the latter 1960s, UNAM was distinctly the more politically active campus. In contrast to the UPR, which has tried to maintain a politically neutral stance since its founding in 1902, the UNAM has had a history of deep political involvement. After the triumph of Juárez over Emperor Maximilian in 1867, the UNAM was closed until 1910 on the grounds that it was a center of reaction. In the 1930s, Eyler N. Simpson, an American student of Mexican history, described the University in the following manner: "the University at the present time is conservative to the point of being reactionary. It is not only out of touch with national life . . . but it is actually engaging in the negative work of raising up a generation either entirely indifferent to the revolution or for which the revolutionary principles are an anathema."[53]

In the following decades and into the sixties, the UNAM was in continual political tempest. For example, in 1944 left-wing students disapproved of the appointment of a new director of the National Preparatory School. Fighting broke out as opposing sides took their stand either for or against the appointment. Two students were killed, and the rector of UNAM as well as his newly appointed director resigned. The new rector, Don Alfonso Caso, a distinguished archaeologist, was acceptable to the left-wing students but not to the right, who accused him of being a Communist because he was the brother-in-law of the prominent leftist labor leader Vincente Lombardo Toledano.[54]

Since then, students have continued to be politically sensitive and active. Student disturbances have accompanied the arrival and departure of UNAM rectors, who, it should be noted, appear to be chosen for the most part on the basis of their political loyalties.[55] There have been strikes and demonstrations in recent years over such issues as bus fares, admission standards, and government policy toward students elsewhere in Mexico. Virtually all of the disturbances centered around issues related to the university.

In 1966 a major strike erupted at the UNAM, the first significant political action there in several years. It lasted more than three and a half months and inspired at least five more strikes in other Mexican universities. The UNAM dispute began in the Law School and then spread to the Schools of Economics, Political and Social Sciences, and to several preparatory schools affiliated with UNAM. The initial demands of the striking law students dealt with changes in the structure of examinations, remedial courses, discipline procedures, and the resignation of the Law School director, César Sepúlveda. Soon the demand for the resignation of the UNAM Rector, Ignacio Chávez was included. The resignations of Sepulveda and Chávez turned out to be the only major results of the strike.

The 1966 strike was significant for other reasons than the resignations of the rector and Law School director. Of major import, was the government's involvement in and direction of part of the strike. As events unfolded the nature of the government's involvement became clearer, and it became evident that its principle goal in the strike was the ouster of Dr. Chávez. There are several pieces of evidence which support this conclusion. First, the strike started in the Law School, the school in which the PRI is reputed to have the most influence.

Second, during the course of the strike, two of the most important strike leaders at the Law School were expelled from the strike committee because of accusations that they represented extra-university interests. The nature of these interests were made abundantly clear after the strike when these two students were feted at a banquet attended by the president of the Chamber of Deputies and the editor of *El Día*, a prominent PRI deputy. Third, the leniency and the tacit compliance of the police toward the strikers was notable even when the striking students spilled off the campus to commandeer busses and force private schools to close. This was in stark contrast to the way in which the government dealt with student strikers at the University of Morelia which occurred about the same time as the UNAM strike. Finally, there was the public statement by the secretary of the interior, Luis Echeverría, who in 1970 became president of Mexico. During the midst of the strike he publicly condemned Chávez.

It is still not clear why the government or the PRI wanted Dr. Chávez removed. It may have been that Dr. Chávez, an independent leftist who assumed the rectorship after a distinguished career as a medical doctor, educator, and administrator, conducted the affairs of UNAM in accordance with his own proclivities without giving the views or interests of other parties or groups, including PRI, much consideration. In fact, his independence and his reforms as well as attempts at reforms had alienated so many persons and groups at UNAM that he had few allies when confronted by the student strikers and the PRI. It is interesting to note that his successor was Javier Barros Sierra, a prominant national political figure who had been secretary of public works during the administration of López Mateos and a man so high in the ranks of the PRI that he had formally been considered by the highest party echelon as a candidate for the presidency of Mexico.

The strike, however, involved more than the PRI and its accomplices among the students. Elements from the student left as represented by the students from the Schools of Economics, Political and Social Sciences, and Philosophy also became quite active. They, too, wanted the resignation of Dr. Chávez but not for the same reasons as the PRI oriented student strikers. The left opposed Dr. Chávez because of his reform measures which included tighter admissions procedures and entrance examinations even for the graduates of UNAM'S own preparatory schools. They viewed his attempts as part of a general plan to restrict university education even further to a middle- and upper-class elite and reduce to a minimum the opportunities for anyone from the lower strata to gain admission to higher education. Ironically, they coupled his efforts with that of the government's because they felt that through low budget appropriations for education and general neglect of the educational system, the government was also trying to reduce the lower strata's access to education at all levels. The left strikers, contrary to the others, were not appeased by Dr. Chávez's resignation. Also, unlike the other strikers, they made attempts to gain public support and bring their case to the people. They were interested in turning the strike from a university issue to a national issue. The conclusion of the strike following the resignation of Dr. Chávez did not bring harmony to the UNAM. The left remained frustrated because the issues for which they had fought were left unresolved, and furthermore they were angered because they felt they had been used by the PRI. All in all the 1966 strike helped to set the stage for the events of 1968.[56]

The intervention of the PRI in the affairs of UNAM in 1966 was not an unprecedented act. Historically and up to the present day, the PRI has rarely viewed the National Autonomous University of Mexico or any other Mexican college or university as being outside of or above politics. It has tried to extend its influence and control over Mexico's institutions of higher education through a PRI youth corps, academicians and administrators with personal ties to the PRI, and undercover agents. Leftist and critical professors from provincial or state universities have been harassed or fired at the behest of the PRI officialdom. The government has sent federal troops into various state universities to quell student disorders or demonstrations. This practice increased during the 1960s. Generally, when the troops withdraw, PRI loyalists and rightist organizations are left in positions of control. The PRI's hostility to the faculty and student dissidents at UNAM grew as that university became the single strongest bastion of PRI critics in the country.[57] UNAM could not be dealt with in the same manner as other universities because it was the nation's leading institution of higher education; it was located in the capital, and it was officially guaranteed autonomy. An attack on the UNAM could not be as open and as blatant as one on a provincial university.

Political activity among the students at the UNAM has, for the most part prior to 1968, centered in the Schools of Law, Economics, Social and Political Sciences, and Philosophy. These schools are physically adjacent to one another and look across the quadrangle at the more "politically quiet" schools of Architecture, Business, and Engineering. There has been considerable political antagonism between students from different schools, particularly between those from the active and those from the nonactive schools. In the 1966 strikes little support came from the latter schools, Architecture and Engineering, for example, were closed for only a few days while students at the more active schools remained on strike for the entire seventy-three days. As a consequence or perhaps a function of this disagreement among the students, there had been prior to 1968 little effort to unify the students into a campus-wide student political or governmental organization. As one student in the School of Architecture expressed it in an interview with Arthur Liebman, "University-wide student elections and a University Student Council would lead to political control by the 'political mafia' here at the University." The political mafia, he went on to explain, were the professional politicians — students, particularly in Law, Economics, and the other politically active schools, who had considerable time available to devote to politics.

The student president of the School of Economics, a leftist activist, saw things from a different perspective. He, too, was opposed to a university-wide student government. "If we ever had such a thing, the right would get control, so therefore, we are better off without it." When asked to amplify his remarks about the right, he pointed to the schools across from him and stated that they contained more students than the schools on his side of the quadrangle.

Before 1968 the UNAM campus was politically fragmented, with issues extending far beyond the differences of the activist and the nonactivist schools. Political divisions have characterized virtually every school. There are a variety of political organizations at the UNAM, most of which are on the left. These include the Communists, Maoists, Trotskyists, Anarchists, Fidelistas, Christian Socialists. There are also rightists organizations such as the Falangists and the Movimento Universitario de Renovadora Orientacion (MURO), a clandestine fascist organization. There are in addition regional organizations that take on political coloring, as well as independent groups unique to the UNAM, such as the Miguel Hernandez organization at the School of Philosophy. Few, if they are youth appendages of adult political organizations, act strictly in accordance with party or organizational discipline and most, in fact, take quite independent stances. At the School of Economics, perhaps the most ideological school at UNAM, seven candidates ran in the election for student president in 1967, each representing a different political position, six of which were leftist. Few organizations cut across any school lines and those that do, like the Communists, have little political power on campus. Only on rare occasions is there cooperation among the various political organizations, and this is also true of the leftist groups that are physically and seemingly ideologically in close proximity to one another. Squabbling and political infighting have been the major continuing features of student politics among the UNAM student activists.

The structure of the university lends itself to this state of affairs. At UNAM, as in most Latin American universities, the individual school is almost a world unto itself. A student takes virtually all of his courses within the walls and with the students of one college or faculty. Many schools have their own cafeterias and each has its own student government. There are no structures on the campus which facilitate meaningful interaction among students from different schools.

Conditions within schools are also conducive to political fragmentation. Every college at the UNAM has morning and late afternoon classes. Generally a student will take all of his classes within a particular session and then leave the campus. Therefore, in many cases morning students will rarely come into contact with afternoon students even though they are enrolled in the same school. In addition, several schools assign a student to a group. This group then takes all of its classes together and by itself throughout the year, thus further reducing widespread contact with other students in that school.

It is not altogether unexpected that student activists, particularly those on the left, should be found divided into a variety of small bickering groups. This was the same condition in which their adult counterparts off campus found themselves. Both the students and the nonstudent leftist organizations were responding to the same forces, specifically the power of the PRI and a rapidly growing but noninflationary economy capable of bringing increasing, albeit unequal, benefits to large segments of the population, the urban population in particular.

Belief in the power of the PRI was probably the one factor that all the student leftist organizations shared in common. In the course of Liebman's interviews with leftist students from different schools and organizations, this emerged as a dominant theme. They believed that the PRI was as strong as it claimed to be. All made clear that the students and their organizations were too ineffectual at the time (1967) to pose a serious challenge to the government. They anticipated a long and arduous process of building an effective anti-PRI force among students as well as nonstudents. Their political analyses clearly revealed their own weakness vis-à-vis the government.

This perception of the political world had consequences for the students' political behavior. One of the more important results was that they, the leftist activists, directed their attention inward toward the campus. This tendency of UNAM students, in general, to focus on the campus has been observed by several prominent American social scientists. In fact, both Robert Scott and Kalman Silvert noted before 1968 that there had been an overall reduction in the political activity of UNAM students in recent years.[58] Increases in bus fares and unpopular academic regulations or administrators were the issues that triggered the UNAM students into action.[59]

National and international issues and events were not very important to student leftists at UNAM Liebman's interviews revealed. They would, of course, loudly voice condemnations of official corruption and various government leaders and policies as well as the United States, but it was as if they were stating these condemnations for some historical record or as a way of presenting their political credentials. It was radical rhetoric because there was little connection between their words and their actual or intended deeds with respect to off campus events and personalities. This is in marked contrast to the Puerto Rican leftists whose orientation and activity have been directed toward the world beyond the campus or toward linking university issues to broader national concerns such as in their anti-ROTC campaign. Our survey data also indicate that, in general, Puerto Rican students were more interested and oriented toward national and international politics than were the Mexican students.

In 1968, starting in July and lasting through December, students from the UNAM and elsewhere found themselves in the midst of the largest and most significant student movement in recent Mexican history.[60] What caused such a radical departure from the normal campus-oriented politics? What transformed a by and large apathetic and cynical studentbody, among whom political activists numbered into the hundreds, into a moral and political force numbering into the tens of thousands that visibly shook a heretofore seemingly impregnable government?

There had been no major changes in the students at UNAM or in academic regulations prior to 1968. The economy experienced no sudden downturn and in fact was growing faster than ever at a rate of 7 percent a year, making Mexico's growth rate one of the world's fastest. There had been no sudden changes in Mexico's foreign policy nor was there any threat of war on the horizon. No social movement or political party had launched a campaign against the PRI in the months before July 1968.

There were some minor political and social disturbances, but for the most part these were not extraordinary and occurred far from the capital. The army moved to quell some peasant disturbances in Sonora state but this had not caused much of a stir. In 1967 the PRI had been shaken by the loss of the mayoralty elections in two state capitals, Merida and Hermosillo, but no one questioned its basic political strength. Probably more disturbing were the speeches and activities of Carlos Madrazo, the former chairman of the PRI. Forced from his party position for espousing liberalization of the PRI in 1965, Madrazo used every available forum throughout the country to attack the PRI openly.

Student disturbances had erupted in the provinces in late 1967 and 1968, but these did not seem out of the ordinary. Even when the army invaded the

University of Sonora in 1968 to quell the students, this had not sparked any response by the UNAM students. Immediately prior to the Mexico City student eruption, there had been bloody student-police confrontations in Puebla, Cuernavaca, and a few other cities, but, again, these failed to evoke a response from the students in the capital. The focal point for these confrontations tended to be local issues and personalities. The UNAM students had been relatively quiet since the strike of 1966. They had not reacted overtly to the cuts in the university budget which followed on the heels of that strike and which contributed to a deterioration in facilities, a growing shortage of professors, and a growth in the size of classes. This, however, undoubtedly helped fuel their hostility to the government.

From the point of view of the government, any real student political problems would come from the students in the capital, the hub of Mexico's political, economic, and social world. The UNAM students gave little cause for concern in 1967 and the first six months of 1968. No one expected any trouble from the other major concentration of students in the capital, the approximately 50,000 who attended the National Polytechnic Institute (IPN) and its associated preparatory or secondary schools. The IPN students were much more apolitical than the UNAM students. In addition, the National Federation of Technical Students (FNET), the official student organization of the IPN, was government-financed and widely considered to be government-controlled. Furthermore, students at the IPN and the UNAM were famous for their rivalry and the possibility of a large-scale concerted political movement based on their cooperation appeared quite slim.

The one new factor in 1968 was the Olympic Games scheduled for Mexico City in October. The Mexican government viewed the Olympic Games as a contribution to its economy and an important boost to its international prestige. In preparation, it had budgeted over $80,000,000. After all, this was the first time that they were to be held in a developing nation. The designation of Mexico as the site was an international recognition of Mexico's well-advertised political stability. It meant that immediately prior to and during the games, the eyes of the world would be on Mexico City as reporters from all over the world arrived; in addition, great numbers of tourists and potential investors would also be on hand. Stability took on added importance as the opening day drew near.

On July 23, 1968, a small number of teen-age students from the IPN and UNAM preparatory schools in Mexico City met in a minor clash. *There is unanimous agreement that politics was not a factor in this disturbance.* It has been attributed to youthful rivalries over schools and girlfriends. This, in retrospect, became the first act in the major drama which then began to unfold. In this disturbance, for some inexplicable reason, instead of the city police who were acquainted with the students and the schools and who had handled such events in the past, the *granaderos*, a special riot corps, were dispatched to the scene. They halted the fracas. However, in the process, the granaderos chased some of the students into a nearby vocational school, one associated with the IPN. The riot police entered the school where they indiscriminately proceeded to beat students, professors, and janitors.

Incensed, the normally complacent IPN students demanded that their oganization, FNET, protest. The FNET responded by calling for a demonstration on July 26 which would urge the government to disband the granaderos or, at the very least, to dismiss their chief officers. By coincidence, July 26 was the date on which another demonstration was planned. This other demonstration involved mainly UNAM students who wished to celebrate the anniversary of the Cuban Revolution. Both demonstrations received the necessary authorization. Much to the consternation of the FNET organizers, the two groups of demonstrators mingled, and large numbers from each headed toward the Zocalo, the main square and the site of the presidential palace, an unauthorized demonstration locale. There the granaderos were waiting and brutally dispersed the students.

Enraged, the students barricaded themselves in nearby preparatory schools, using commandeered public buses for their barricades. For three days the situation was tense. Then on July 29, claiming that public safety was endangered and that arms were being smuggled to the students, the police and the army moved to disperse and arrest the students. Other schools were occupied by the army and the police to prevent their use by student demonstrators. The UNAM and the IPN were ringed with troops. The fighting, which did not subside until July 31, resulted in many arrests and injuries as well as several student deaths. The government charged that the Mexican Communist party (PCM) was behind the disorders and arrested seventy-six of its leading members on July 31. The PCM officially denied any responsibility and at one point accused the CIA of provoking the students. For the next few months the PCM cautiously remained relatively uninvolved.

Meanwhile, strikes spread throughout Mexico City's schools, supported by students and teachers alike. A National Strike Council (CNH) was formed, consisting of representatives from each of the schools and colleges of the IPN and the UNAM. The rector of UNAM, declaring the University's autonomy in danger, led an authorized protest demonstration of from 50,000 to 100,000 persons from University City into downtown Mexico City. On August 5, the director of the Polytechnical Institute led an even larger demonstration on behalf of the missing students who were presumed dead.

The strike spread and grew in intensity. The CNH formulated its demands for a settlement: (1) repeal of Articles 145 and 145 *bis* of the Mexican penal code, the "Law of Social Dissolution," which permitted the government to imprison for a maximum of twelve years anyone convicted of circulating ideas that lead to "rebellion, sedition, riot or insurrection"; (2) freedom for all political prisoners particularly Demetrio Vallejo and Valentín Campa, who, as previously mentioned, were convicted in 1958 under the Law of Social Dissolution for leading a railway workers' strike; (3) dismissal of the Chief and the Deputy Chief of Police of Mexico City; (4) establishment of responsibility for those who authorized the use of the granaderos and the army against the students; (5) abolition of the granaderos and the dismissal of their chief; and (6) compensation for wounded students and the families of students killed in the disturbances. These remained the basic demands of the students throughout the turmoil. At various times, the student strike leaders also demanded that any negotiations between them and the government be carried live on television and radio.

The month of August was a period of intense political activity. Perhaps more overt anti-PRI and antigovernment activity took place during that period than in any other comparable time since the PRI came to power. The CNH organized student brigades which fanned out into the factories, parks, stores, buses, and nearby villages. These brigades told the students' version of the events, mobilized public support, and raised funds. Health and political as well as information brigades were also formed. Public opinion, although difficult to gauge, appeared to be growing on the side of the students, and in several factories strike votes were scheduled. During the same period, four major demonstrations were held in Mexico City, each successively larger, more inclusive, and more hostile to the government. The last, on August 27, organized by the CNH, totalled from 200,000 to 400,000 persons including large numbers of nonstudents. It ended at the National Palace. During these demonstrations, speakers in front of the National Palace publicly denounced President Gustavo Díaz Ordaz, a feat which broke with the well-entrenched political tradition of never publicly criticizing the Mexican head of state.

On August 28, after several weeks of self-restraint, the government felt that the situation had gone far enough. The army was called out and occupied strategic points throughout Mexico City. There were some attempts at negotiation, but when these failed, troops were on September 18 sent on the grounds of the National Autonomous University of Mexico, the first overt and concerted violation of that university's guaranteed autonomy in forty years. Several thousand students as well as scores of their teachers were arrested. Sporadic street fights took place for weeks thereafter, but the government was clearly in charge of the situation. Then, on October 2 during a peaceful but unauthorized student rally at Tlateloco or the Plaza of the Three Cultures, the army apparently upon prearranged signals from government agents proceeded to fire indiscriminately into the crowd, killing dozens of students, women, and children and wounding hundreds of others. Many were arrested, including foreign correspondents in attendance. This was the last public demonstration. The Olympic Games were held without further significant disturbances, and as the year progressed increasing numbers of students returned to their classrooms. By the end of the year, there was little political activity. The Mexican student movement of 1968 ended with seemingly few enduring things to show for itself other than several hundred deaths, several hundred student activists and some professors in jail, and scores of others in exile. The PRI government remained in power although it had experienced its most severe political shock in decades.

Why and how did this major student movement occur? Had the Mexican students or the political situation changed so drastically in the months preceding 1968? The answer is no, neither the political conditions in the country nor the students had changed very much in that period. The economy continued to boom, the PRI remained seemingly as powerful as ever, and the student activists as few and as fragmented as ever. The Mexican students or any particular political group among them did not plan to launch any movement in the latter half of 1968. There was no group that defined itself as a "detonator" such as Daniel Cohn-Bendit's Movement of March 22nd or the SDS in the United States. There was nothing to indicate that any student organization had changed its basic position on the relative strength of the students versus the government.

In fact it would be a mistake to focus solely on the student activists and their organizations in order to explain what happened in Mexico during July and the following months. When the student rebellion began and during its height, the organizational radicals and the long-time activists were not at the forefront. During those periods it was the younger students and those who were not previously involved in politics who rose to head the movement. It was this that proved so frustrating to the government in its attempts to arrange a settlement. The PRI was accustomed to dealing with leaders of organized groups among the students and to entering into mutually satisfactory bargains as the most effective way of settling student grievances. The novices, however, refused, for the most part, to follow this tradition. They publicly announced their six basic objectives and stuck to them throughout. The call for televised negotiations with the government sprang from their knowledge of how political settlements had previously been reached. They feared that, like other student leaders, the PRI would co-opt or in other ways compromise them.

It was the moral outrage of thousands of students of this type that was the major force behind the movement. They were not constrained in their actions by ideology, reasoned political analysis, or organizational involvement. Politically and structurally they were free; free to express and act out their moral feelings. Thus, when the granaderos brutally dealt with some innocent teen-age students, they could and did react. The seasoned activists and the traditional leftist organizations, such as the Communists, hesitated for weeks before actively participating. Their reasoned political analyses had led them to believe that involvement in the disturbances would yield few positive benefits. Conversely, such participation, from their point of view, would be much more likely to have negative consequences both for themselves and for their oganizations. They did not want to endanger their organizations or risk prison by being drawn into a fracas which they had not planned and from which they had few hopes of significant benefit. Therefore, eschewing "adventurism," these leftist leaders and organizations generally did not, during the early phase, seek positions on the National Strike Committee and these leadership posts were filled by students who had not been politically involved before July 1968.

Later, as the movement grew and endured, the situation began to change. The traditional activists and organizations realized that what they had thought to be a short-lived spontaneous student disturbance had begun to take the form of a rather significant political movement. They, therefore, started to strive for leadership and with the passage of time the more traditional and experienced student politicians and organizations succeeded in moving into positions of prominence and influence. Their accession to these offices was aided by the fact that many of the earlier leaders had been arrested or forced to flee the country. Other leadership positions were vacated because their incumbents had been undermined by government paid agents or had just wearied of the intense and constant political struggle.

Another important feature of the Mexican student movement, again during the first two to two and a half months in particular, was the unity of the participants. The movement was unique in that it encompassed a wide political spectrum from center to left. For the first time, the IPN and UNAM students set aside their rivalries and disagreements to work together politically. At the UNAM, students from all schools joined in the common effort. Although a disproportionate share of the leaders and activists came from the School of Philosophy and Letters, students from schools not previously noted for their political activity, such as the School of Engineering, were also at the forefront. An important factor underlying this unity was the fact that the moderates remained in the coalition and the leftist students who were involved chose to educate, lobby, and push from within rather than to force the moderates out. The aforementioned hesitancy of the established leftwing organizations to become involved also helped give initial unity to the movement. The demonstrated unity, cooperation, and camaraderie of the students during those turbulent months were truly impressive to anyone familiar with the fragmentation and political divisions that had characterized the Mexican students prior to July 1968.

The absence of *the* leader was another facet of the Mexican movement of 1968 that made it unique. Throughout the course of events, direction was in the hands of a collective leadership. The Mexican student movement did not produce its counterpart of Mark Rudd, Mario Savio, Daniel Cohn-Bendit, or Rudi Deutschke. This was yet another reason why the PRI government had so much difficulty in trying to reach a settlement.

The immediate cause of the movement was the use and the brutality of the granaderos. In the initial disturbance on July 23, virtually no one believed that that trivial incident had merited the dispatch or the excessive force of the granaderos. Then there was the repeated use of these riot police and their repeated brutality as well. At Berkeley, Columbia, and Harvard universities, the *violent* aspect of the student-police confrontation was for the most part either quick, removed from public view, or a single occurrence. In Mexico, the brutality of the police had none of these characteristics. The granaderos beat the students repeatedly and quite openly. Another aspect which caused considerable resentment was that students, particularly younger ones, were beaten while involved in a typical schoolboy fracas, while attending a peaceful demonstration, or while they were standing too near these occurrences. The fact that the granaderos' very existence was felt by many students and nonstudents alike to be a violation of the Mexican constitution increased the anger. Finally, the granaderos' and the army's invasion of preparatory schools associated with the IPN and the UNAM further exacerbated the situation. The government's hesitancy to continue the crackdown on the students after the period from July 26 to July 30 gave the students time to organize and build a movement.

The nature of the government's involvement as well as strong antipathy to the PRI helped shape the events which made this particular Mexican political student movement so unusual. In previous student strikes or demonstrations, the focus had been on concerns directly related to student life, such as examinations, course requirements, or bus fares. When these disturbances escalated and spilled off the UNAM campus, the police would act but the authorities never came onto campus. It was very much like a game between the students and the government with both sides adhering to the governing rules. On campus and with respect to campus-related matters, students had leeway to act in almost any manner they pleased without fear of intervention by the government. If the students violated the rules of the game by going off campus and being destructive, the authorities could punish them and push them back on to the campus. In July 1968 the students felt that the government had seriously violated this unwritten agreement and had dealt harshly with them without cause. As a result the focus of the student protest lie outside of the university as evidenced by the strikers' six demands, not one of which was related to a "university" issue. The demands did not pit students from the more radical schools against those from the more conservative ones as had been the case in earlier internal disorders, but instead helped to unite all of the students against an external enemy perceived as attacking students for no reason except that they were students.

The students were also quite aware that the repression they experienced could not have occurred without the knowledge if not the approval of the highest levels of the federal government. They also knew that the government was anxious about the Olympics and the huge expenditures made to prepare for the games. This was juxtaposed to the budgetary difficulties of the UNAM which had resulted in lowering the quality of education at that university. It should also be pointed out that prices all over Mexico City had been raised prior to the Olympics in anticipation of the tourist influx and that the tickets themselves were priced far beyond the reach of the average Mexican. These factors helped engender student hostility directly against the PRI government. It must also have seemed natural to them after the events of late July that a government which had made such a huge commitment of money and pride would be more than willing to protect its investment with the use of granaderos and troops against students.

Recall, too, the historical underlying hostility toward the government which although by itself did not give rise to a movement certainly paved the way for it. The students knew of the graft and the corruption that abounded in the PRI and were troubled by the fact that the PRI had made graft and corruption an intrinsic part of the way of life of the Mexican people. They were cognizant of the role of bribery and contacts in the competition for jobs. They had intimate knowledge of the low professorial salaries and the poor education they received in the public universities because of the government's limited fiscal support. Each inequity and relative neglect of basic worthwhile needs of so many sectors of the Mexican population, particularly those of the poor and the *campesinos* as well as the students, raised the students' level of hostility toward the government. Finally, the spectacle of a corrupt and authoritarian government constantly mouthing revolutionary phrases and slogans raised the ire of the students even higher.

One lesson to be drawn from the 1968 student uprising is that given an appropriate level of discontent, a crucial provocation can evoke a spontaneous reaction that may create in its wake an entire new set of political relationships. The Mexican student movement supported the contention of Camus and Debray that political consciousness can flow from intense political action. This is more likely to be true when the participants are political neophytes holding positions allowing a wide latitude of political behavior.

The Mexican student rebellion revealed the existence of a large disaffected element in Mexican society whose numbers included more than just students. Prior to July 1968, there had been extremely few ways in which this disaffection could manifest itself in the normal operation of society. The students and their movement represented an available channel through which to express hostility toward the government. Given the power of the PRI and its control over the meaningful secondary associations, hostility and frustrations against the government were unable to find an acceptable outlet. The students represented the one important sector of the society that the PRI had not been able to effectively co-opt or dominate. In 1968, however, students proved able to dispense with their petty squabbling, overcome their fears of government sanctions, and resist the government's attempts at manipulation and co-optation. They then began to function as a magnet and a voice for other dissidents. The government found, on its part, that it could not translate huge electoral majorities into actual and effective support during a crisis period. In France, during the 1968 student disorders there, progovernment supporters backed their government and held mass rallies. In Mexico the one progovernment rally that was held consisted of dragooned public office workers for the most part who had to be forcibly dispersed by the army when they began shouting prostudent and anti-PRI slogans. Reliance on the army in response to the growing antigovernment demonstrations numbering in the hundreds of thousands revealed to all of Mexico the considerable weakness of the PRI regime.

The students, however, did not win their struggle although several of their basic demands were eventually realized. In July 1970, two years after the beginning of the student movement, the Law Against Social Dissolution was repealed and Demetrio Vallejo and Valentín Campa, the aforementioned labor leaders, were released from prison. At the same time, however, a new penal code was drafted into law, carrying with it longer prison sentences than the law which it replaced and defining in greater detail the crimes of sedition, treason, sabotage, and "conspiracy against the nation." In another gesture an ammendment was passed lowering the voting age from twenty-one to eighteen for unmarried Mexicans. Married Mexicans from eighteen to twenty-one already had the franchise. There have been other changes and measures designed to assuage the students without basically changing the situation very much. The UNAM rector, Javier Barros Sierra, a man never very popular at the UNAM campus since his appointment under dubious circumstances in 1966, was replaced as rector. His successor was Pablo González Casanova, a prominent Marxist economist and professor of economics at the UNAM. During the 1968 student movement he accused the United States Central Intelligence Agency of instigating the disturbances.

In the 1968 confrontation with the students the PRI government won, although it did sustain some losses, which eventually may prove to be far from negligible. Prior to July 1968, Mexico had an international reputation for political stability. It was also hailed as a democracy whose governing party had a broad base of popular support. Internally, the PRI's claim to be the institutional embodiment of the Mexican Revolution generally went publicly unchallenged. These, particularly the latter, were the basic ideological underpinings of the PRI regime. The Mexican student movement called each of these claims into question. A secure and democratic government does not dispatch riot police to quell a schoolboy disturbance nor does it sanction the army's indiscriminate firing into a peaceful demonstration. Reliance upon riot police and soldiers in the capital city to repress the most talented and best educated youth in the country revealed that Mexico's much heralded stability and democracy were a fiction. Far from being unique, Mexico was shown to be very similar to most of the other countries in Latin America and in the developing world in that it too proved heavily reliant on its police and military for support. In 1968 the students together with other dissident elements came close to challenging the rule of the PRI, a feat hitherto regarded as extremely unlikely. Since 1968, opposition to the PRI has become a more realistic possibility; the PRI is no longer an omnipotent ruling party whose legitimacy is solidly based in revolutionary and democratic myths. In 1968 the Mexican government revealed itself in full public view as a government of ordinary men, desperately concerned with protecting their vested interests in a similar manner to any other corrupt Latin American regime. This may be one of the more important legacies of the 1968 student movement.

From the end of 1968 through the early months of 1970, student activism has continued but primarily on a covert and restricted level. Many of the leaders and activists are either dead, in jail, or in exile. Arrests of students, it should be pointed out, did not end in 1968 but continued through 1969. Government informants are believed to be placed throughout the schools and university community. Authorities have made it quite clear that the resumption of mass student activism will neither be tolerated nor permitted. At various times troops have been positioned throughout the capital in order to discourage student demonstrations.

The focal point of the sporadic political activity that has occurred since 1968 is the fate of those imprisoned as a result of their alleged involvement in the 1968 student disturbances. Although 121 of those arrested were released by presidential order shortly before Christmas 1968, an almost equal number have languished in jail for over two years without bail or trial. On December 10, 1969, about 87 of these political prisoners began a hunger strike to protest their illegal treatment and draw public attention to their plight. During their fast which lasted more than 40 days, prison guards provoked other prisoners to attack them. The Mexican public has learned little about the situation from the media, as a government ban has prevented the dissemination of news dealing with the prisoners.

The hunger strike and the condition of the fasters appeared to stir student unrest. Student leaders at the UNAM and the IPN called for a two day strike by the students to begin on January 15, 1970. Various intellectuals and priests, including the Bishop of Cuernavaca, were scheduled as speakers on behalf of the imprisoned students. In February students spread out through the city distributing pamphlets and making house to house visits in order to rally public support for the cause of the political prisoners. Shortly thereafter, activism again subsided. Although there was some effort to launch a furtive boycott campaign against the presidential elections scheduled for July 5, 1970, much of the overt and clandestine student political activity for the prisoners and against the regime was suspended several months prior to the elections. This was done as a calculated political tactic designed to favorably influence the PRI candidate and future president, Luis Echeverría Alvarez, to release the prisoners. It should be noted that Echeverría in his capacity as Minister of the Interior in 1968 was one of the men directly responsible for the treatment of the students during the 1968 student movement.

It was evident from government actions that the student activity on behalf of the political prisoners coupled with the public support that they managed to obtain have made some impact. In December 1969, President Gustavo Díaz

Ordaz, no friend of youth during his term of office, signed an amendment to the constitution granting voting rights to all Mexican citizens who were at least eighteen years old. Previously the minimum voting age had been twenty-one. This gesture was widely interpreted in Mexican political circles as a concession to the student demands for more participation in the nation's political life. Other conciliatory measures were taken after Echeverría's election, in which he received 86 percent of the vote. These measures reflected Echeverría's influence, for once a person is officially designated as the presidential candidate of the PRI he becomes the major determinant of important political decisions even prior to his election. In July 1970, Article 145, the law of "social dissolution" was repealed, fulfilling one of the students' principle demands. On July 29, 1970, labor leaders Demetrio Vallejo and Valentín Campa, imprisoned since 1958 under the provisions of Article 145 were released from prison, complying with another of the 1968 student movement's demands. Less than a month later on August 14, 45 persons arrested during the 1968 disturbances were freed from prison. After assuming office on December 1, 1970, President Echeverría contined to release imprisoned students, professors, and intellectuals and to allow those in exile to return. The *New York Times* predicted that before the end of 1971 all of those arrested because of their political activities during the 1968 student movement would be freed.

In addition to releasing the large proportion of student prisoners, Echeverría took other steps to bring about a reconciliation between himself and the students. He has periodically met with students throughout Mexico to listen to their problems and grievances. In June, he intervened in a dispute at Nuevo León University in Monterrey between the students and professors on the one hand and the university rector and the governor of the state on the other. The issues concerned the right of the students and the professors to appoint their own rector and the demand for an effective degree of autonomy. The governor, Eduardo Elizondo, imposed his own candidate upon the students and influenced the state legislature to pass a law ensuring government control over the university. The students resisted, clashes between students and police ensued, and many were arrested. Echeverría intervened in the dispute at that point securing the resignation of both the governor and his appointed rector. A new law was passed in the state legislature granting the students many of their basic demands.

Paradoxically, despite these conciliatory gestures, the intermittent release of student activists and the return of exiles from abroad led to the firing up of the student movement. These leaders and activists returned to the universities and promoted demonstrations and protests for the release of those still in prison as well as against various policies of the Echeverría administration. Less than a week after the President's successful intervention at Neuvo León University, leftist student leaders issued a call for a mass street demonstration through Mexico City, the first since the massacre at Tlatelolco in 1968, to be held on June 10. Ironically, a major purpose of the demonstration when originally planned was to have been the support of the Nuevo León students in their struggle.

Shortly after the demonstration had commenced, riot police ordered them to halt and disperse. The demonstrators refused, citing their constitutional rights. Then, suddenly, a number of grey buses and trucks appeared, coming through police barricades. Immediately, hundreds of well-armed youth jumped from them and began to beat and shoot the demonstrators. The shooting and beating went on for about five hours with the attackers pursuing the student demonstrators into stores, theatres, and even into ambulances and a Catholic hospital. All of this time the police made no move to interfere. By the time the affair ended more than 11 student demonstrators were dead and more than 200 wounded.

A wave of protest immediately began. The attackers were identified as the *Halcones* or Hawks, a band of paramilitary toughs who were associated with the police. In fact, according to the *New York Times*, the Hawks had been trained by the police in karate and the use of firearms and during the actual attack had used police and city vehicles and radio equipment. The police chief as well as the Mayor of Mexico City, Alfonso Martinez Dominguez, a powerful figure within the PRI, were accused of involvement in the attack. They denied it, but on the following day resigned, apparently under pressure from Echeverría, and an official probe of the entire affair as well as the city government was announced shortly thereafter.

It quickly became evident that the entire episode had been planned by individuals and groups in important positions within the PRI and the government. The President himself told a group of foreign correspondents that "mercenaries connected with 'inferior' elements in the government were responsible for the attack on the students." The whole affair was seen as part of a right-wing group within PRI and allied with important businessmen to embarrass and discredit Echeverría. This conservative or right-wing element disliked his attempts to conciliate the students and enter into a dialogue with them. They were also displeased with his advocacy of university autonomy and his tolerance of what seemed to them growing student dissent throughout the country. Furthermore, the conservatives in and out of the government were disturbed by his encouragement of greater press freedom and by his public attacks on corruption in government and state controlled industries. The president also aroused their anger by his charge that Mexican capitalists did not have the interest of their country at heart as well as by his plans to introduce liberal economic and social legislation. The attack by the Falcons was seen within this context as being a dramatic attempt by the right to signal the president that he must halt his overture to the left. At this date it is not clear what the outcome of this struggle will be even though the official probe of the Mexican attorney general found no proof of any official involvement in the June 10 disaster. The president, however, has continued his dialogue with student dissidents and other sectors such as peasants and has encouraged them to reveal their grievances and instances of corruption by government officials.

Numerous observers, including James Goodsell, the foreign affairs editor of the *Christian Science Monitor*, have attributed Echeverría's move to the left to his long and vigorous election campaign. They assert that he was obviously quite moved and impressed by the poverty, squalor, and neglect that he personally came into contact with for the first time. After witnessing such conditions he became determined to institute reforms to ameliorate the conditions. He also expressed the feeling in private meetings with selected journalists that the charges that the students were the forgotten men of Mexican politics had some degree of validity.

However, puting aside President Echeverría's personal and political conversion, the events since 1968 indicate that the Mexican students have moved on to the center of the national political stage. Prior to 1968, they were political nuisances but nuisances who did not present much cause for concern by PRI and government officials. The government by its repressive measures in 1968 changed the student situation dramatically. It inspired unity and cooperation among the students that few students or nonstudents had previously thought impossible. Despite some friction and bitterness, particularly pertaining to the Communists for their nonparticipatory role in the 1968 upheaval during its most dangerous moments, the student political scene did not revert back to the status quo prior to 1968. The student movement of 1968 in itself and particularly the political prisoners associated with it have served to unify the students and also provided them with the impetus to sustain an ongoing movement. In an unprecedented fashion, students at UNAM and IPN have formed ties with their compatriots in provincial universities and have established links with adolescents still in high school in order to defend and promote common interests which are still in the process of being articulated.

Reactionary elements in and out of the government and PRI, as well as President Echeverría, appear to have become cognizant of the actual and potential strength of a unified and a politicized body of students numbering in the hundreds of thousands. These rightist forces, in addition, are fearful that either Echeverría through his policies and activities will gain their political support or worse that the students will fall under the leadership of the radicals. These rightists, in addition to attempting to block the movement toward a reconciliation between the president and the students, have attempted to sew seeds of discord among them by actively agitating and supporting reactionary elements within student bodies throughout the country. As a result there have been numerous incidents of bitter fighting between rightist and leftist students, a large proportion of which took place after Echeverría had won the election. It should be noted that there have always been conflicts between leftist and rightist students on various campuses, particularly at UNAM. But at the present time under the very active tutelage and sponsorship of the rightist forces outside of the universities, these conflicts have been escalated in number and intensity.

Nonetheless, despite the efforts to activate rightist students, Mexican students, on the whole, are more unified now (1971) than at any time in the recent past. Their influence appears to extend beyond those in universities and secondary schools to other segments of youth, including persons who have never enrolled in secondary or postsecondary educational institutions as well as recent high school and university graduates. The influence of politicized and politically disaffected youth is an object of concern to the various ideological sectors of the PRI and government, particularly the moderates and the rightists, as well as to big business interests. Already there are students who were active in 1968 who occupy government positions. Knowledgeable Mexicans have commented upon the existence of youth cliques within government bureaucracies and business organizations, who, increasingly dissatisfied with the status quo, are organizing to push for meaningful political, economic, and social changes. The constant addition to their ranks of politically embittered and alienated graduates will make these youthful groups more potent. In addition, there have been a small but apparently increasing number of students who have organized or joined guerrilla bands. The 1970 census revelation that 55 percent of Mexico's population was under twenty years of age indicates that students and other youthful dissidents will have a large pool from which to draw recruits.

The students and youth are not the only sectors of society with grievances. Mexico's poor, particularly the peasants among them, represent a large proportion of the population whose interests and needs have long been neglected. It was the fear of the students acting as a catalyst for other aggrieved sectors of the Mexican populace that in large measure prompted the government repression of the 1968 movement. If a unified and politicized student force can make common cause with these elements, the nature of Mexican politics would be drastically altered. For now and for the foreseeable future, the students, who only a few short years earlier had seemingly been concerned primarily with campus matters and bus fares, are and will be a national political force to be reckoned with.

PUERTO RICAN STUDENT POLITICS

Throughout the late 1960s, student politics in Puerto Rico has been in a state of flux.[61] However, this instability followed a period from 1948 to 1964 in which there was virtually no student political activity among Puerto Rican university students. In 1948, after a student strike over the barring of Nationalist leader Albizu Campos, the chancellor of the University of Puerto Rico took stern measures that had repercussions for almost two decades. Many of the politically active students were expelled or suspended. Others lost credits for a year of college. University-wide student government was dissolved and the student newspaper was shut down. All partisan political activities were banned from the campus and outside political speakers were denied admission to the campus. Student organizations and meetings were allowed on university grounds only if they did not engage in partisan propaganda and demonstrated, from the administration's point of view, a sincere attitude toward good politics. In addition, class attendance was made obligatory.

During the ensuing years, there was very little political activity among Puerto Rican students. Chancellor Jaime Benitez's guiding philosophy of a university as a "house of studies" became the main orientation of the University of Puerto Rico. The years from 1948 to 1964 were also those in which Muñoz Marín and the Popular Democratic party consolidated their power and in which the electoral fortunes of independence forces declined to their nadir. It was also a time of rapid economic progress and relative prosperity. All of these factors made Puerto Rico barren soil for left- and right-wing politics as well as for student politics. The growth in the enrollments at the UPR, especially in the fields of business and education, brought into the university increasing numbers of first generation college students for whom jobs and status became principal concerns. For these students, politics was either a nuisance or a possible impediment to the achievement of their materialistic goals. Thus, by the mid-1960s social scientists and other observers of Puerto Rican students viewed them as archetypical examples of apolitical, status-striving students. The data in our survey present a cross-sectional picture of these students at that time.

The University of Puerto Rico was, however, not totally devoid of student politics during this period. In 1956 the University Federation for Independence (FUPI) was organized. FUPI was a militant advocate of independence and greater student political rights. However, until 1964 it made little impression upon the campus community. Few joined, as FUPI's ideological arrogance, loud commitment to Castro and other world revolutionaries, and accusations of harassment by school and government officials either repelled or frightened the students, even those sympathetic to independence. By 1965, when FUPI leaders were interviewed by Liebman, the organization had a membership of about 300, of whom approximately 60 to 100 were active members, in a total student body of over 18,000. FUPI's major base of support was located in the Schools of Social Science and Humanities. FUPI, despite its small numbers, has been able to make a significant impact on the UPR community. Its leaders during its early years were drawn from families whose members had been quite active in various independence movements and organizations. Thus this FUPI elite was no stranger to oppositional politics and in addition had the support of their families for their political activities. Also, even their foes in the student body and administration acknowledged that the members of FUPI were among the brightest students on the UPR campus. And, FUPI activists worked long and hard both on and off campus. All of these factors plus the fear that eventually FUPI would politicize large numbers of students caused the UPR administrators to worry about FUPI and its activities.

FUPI's very existence spurred into being the University Federation of Anti-Communists (FAU) during the 1963–1964 academic year. This small group provided the major opposition to FUPI and existed almost solely for that purpose. In later years it merged and became the driving force behind the University Association for Statehood (AUPE). Both FAU and AUPE are committed to statehood, as the best solution to the status issue and as the most effective way of preventing a Communist takeover of Puerto Rico. The members of these organizations also feel that the University of Puerto Rico administration and faculty contain too many who are "soft" on communism. They cite as evidence for their contention that the university has failed to deal harshly with FUPI. Both FAU and AUPE draw their largest support from students at the School of Business. A great deal of their members' time has been spent in rallies denouncing FUPI and the UPR administration, and there have been frequent physical confrontations with FUPI members, increasingly in the late 1960s. However, despite these organizations and their rivalries, there was still very little political activity at the UPR into the mid-1960s.

Nonetheless, there were forces at work in the UPR during the latter 1950s and early 1960s which rose to the surface by the mid-1960s and helped to politicize an increasing number of students. In the 1950s various advisory and study groups as well as the Middle States Association of Colleges, the accreditation agency of the UPR, issued reports highly critical of the UPR, particularly its organizational structure. In essence, they found that far too much power was concentrated in the hands of Chancellor Benitez and as a result there was poor planning, lack of coordination, wastage of funds, and in general ineffective administration of the university. Also, the fact that both the students and the faculty lacked their own organizations as well as an effective voice in decisions affecting them and the university was also alluded to in these reports as a shortcoming of the UPR.

In part as a response to these official and semiofficial criticisms and in part due to the anticipation of a significant and independent movement for university reform emerging, particularly among the students, the UPR administration decided that it should guide the development of university reform. In 1962 it selected a group of students whom the administration considered highly responsible for the purpose of drafting reform proposals. Unexpectedly, this "safe" group drew up a set of demands and reforms which the administration defined as too radical and too far-reaching. The proposals were turned down and the group dismissed by the UPR authorities. However, instead of calmly returning to their studies and previous pursuits, these students, disturbed and politicized by their experience and treatment, became increasingly active on their own in the cause of university reform.

Developments came to a head in the Fall of 1964, marking a significant turning point in student politics at the UPR. As the administration had predicted and unexpectedly promoted, a movement for university reform had emerged and by 1964 it had attracted a relatively small but growing number of students and faculty. They demanded an academic upgrading of the UPR, competitive hiring of professors on the basis of ability, increased rights for students, and the reduction of the nearly absolute power of Chancellor Jaime Benitez. Although the reform group was comparatively small and its demands moderate, indeed many closely resembled recommendations urged by the aforementioned study and advisory bodies, both the group and its demands struck sympathetic chords within the UPR community and began to attract growing numbers of sympathizers and supporters. Through its use of the sit-in, the reform group further politicized the atmosphere at the UPR campus. However, its very existence represented another addition in the growing politicization of the, for the most part still quite apathetic, student body.

The activities of the reform organization were not the only factors raising the political consciousness of the UPR students in the Fall of 1964. The gubernatorial campaign was in full swing and more important than in previous years because for the first time since 1940, Luis Muñoz Marin no longer headed the PPD ticket. FUPI was conducting a vigorous campaign for an electoral boycott, arguing that the election was a farce and could not represent the real will of the Puerto Rican people.

FUPI was also interested in university reform, although this was not very high on its list of organizational priorities. Unlike the reform group, FUPI leaders considered university reform as a means to an end, a decidedly political end, rather than an objective in itself. In their view, the UPR was a highly strategic institution, one on which important societal sectors and other institutions depended for social, economic, and technological guidance and assistance. FUPI militants saw university reform as a device through which their organization might radicalize the university and then utilize it as a lever with which to change the entire society. Nonetheless, despite this analysis, FUPI did little to aid the cause of reform other than give its formal endorsement. FUPI did not work closely with the reform group nor for that matter with any other student organization. Its definition of itself as a vanguard organization with an almost sacred mission inhibited alliances or close cooperation with other student groups, regardless of how sympathetic they might be to FUPI's causes.

On October 27, 1964, a series of events commenced that changed FUPI's working relationship with the university reform group as well as its campus image. On that day, two FUPI hecklers at an FAU rally were injured by FAU supporters. In protest, FUPI scheduled a rally of its own for the following day. Shortly before it began, in violation of university regulations, FUPI members marched through the campus urging all to attend. The administration ordered the FUPI marchers off its grounds and summoned the police. The FUPI students refused and proceeded to sit down, soon attracting the attention of hundreds of curious students who gathered nearby to watch the FUPI-police confrontation. After several hours, the police appeared to lose their patience and charged into the students, injuring a few. Some observers claimed that the non-FUPI students on the scene received the brunt of the police attack. The students dispersed throughout the campus and fighting between police and students continued into the night. Eventually calm was restored, ironically with the assistance of Juan Maris Bras, secretary general of the militant Pro-Independence Movement, who as a student leader had been expelled from the UPR for his part in the 1948 disorders.

The events of October 28 galvanized the university community. FUPI, for once, had a sympathetic image as an underdog. The proponents of university reform made common cause with FUPI in protesting both the decision to call the police onto the campus and police brutality. Other previously uninvolved students and faculty were also angry over the presence and conduct of the police on the university campus. A protest march from the UPR grounds to the Capital Building and the governor's mansion was organized and held on October 29. About 5,000 students and faculty drawn from virtually all of the UPR schools took part including FUPI and non-FUPI students, supporters of reform, and opponents of Benitez. This was the largest political demonstration emanating from the UPR in the post-World War II era.

These events did not have the immediate effect of transforming the UPR into a caldron of politics. In March 1965 a student referendum was held on the subject of student political activity. At that time the UPR students were asked to vote on two alternatives pertaining to student political conduct:

(A) The freedom of expression, association, and assembly that are in the Constitution are guaranteed to students on the campus.

(B) The freedom of expression, association, and assembly that are in the Constitution are guaranteed to students on the campus but political activities should be regulated. Demonstrations, pickets, and public meetings on the campus that disturb scholarly activities or are contrary to the norms of the institution are prohibited.

Alternative B won by better than two to one (2,963 to 1,375). This meant that more than two out of three students voting were in favor of placing restrictions on their own political activities. The fact that 76 percent of the eligible students chose not to vote in this 1965 referendum was also indicative of the Puerto Rican students' continued indifference toward student politics. In the 1967 student elections, only in one school, Business, was the turnout more than half and in most other schools between 10 and 20 percent either voted or participated in the nominating procedures.

However, despite the apparent lack of change in the political attitudes of the student body at large as indicated by the March 1965 referendum and the 1967 student election, significant changes continued to take place, having an immediate political impact first upon a growing student minority, and then in a relatively short period of time, upon the large majority of students. On January 20, 1966, Governor Roberto Sánchez Villela signed into law a legislative bill reorganizing and reforming the University of Puerto Rico. Under its provisions the UPR was divided into three autonomous units, Rio Piedras, Mayaguez, and San Juan, with each having its own chancellor and the entire university administered by a president with limited powers. It provided for academic senates and called for elected campus wide student councils in each of the three units. The law also liberalized the rules and procedures pertaining to student political activity on university grounds.

After the law was enacted, in 1966 Jaime Benitez was chosen to be the first president of the UPR and Abrahán Díaz González was appointed to the chancellorship of the Rio Piedras campus. Chancellor Díaz greatly differed from his predecessor in his attitude toward student rights and politics. He encouraged students to participate in university affairs at meaningful levels. He initiated student representation or participation in various university deliberative bodies including the Academic Senate. Although strongly opposed by President Benitez, Chancellor Díaz permitted peaceful picketing by students on the campus. In general, it was his contention that there should be no absolute prohibitions on student political expression within the university and that the ensuring of liberty on campus merited the taking of risks, particularly increased student political agitation, a major concern of President Benitez.

After the passage of reform legislation and the liberalization of the campus at Rio Piedras by Chancellor Díaz, the number of political incidents and demonstrations increased. Invariably, they involved clashes between FUPI and AUPE members. One such clash reached major proportions on September 27, 1967, and led once again to the presence of police on campus. In this disturbance, a taxi driver watching from university grounds was shot and killed and two students were wounded.

Since 1967 and especially after the election of statehood advocate, Luis A. Ferré, as governor in 1968, political activity among growing minorities of students has increased both in number and intensity. Other significant student political groups in addition to FUPI emerged on campus. During 1968–1969 *Acción Progresista* (AP) was organized at Rio Piedras and in effect became the successor organization to AUPE. AP like AUPE is rightist , in favor of statehood, against the abolition of the ROTC on campus, and militantly opposed to the politics and activities of the independentistas, particularly FUPI. The AP is alleged to be closely associated with the right wing of Governor Ferré's New Progressive Party (PNP). The AP has generally been a strong supporter of President Benitez in his disputes with FUPI and other independentistas.

About the same time that AP came into being, the Juventud Independentista Universitario (JUI) was organized at the UPR. The JUI is the youth wing of the Puerto Rican Independence Party (PIP). Following the lead of its rejuvenated and now activist parent organization, JUI has taken an activist stance, one informed by a leftist and pacifist political orientation. Like FUPI, JUI is ardently proindependence, but unlike FUPI JUI has adopted a more flexible and pragmatic position and has therefore been able to attract considerable numbers of proindependence sympathizers and even former supporters of the Popular Democratic Party (PPD) to its ranks, who had previously been alienated and kept at arm's length by FUPI. In addition, JUI has strengthened its support among the students by taking an active interest in university and student matters and in general becoming the campus's most forceful and innovative advocate of student rights and interests. This occurred as FUPI was purposefully trying to transform itself into an organization oriented toward working-class students in particular and the working class in general.

Another student political organization that emerged about the same time as AP and JUI was the *Liga Socialista*. The Liga Socialista has never been able to attract many members or supporters. It is an avowed Maoist group, very militant and extremely action oriented. The Liga's very existence however has helped to heighten political tensions on campus.

The focal point for much of the political activity among the students from the latter 1960s through 1971 has been the FUPI led campaign for the abolition of ROTC from the UPR. In October 1969 the intensity and support for this effort was increased by the sentencing for draft evasion of a UPR student, who took the position that the drafting of Puerto Ricans was unjust and immoral and an example of the colonial status of Puerto Ricans. After the sentencing, FUPI led an attack against the ROTC buildings on the UPR campus, setting the main ROTC structure afire. Chancellor Díaz refused to call the police onto the university grounds fearing a possible massacre and the unification of the student body into a massive oppositional force. After a quiet weekend he suspended 7 students, including the President of FUPI, for 90 days for inciting the disturbance. The independence and leftist dominated student councils of the Schools of Social Science and Humanities sided with the activists and condemned both the draft and the ROTC program. And 3000 students marched in support of the convicted student draft evader. Shortly thereafter the Academic Senate voted to phase out the ROTC program on the Rio Piedras campus.

The right, in response to the actions of the left and the Academic Senate's decision, organized its own demonstration. The demonstrators appeared to be ROTC cadets, members of *Acción Progresista*, partisans of the right wing of the PNP, and allegedly thugs and ruffians recruited by the latter group. This procession marched through the Rio Piedras section and toward the UPR campus where Chancellor Díaz and concerned faculty members were able to dissuade them from coming onto the campus and to keep leftist students from leaving the university grounds in order to confront the rightists. The rightist procession them marched five blocks to the headquarters of the Proindependence Movement where about 200 tried to charge the building while others threw Molotov cocktails and rocks. The police, although present in force, refused to intervene. One policeman claimed to a shocked Protestant minister that he and his associates had received orders not to interfere with the mob attacking the MPI. Shortly after the fury of the mob had decreased, proindependence students emerged from the burnt building to demand police protection. They were then beaten and dispersed by the police while members of the demonstration threw more rocks and Molotov cocktails at them. The entire scenario had an aura of official inspiration similar to that of the June 10, 1971, "riot" in Mexico City.

In the wake of the anti-ROTC demonstration, the demand for the dismissal of Chancellor Díaz mounted. Governor Ferré and prominent members of his New Progressive Party accused him of being too lenient with FUPI and other militant independentistas. He was also charged with being too openly proindependence for Puerto Rico and with surrounding himself with high level administrators with the same political tendency. A bitter campaign was launched against him in the press with one paper asserting that he was "turning the school [UPR] into a haven for Castro Communists." On December 22, 1969, after a bitter six-hour meeting, the Council of Higher Education voted five to two for his dismissal. Four of the five voting against Chancellor Díaz were recent appointees of Governor Ferré. After he was fired, several faculty and members of the UPR administration resigned in protest, a rare deed in the annals of Puerto Rican higher education given the paucity of equivalent and alternative employment outside the UPR system. This action against a popular chancellor embittered the students as well as demonstrating to them the intimate interplay between on and off campus politics.

Shortly after the sacking of Díaz, Governor Ferré attempted to placate his student opposition. In his State of the Commonwealth address in January 1970, he called for lowering the voting age to eighteen. In addition, the governor also urged that students through legislation be given the right to participate in the governance of the university. These gestures, however, seemed to have little impact upon the UPR students, particularly the various independentista groups.

Three months after Ferré's speech, the anti-ROTC campaign which had continued unabated reached new heights on March 4, 1970. On that day several hundred coeds, members and supporters of FUPI, marched to the campus ROTC buildings where they became embroiled in fights with ROTC cadets. Soon a full scale riot broke out involving more than 3,000 students and the special riot police the, *Fuerza de Choque*, were called onto campus. In the ensuing melee, Molotov cocktails were thrown and shots were fired resulting in the death of a nineteen-year-old female student, Antonia Martinez, as she stood on a balcony watching the disturbance. Three other persons were wounded by bullets. One reporter on the scene claimed that the Fuerza de Choque, Puerto Rico's version of the granaderos, fired directly into the students virtually without provocation.

An angered and aroused UPR student council called for a mass meeting to discuss the possibility of a general strike, the ouster of President Benitez, and the dropping of ROTC from the university's curriculum. Out of these discussions, the idea for a university-wide student referendum emerged and quickly came to fruition on March 21, 1970. The results as well as the size of the turnout attested to the increased politicization and radicalization of the students since the earlier referendum in 1965. Eighty percent of the students voted, a record for any student election or referendum. Furthermore, to the dismay of government officials and editorial writers, slightly more than half voted for the abolition of the ROTC. On a second issue, 71 percent supported demands for an "effective" student role in campus affairs. In a third item dealing with the fate of President Benitez, 51 percent of the students voted against his dismissal.

One might argue that the referendum results and turnout were in large part a function of the crisis situation prevailing on the campus at that particular time and thus not valid indicators of the political attitudes of the UPR students during more normal periods. This does not appear to be the case. Various university professors and administrators have testified to the rise in the numbers of proindependence students during the latter 1960s and into the early 1970s. In addition, a survey of the 1969–1970 University Student Council whose membership reflects the political weight of the various parties, organizations, and ideologies throughout the entire campus at Rio Piedras clearly indicates the degree of radicalization as well as politicization that had taken place at the UPR since 1964. Ninety-five out of 130 members of the Student Council responded to questions dealing with their politics. There is no indication that those not answering were in any way different from those who did respond. Of those who had an affiliation with an island political party, 68 percent chose a left party, the bulk selecting PIP. Only 3 of the 95 claimed an affiliation with Ferre's PNP, the party furthest right on the political spectrum. A similar question was also asked dealing with student political parties, but 56 out of the 95 or 59 percent responded either with "no answer" or "no political affiliation." Of the 39 who did answer, 34 or 89 percent claimed an affiliation with JUI (22) or FUPI (12). Only one council member identified with a right student party. Another item tapped their attitude toward protests. Here, all but 3 of the 95 respondents asserted that they approved of illegal protests on behalf of justified causes. Almost two-thirds were willing to approve of civil disobedience or under exceptional circumstances violence on behalf of such causes. Thus, these survey findings plus the referendum results as well as the growth of independentistas on the campus strongly indicate that substantial political changes, generally in a leftist direction, have taken place among the UPR students from 1964 to 1970.

Since 1970 the politicization and bitterness of the students has appeared to increase. After the March 1970 shootings, increasing numbers of students have begun to carry firearms on to the campus. Many faculty members, particularly the liberal or left ones, who used to help mediate disputes and in general served as a cohesive force under Chancellor Díaz have refused to play the same role under his successor, Pedro José Rivera. The new chancellor, for his part appeared to have adopted the position that campus political problems were in large measure due to the activities of a small core of troublemakers within both the student body and the faculty. Consequently, he chose to pursue a much harder policy toward dissent than Díaz. The atmosphere engendered by these factors further heightened the political tensions at the UPR.

At the same time, FUPI and JUI have continued their campaign against the draft and ROTC, which despite the adverse referendum vote and the decision of the Academic Senate still remained part of the UPR curriculum, because it had the support of the Council of Higher Education. The Acción Progresista together with the ROTC cadets, for their part, have intensified their own efforts primarily in defense of the ROTC program. Given the nature of the campus environment and the bitter rivalry between the leftist and rightist student groups, the student body in addition to becoming more politicized became increasingly polarized as well. Fist fights and heated arguments became a more frequent occurrence on campus.

An additional element further contributing to the growing political tension and divisiveness on the campus was the increasing numbers of Puerto Rican style "hippies" or as they are called at the UPR, "the Peyton Place people." They were predominantly freshmen students from the School of General Studies. The Peyton Place people claimed to be anarchists and independentistas but in reality did not appear to be very political. They abhored theoretical discussions or involvement in organizations. Instead, they were advocates of action seemingly almost for its own sake. The Peyton Place people were, of course, very hostile to the rightist students and the ROTC cadets.

Tensions and divisions on campus appeared to reach their height in early March 1971. The immediate flash point was the commemorative rally held on behalf of Antonia Martinez, the student slain a year earlier. The rally was sponsored by the Student Council, FUPI, JUI, and other liberal and left organizations. Unexpectedly, the rally went on virtually without incident and it appeared that with each passing day the tensions were subsiding. This, however, proved not to be the case.

On March 11, 1970, the heightened bitterness and polarization of the students became manifest. It started with an argumem in the student cafeteria between some fraternity members, who generally had managed to stay out of the political fray, and ROTC cadets over the respective merits of Muhammed Ali and Joe Frazier. As the argument became more heated with fist fights developing, the fraternity students sought support from nearby FUPI members and then the Peyton Place people. At that point the manager of the cafeteria ordered everyone to leave the building, placing a considerable number of people in the middle of the fights. The chaos and confusion was further escalated by the increased participation of the Peyton Place people in the dispute, primarily in the form of rock throwing. The situation appeared to be getting out of hand and the chancellor then decided to summon the riot police. When they arrived at the scene, shots were fired resulting in the death of two riot police and one ROTC cadet and the wounding of numerous others, both students and police. This proved to be the most violent disturbance that had ever taken place on the UPR campus.

In the aftermath of the riot and killings, the UPR administration apparently decided to pursue a strict policy with dissidents and potential dissidents among the faculty and students, the targets in many cases being the active independentistas, such as the pacifist president of the Puerto Rican Independence Party, Ruben Berríos Martinez, a professor at the School of Law. At the same time Governor Ferré's Secretary of Instruction, Ramon Mellado, publicly attacked segments of the UPR faculty, primarily independentistas for abusing and attacking academic freedom within the university. In accord with these policies and attacks, students have been expelled and suspended and many faculty members have either been notified of their dismissal or given a warning about any future activities. By any measure the situation seems less than promising for the immediate future of the University of Puerto Rico.

Let us now drawback from this narrative of campus events and try to explain the reasons for the rapid growth of militancy within a student body long noted for its apathy. The sources of this change in political attitude and behavior are to be found both on and off the campus. It should be pointed out, however, that although it is analytically possible to differentiate between on and off campus sources of student militancy in actual practice it is difficult. This is due to the nature of the University of Puerto Rico and the close interaction between university and non-university events and politics.

The UPR is tied into the politics of the island in a variety of ways. The most explicit one is through the Council of Higher Education, the Puerto Rican equivalent to the Board of Regents of a public university in the United States. It is composed of persons who are selected and influenced by the Governor. The island's legislature is also another way in which politics intrudes onto the university community from an outside source. The legislature is the final determinant of the university's budget and it is also responsible for the legislation under which the UPR operates. Therefore, if any sector of the university desires a reform of substance, this of necessity involves the legislature and lobbying activities.

It should also be recalled that the University of Puerto Rico at Rio Piedras is the major university on the island. It provides the personnel for important political, governmental, and business positions through both its graduates and staff. The intellectual leadership of the island is centered there as well. It is continually in the public limelight because what goes on there is of great interest to politicians, government leaders, students in other colleges on the island, high school students, and the mass media. The UPR students, particularly the activists, are well aware of their center stage position and this figures prominently in their plans and tactics even in matters that appear to be purely university-related.

One of the initial impetuses to the politicization of the UPR students was the aforementioned university reform legislation of 1965 and the events surrounding it. The reform, passed in part due to student political pressure, afforded the students more political expression within the university than they had had since 1948. At the same time it provided the students with legitimate political structures such as a university wide student council through which they were encouraged to become politically involved. In addition, as previously noted, the university reform had the immediate and practical affect of removing Chancellor Jaime Benitez, no friend or supporter of student political activity, from direct supervision and administration of the Rio Piedras campus. The new chancellor, Abraham Díaz González, differed from Benitez and encouraged as well as allowed increased student political activity in a variety of different areas and spheres previously closed to students. Chancellor Díaz's statements, policies, and actions, in contrast to those of his predecessor's, legitimized student political activity, removing an official onus or stigma from those who chose to participate and replacing it with a virtual seal of approval. He did not, however, eliminate all restrictions nor call for complete student cogovernment on equal terms with faculty and administration. In a sense, it was both what he and the new law did as well as did not do or state that encouraged the rise of politics and militancy among the students.

Partial liberalization of the rules regulating political conduct, especially when viewed by the students as a response to student political pressure, served as an incentive for the activists and to some extent the general student body to expand their political activities even further. First, the reform measure demonstrated that the university authorities and the legislature would make concessions in the face of student demands and as such it established a new and important precedent at the UPR. Second, for those students who had been politically inactive or relatively inactive, the new rules as well as the actions of the new chancellor legitimated if not formally sanctioned increased activism on their part. Third, whereas the new rules and procedures established new outerlimits for the nonactivists, for the activists they meant a new center base from which they could push even further. Fourth, once the reforms were enacted the authorities' ideological position was weakened vis-à-vis the activists. It is easier to legitimize a total ban on student political activity than it is to justify a partial ban. Once certain restrictions are lifted and specific political activity permitted, the moral grounds for the continued prohibition of political efforts in other areas becomes shaky when they come under attack by the activists.

Also, again particularly at Rio Piedras, the campus can not be insulated from the major political issues and struggles of the island. And with the legitimation of political activity of the students, albeit restricted, it was highly improbable that the basic political issue of Puerto Rico — the status issue — could have been kept outside of the area of their concerns. Conversely, the lifting of much of the previously imposed political restrictions encouraged off campus political forces to become more interested in the students.

The period of the reform and the chancellorship of Abraham Díaz González can not be isolated from the significant political changes taking place off campus during the same years, 1965 through 1969. The UPR students have always responded to the same forces affecting the entire Puerto Rican populace. However, due to the lack of permanent depoliticizing commitments such as family and occupation as well as to their heightened political sensitivities stemming from their status as students, especially after the reform, the UPR collegians tended to respond more quickly and in a more exaggerated manner to these forces than did other segments of the island's population. In addition, each of the major political changes or factors had a unique dimension which affected the students directly.

The most significant off campus political events which furthered the politicization of the UPR students as well as sectors of the society were the split and decline of the Popular Democratic Party (PPD) and the election in 1968 of an ardent advocate of statehood as governor, Luis A. Ferré which followed in its wake. The PPD had been the governing party for almost thirty years and for almost all of that period Luis Muñoz Marin had been the governor and the effective political leader of his party and the country. In 1964 Muñoz Marin decided not to run for re-election and designated Roberto Sánchez Vilella as his successor. Sánchez Vilella won, but almost immediately the various problems and factions that Muñoz Marin had coped with fairly effectively began to rise to the surface and grow worse during the Sánchez Vilella administration. In 1968 the splits within the PPD came to the surface and Sánchez Vilella denying his party's nomination ran as an independent, ensuring the victory of Luis A. Ferré.

The election of 1968 not only formalized the weakness of the PPD but also signalled the re-emergence of the status issue as a vibrant factor in Puerto Rican political life. Without the near charismatic figure of Muñoz Marin at the head of a strong and unified PPD, the conflict over status which he and the PPD had managed to contain for almost three decades burst back into the political arena. The victory of Ferré and his statehood oriented New Progressive Party exacerbated the situation and accelerated the divisiveness as they made little effort to disguise their ultimate goal.

Since 1968 there has been a rapid polarization of Puerto Rican politics. The Commonwealth solution, the long term position of the PPD, has begun to lose its political viability. Increasingly the choice that Puerto Ricans are confronted with is between the diametrically opposed ones of statehood or independence. Even Muñoz Marin, who for so long has been a moderating force on this issue, has become so aroused by the tactics and position of the Ferré administration that he has publicly called upon the Puerto Rican people to "defend their cultural heritage" from the attack of Ferré and his supporters.

The ideological lines have hardened and grown sharper both on the left and the right. Various elements in the PNP to the right of Governor Ferré, similar to the situation in Mexico with President Luis Echeverría, have attempted to pursue their own policies at the expense of their party and government leader. Often these elements, again in both Mexico and Puerto Rico, have recruited and agitated among sympathetic students and youth furthering and hardening the polarities already in existence within these strata. At the same time, clandestine terrorist organizations, primarily leftist and proindependence in orientation, have appeared. During the period from 1969 to 1971 there have been over 150 acts of sabotage committed against American owned stores, businesses, and tourist hotels. All of these events and the manifestation of bitter ideological divisions have had a significant impression upon the students' political ideas, concerns, and involvements especially since they have occurred almost simultaneously with a period of heightened political consciousness with respect to university related matters.

The election of Luis A. Ferré and the triumph of his New Progressive Party directly contributed to the polarization and the heightening of political tensions on the campus. During the administrations of Muñoz Marin and Sánchez Villela, student militants while not exempt from criticism were generally dealt with rather gently. However, under Ferré and the PNP, militants as well as activist independentistas have been subject to a barrage of strong and constant criticism from the governor, the Secretary of Instruction, and other high government and party officials. Ferré and his appointees in the government and in the Council of Higher Education have influenced the direction of university policy with respect to politics and the dismissal and selection of professors and administrators, most notably the aforementioned firing of Chancellor Díaz. The tactics, policies, and statements of Ferré and his officials have made the students more aware of their own political feelings as well as more cognizant of the lack of boundaries between the university and the political community.

The Vietnam War and the draft have increased the level of student militancy in Puerto Rico in a manner similar to that in the United States. However, in addition to the more universal issues of the morality, legality, and purposes of the war, there is a unique Puerto Rican dimension upon which the various independentista spokesmen have skillfully focused. The Vietnamese war has been constantly portrayed as a "foreign" war having no significance for Puerto Ricans. Also, the war and the draft cast the second class citizenship status of the Puerto Ricans into sharp relief. As citizens they are obligated to fight and perhaps die for the United States but unlike other citizens they are denied the basic mechanisms of affecting or at least seeming to affect policy and legislation on the war or draft because Puerto Ricans cannot vote for members of the United States Congress or for president. Because of their youth and potential availability for the draft as sensitivity to the war, this entire issue has made a significant and direct impact upon the UPR students.

The close identification of the student independentista groups such as FUPI and JUI with the antidraft campaign has redounded to their benefit. Students previously politically uninvolved or unsympathetic to these groups have been forced to adopt a more positive position toward FUPI and JUI if they are at all negative toward the war or especially if they are concerned about the draft. This positive disposition to the activist independentistas could not help but increase when it became evident that their antidraft campaign had born fruit. The federal government in the face of resistance to the draft in Puerto Rico apparently has decided to ignore rather than prosecute draft resisters and evaders. Also, even President Benitez has lent his support to the independentista efforts by publicly urging the government to grant conscientious objector status to Puerto Rican youth who favor total independence of Puerto Rico.

In 1970 and 1971 an important adjunct of the campaign against the United States' military in its relation to the Puerto Rican people crystallized around the issue of the United States Navy's use of the island of Culebra as a firing range. For the Puerto Rican Independence Party (PIP), the party which directed the campaign, Culebra also symbolized in a very concrete fashion the exploitative and insensitive nature of the relationship between the United States government and Puerto Rico. The Navy's bombardment of the populated island endangered the lives and economic livelihood of the islanders, yet they were powerless to make the Navy stop. The reality of second class citizen came sharply into focus. Also, the PIP constantly pointed out that the total American military bases on the island occupied about 13 percent of Puerto Rico's scarce arable land.

The campaign reached its height in mid-January, 1971 with the arrest of Ruben Berríos Martinez, the new and youthful president of the PIP, and several others for trespassing on the firing range during a civil disobedience action. The whole affair attracted much attention and became a *cause célèbre* on the island, as even the media hostile to independence gave the demonstrators favorable coverage. This issue further aroused the UPR student independentistas and their own campus campaign against the military which centered around opposition to ROTC. The Culebra actions also had special relevance to the UPR students particularly those who were members of the youth wing of the PIP because Ruben Berríos Martinez, the principal architect of the affair was a law professor at the UPR. It was also significant for the further general movement towards political activism in that Culebra marked the first time that the PIP, much less its president, had launched a civil disobedience action in the face of imminent arrest. The March 11 student disturbance growing out of a fight between ROTC students and independentistas was not unrelated to the feelings and emotions surrounding the actions in Culebra.

The presence and political activities of the Cuban émigré community has increased political tensions on the island and among the UPR student body, also. The Puerto Ricans had no official voice in the decision which led to the emigration of over 50,000 Cubans to an already overcrowded island. In Puerto Rico the newly emigrated Cubans had much success in business and many have moved into position of economic prominence. However, at the same time they have not been overly circumspect in the expression of their views concerning Puerto Ricans and Puerto Rican politics. They have made known their disdain for Puerto Ricans. As one Cuban émigré expressed it in an interview with Arthur Liebman after first giving his name: "I am Cuban, not a Puerto Rican. I work."

Politically, the Cubans are ardent supporters of statehood and adamant opponents of independence, which many feel to be an interim step on the way to a Communist takeover. The more militant Cubans have formed a clandestine terrorist organization, "Cuban Power," in order to combat the proindependence forces. FUPI and the other student independentista activists at the UPR have frequently evoked the wrath of various Cuban émigré organizations not only for their proindependence activities and positions but, in addition, for these students' avowed admiration of Fidel Castro. On the campus of Rio Piedras itself, Cuban refugee students have been among the more militant opponents of FUPI.

In the midst of these various political developments, the economy since 1969 has been in a growing slump. Tourism has declined and factories have closed. From 1969 to 1971, 122 plants have shut their doors eliminating the jobs of 4,000 workers. In 1970, 3 luxury hotels went out of business causing 600 hotel workers to lose their positions. Fomento, the aforementioned Economic Development Administration of Puerto Rico, in 1970 for the first time since its creation not only failed to generate more jobs but also witnessed the net loss of 1800 workers in plants associated with it. The economic downturn has even affected the petrochemical industry. As a result of the economic slowdown unemployment has grown considerably and the immediate prospects are that the situation will get worse. Given the economic situation, which the *New York Times* predicted would soon reach crisis proportions, there is little doubt that there will be serious political consequences further unsettling an already problematic political scene.

The major beneficiary of this economic slump will in all probability be the independentistas. They now can more effectively undercut the arguments of the statehood supporters with the assertion that close association with the United States is not a guarantor of Puerto Rican economic well-being and, in fact, can be detrimental to the Puerto Rican economy. As for the students, the curtailed prospects in the job market cannot fail to further embitter them, especially in their attitude toward the United States, the apparent cause of their economic woes.

Puerto Ricans, furthermore, particularly those who have politically come of age in the middle and latter 1960s can not help but be politically affected by events taking place on the mainland. They have had intimate and massive exposure via the United States' mass media to the struggles of the blacks and students and then later of the Mexican-Americans and Indians. The daily lessons witnessed on the omnipresent television screens began to strike responsive chords as the situation of the Negroes and later other ethnic groups was seen as having some relevance to the condition of the islanders. The media made the Puerto Ricans, again particularly the young, more aware of the increasing importance of the ethnic in American life and the ways in which ethnic groups in America were beginning to proudly claim their heritages and identities as well as political rights.

The students have learned much about the tactics and political philosophy of American student militants through the media. In addition, cheap and quick transportation between the mainland and the island has facilitated personal contact between Puerto Rican students and youthful activists from the mainland. In fact, on January 26, 1967, Stokely Carmichael as the official representative of the Student Non-Violent Coordinating Committee (SNCC), signed a "protocol of cooperation" with the president of FUPI, recognizing FUPI as an equal and an ally in the common struggle against American imperialism. In the latter 1960s and early 1970s, there has been considerable interaction between Puerto Rican student activists on the island and youthful Puerto Rican militants on the mainland, especially the members of the Young Lords Party. All this has contributed to the growth of militancy among the UPR students.

From 1964 to 1971, despite different historial, political, and socioeconomic contexts, students in both Mexico and Puerto Rico have represented major political problems for their respective governments. Spurred into action by similar as well as dissimilar forces, student activists in both societies have demonstrated to themselves, and to other oppositional or potential oppositional forces, the vulnerability of the Mexican and Puerto Rican political structures.

In Mexico the students mounted the first effective challenge to the ruling Institutional Revolutionary Party in recent history. The 1968 Mexican student movement was brutally suppressed but not eliminated. The 1968 student movement in retrospect now seems to have been but the beginning of a larger and potentially more potent student political force. The government and rightist elements unwittingly helped bring this force into being through their under-estimation of the students as well as through their repressive measures. Students together with other sectors of youth throughout Mexico have, to a significant extent, been politicized and radicalized by the events of 1968 and the treatment of the students, particularly those in prison, in the following years. However, the students by 1971 have moved beyond the student and campus concerns that previously occupied their attention to occupy a major position in national politics. Various political forces including the president of the country are vying with one another in order to influence the direction in which they, the students, will move. The students, particularly if they can reach and mobilize other groups and strata while maintaining their newly found unity and sense of mission, have it within their power to significantly reorient Mexican politics back into leftist paths reminiscent of the Mexican Revolution.

In 1971, university students in Puerto Rico, as in Mexico, constitute one of the most significant bases of opposition to the government. Despite the increased political potency of the Mexican students, the Puerto Rican student activists appear to be in a better strategic position than their Mexican counterparts. The Puerto Rican students are already part of a larger force located outside the university and in a society where fundamental polarization is taking place at an increasing rate. The Mexican students simply do not have so basic a source of political instability and division as the status issue available to them. As the status issue resumed its foremost position in Puerto Rican politics in the 1960s and early 1970s, the student independentistas who had so closely identified with it became an increasingly significant force both on and off campus. Thus the militants were transformed from a small band of relatively isolated political deviants and bravadoes to the vanguard of an important student movement in the years from 1964 to 1971.

Governor Luis A. Ferré and his administration appear to be in a quandry as to how to deal effectively with the student independentistas. The use of force against them has solidified support for these students and has gained them sympathizers. Because of their identification with a solution to the status issue that a significant number of Puerto Ricans hold to varing degrees, it is difficult either to deal harshly with them or to isolate them. Their increasingly audacious activities preclude the possibility of ignoring them. It is these student independentistas working in tandem with their nonstudent allies who consistently dramatize and crystallize political issues and dilemmas. They have reached beyond the confines of the UPR campus and begun to have had an impact upon high school students and other youthful groups. And similar to the situation in Mexico, their ideas and basic position, independence for Puerto Rico, have attracted numerous sympathizers among young, highly educated adults who have begun to enter strategic positions in the government, professions, and businesses. Thus, sustained by an ideology rooted in Puerto Rican history and population, supported by off-campus groups and organizations, and situated at the head of an increasingly politicized and militant student body, the UPR independentista activists represent a force, similar to their Mexican counterparts, which will deeply affect the course of politics in their society for decades.

7 Conclusion

Since the Córdoba Reform Movement of 1918, Latin American university students have been a significant social and political force in their countries. They have been at the forefront of movements aimed at eliminating basic inequities in their societies. They have identified with the masses of the rural and urban poor and have often provided short-term leadership for the struggles of these groups against foreign and native elite domination. University students have been instrumental in opposing authoritarian regimes, and have worked for the overthrow of such governments. National politics has not been the sole object of their concern nor has it been the only vehicle for the expression of their values. Concerned students have employed their professional skills in the urban slums and rural villages in order to aid the sick, to save lives, and to improve the general quality of life for the less fortunate in their societies. Since 1918 students have been intimately involved in the fight to reform their universities, to make them into more democratic institutions, and to demand that they be relevant to the needs of national and economic development. Above all, regardless of the nature of the government, left or right, students have persistently functioned as critics of society and as moral and ideological vanguards.

The student role, which shall be our central concern here, is, in Max Weber's terminology, the ideal typical one. Its prime function is to serve as a methodological device to give us further insight into the behavior, values, needs, and expectations of the actual students. The committed visionaries and reformers among the Latin American students who most closely approximate the ideal typical role represent a minority of their stratum. Such individuals are always a relatively small group because majorities are rarely willing to take significant risks, either for a vision or for others outside of their social stratum. However, there is no other societal group in Latin America that contains as high a percentage of critical idealists and activists as is to be found among the students.

This minority concerns us because it includes those who have been the makers of history throughout the twentieth century. They have defined the political and social goals for their student peers since Córdoba.

FACTORS WHICH HAVE SHAPED THE ROLE

Students in Latin America are expected to be idealists, activists, and even rebels. Camilo Torres, the slain Colombian guerrilla, priest, and sociologist, argued that being a revolutionary is the "historical vocation" of the Latin American student. Contemporary governments as diverse as Brazil and Cuba have publicly taken note of the critical idealism of students and have attempted to redirect it and the energies associated with it into approved channels. These attempts have rarely met with success for any length of time. Whatever the nature of the governmental reforms and programs, students have refused to surrender for long their dreams for a better society to any regime.

The nature of the students' university experience is crucial in shaping their visionary political role. The students' tenure in the university is short, lasting about three to five years. Latin American students are aware that once they leave the university their freedom of action will be severely constricted. After their student days they inexorably move into restricting occupational and familial roles. In addition, students often feel that there are no significant, uncompromised groups or organizations outside the university which are committed to student goals and ideals. Thus, whatever is to be done must be done during their brief stay at the university. This short time perspective promotes a disproportionate emphasis on goals as opposed to means.

The elite status of the students is a related factor affecting their political views and the nature of their involvement. They are recognized as an elite and receive respect from all sectors of society. Thus, students feel imbued with the responsibility not only to point to the future directions of social change but also to demand unearned leadership roles in the overall process. While voicing the necessity of understanding and working with the least privileged strata in order to bring about changes, students infrequently seize the opportunity to expose themselves systematically to the deep-seated wishes, needs, and fears of these disadvantaged persons. Students, furthermore, are generally not interested in committing themselves to the long-term organizational effort necessary to build an effective base for their position. Youthful elites often do not see the daily performance of such tedious tasks as part of their historic vision of themselves.

As elites and incipient intellectuals, students have had rather limited experience with long-term self-discipline or the day-to-day aspect of actual social problems. In addition, the Latin American educational system does not make strenuous intellectual demands on most students nor does it require daily self-discipline which might carry over into the students' political and social concerns. Rhetoric and abstractions as opposed to research and tedious study are the usual fare in the university. This lack of research orientation and of concern with the mundane affairs of their society often emanate from the numerous professors who devote themselves neither to research nor to teaching. Students tend to be critical of these professors and their practices but at the same time appear to emulate them. It is the persistent educational experience of dealing with abstractions and logical analyses that are neither grounded in reality nor subjected to empirical testing that distorts the students' view of what the world is like as well as what they are prepared to do in it.

The university also colors the students' perception of the political process in another fashion. Politics conducted by students within the confines of the university rarely exposes student activists to great risks. There they are relatively free to criticize the government and to issue revolutionary manifestoes without much fear of official reprisals. Students are also aware that their actual or potential role models – the older intellectuals and politicians – disproportionately emphasize words and rhetoric at the expense of political action.

Political experience within the university helps foster a somewhat unrealistic view of politics in an additional area. The very ease of being a student politician suggests that nonuniversity politics may be just as prone to reward rhetoric and passion. At the university the student politician is surrounded by large numbers of potential adherents who are within easy range of his voice. Relatively little work is required to reach or to influence them. Students are more readily mobilized than nonstudents, who are tied down by family and occupational responsibilities. Not only does this increase student availability but it also means that they are more easily moved by words and grand visions. This type of political experience poorly prepares the student activist interested in sweeping reforms or revolution should he decide to remain politically involved after leaving the university. For those who do enter the political world there is often a period of rapid exposure to more practical techniques and styles before they can become effective. This failure by students to do arduous, practical, and persistent political work has evoked strong criticism by revolutionary leaders including Fidel Castro and Camilo Torres.

There are times, however, when the students' very propensity for visionary politics becomes an asset for revolutionary or rapid political change. The very existence of such students and the goals which they promote can keep the idea of an alternative to an unresponsive political and economic system visible to their fellow countrymen. This is particularly the case in countries with highly authoritarian regimes where student visionaries may represent the total of active opposition to the government. During periods of crisis or major societal disturbances, it is the student idealists who speak most clearly to the needs and interests of their self-chosen constituencies, the poor and the disadvantaged. Their political style and their relative freedom to act enables the students to perform on grand scales to fill political vacuums which arise when other groups are restrained by their real and permanent interests and fears. On these occasions, the limitations inherent in the student role become sources of effective politics. Rarely if ever do the students themselves immediately move into positions of governmental power, rather they help to open the way for new groups or segments of the military. Then as the new government stabilizes the situation, the students return to their visionary and seemingly ineffective traditional political roles.

STUDENT-GOVERNMENT TENSION

Throughout Latin America there are substantial differences between the goals and the visions of the more committed students, on the one hand, and the government on the other. Indeed with the advent of military dictatorships in Argentina and Brazil and the hardening of government positions in other countries such as Uruguay, the distance between student goals and the possibility of their realization has been increased. Nonetheless, there have been at the same time, counter tendencies which have reduced the gap between university and postuniversity experience, both in the realm of politics and in the world of work. Thus, at the university level there has been an increase in more knowledgeable and more committed professors who have brought with them a higher level of teaching as well as a greater research involvement. In these instances the university has started to become a meaningful training ground, uniting the professional and political concerns of students, while at the same time preparing them to be more realistically integrated into their respective societies than were their counterparts of earlier decades.

There have also been some important changes at the national political level which have narrowed the ideological differences between the state and the student activists in, for example, Cuba and Chile. Cuba no doubt is the clearest example. There the Castro government has attempted to implement some of the goals that visionary students throughout the hemisphere have proclaimed for decades. As part of this program, the Cuban political elites have explicitly attempted to mold the educational system, especially the university, into an instrument of national policy. One immediate manifestation of this policy was to change arbitrarily the proportions of enrollments in different fields through enrollment limitations and differential allocation of resources so that the universities would produce more graduates in the scientific and technical fields and less in the humanities and liberal arts areas. Another outgrowth of this policy of the abolition of university autonomy as the overall official goal was to tightly integrate both the students and the universities into the government's national development program.

Friction and tension between the government and the students were inherent in the official educational policies and this became increasingly evident as the policies were implemented and the students' educational decision-making powers were restricted. The students, from the earliest days of the Castro government, questionned, criticized, and even protested against different educational policies as well as various political and economic policies of the state. The government has responded to these actions by the students in a variety of ways. One method has been to tighten political control over the students through pro-Castro student organizations. Another mechanism has been to alter student selection procedures to ensure at the same time a more politically reliable student body and a higher proportion of students from working-class backgrounds. At various times student critics have been expelled and in the case of the University of Oriente in 1971 an entire university was closed and student protest leaders there were dispatched to disciplinary farms.

Despite the punitive measures taken against recalcitrant students and despite the significant progress the Cuban government has made in educating and improving the living conditions of the Cuban masses, Cuban students have not relinquished their critical function. They, together with intellectuals, have continued to prod, question, and criticize the regime's policies and personnel, including Fidel Castro himself. However, a major difference between the Cuban student visionaries and their counterparts elsewhere in the hemisphere is that the Cubans rarely question their government's legitimacy or sincerity or the validity of its fundamental goals and ideals. Instead the bulk of the student dissatisfcation appears to be focused upon the regime's short-term policies and primarily the methods and mechanisms used to implement the state's professed objectives. The government, for its part, appears to be cognizant of the basic loyalty of the students to the ideals and goals of the revolution. Fidel Castro's frequent appearances on university campuses and his numerous dialogues and debates with students are indicators of his esteem for them, his recognition of their importance, and his desire to gain their support for his policies. Both the regime and the students in Cuba are aware of each other's importance and their mutual goals but neither party will allow the other to pursue its interests, regardless of how worthy, at its expense without some type of critical response. The tension and conflict emerging out of the interaction between students and the state in Cuba has led to difficulties for both but eventually it could lead to a more positive and creative relationship than in most of the other Latin American societies where there is a much more fundamental conflict between students and their governments.[1]

It is still too early to assess the situation in Chile. The fact that a Marxist president, Salvador Allende, was elected with strong student support in 1970 indicates that the Chilean government's relationship with the students may be more harmonious than it was during the last years of the administration of President Eduardo Frei. President Allende has recognized the need for student support to achieve his programs, many of which the students had enunciated in earlier decades. There has also been a major effort in Chile to obtain a convergence of the two major student roles — the professional and the political. Politically conscious students are being called upon, as they were under President Frei, to utilize their professional knowledge toward the solution of crucial societal problems.

President Allende, the first popularly elected Marxist president in Latin America, is keenly aware of the importance of students for the goals of his administration. Speaking at the National Stadium in Santiago on November 5, 1970, shortly after his inauguration, Allende made the following dramatic offer:

Precisely on this solemn occasion I wish to speak to the young people, to those standing on the lawn, who have sung their songs for us. A rebellious student in the past, I will not criticize their impatience, but it is my duty to ask them to think calmly. Young people, yours is that beautiful age during which physical and mental vigor enable you to undertake practically any endeavor. For that reason you are duty-bound to help us advance. Turn your eagerness into more work, your hopes into more effort and your impulsiveness into concrete accomplishments. Use your drive and energy to be better — the best — students and workers. Thousands upon thousands of young people have demanded a place in the social struggle. Now they have that place. The time has come for all young people to participate in the action. To those who have not yet taken part in this process, I say, "Come on, there's a place for everyone in the construction of our new society."[2]

The success of President Allende's appeal and the enthusiasm generated by the vigorous effort of the new administration to solve major national problems resulted in the participation of more than 20,000 young people in the government's Volunteer Summer Work program in February 1971. Students from all major political groups, with the exception of the right, provided a variety of medical and educational services while at the same time engaging in construction work. This action was described by the International Institute of Studies on Education as "an extraordinary display of energy and enthusiasm."[3]

However, the Allende administration has not been free of student criticism. In the first weeks of the new administration, the Leftist Revolutionary Movement (MIR), an important student revolutionary group which was vocal and active in condemning Frei's policies, made clear that it had no intention of ceasing its opposition to selected government policies, even if that government was one headed by a Marxist. The actions of the MIR have transcended vocal and organizational criticism. It has organized and aided peasants in the illegal seizure of farms. An offshoot of the MIR, the Popular Workers Vanguard has also seized university buildings. In addition, there has been criticism of the government from other students and, as noted previously with regard to the election for rector of the University of Chile, a majority of the students voted against Allende's candidate and for Edgardo Boeninger, the incumbent rector, an independent Christian Democrat who argued that the university "should maintain 'a critical position' toward the Government and society."[4]

To date, the Allende administration has generally limited itself to moral suasion when dealing with its student critics and opponents. It is doubtful whether the Chilean government will resort to the strong measures applied by the Cuban government with respect to its universities. Allende was elected by a minority vote and is constricted in his political maneuverability by democratic parliamentary considerations and an independent army. In addition, the universities were and are major bases of Allende's support. He also has strong societal and university traditions of positive student involvement and commitment upon which to build. It is this latter factor especially which may bring a large measure of success to the new government's efforts to unify the political and professional roles of concerned students on behalf of Chile's economic and social development.

In most of the other countries of Latin America there is little opportunity for the convergence of these roles. Military dictatorships such as those in Brazil and Argentina try to eradicate the political or the visionary components rather than fuse them with the professional as Chile and Cuba are seeking to do. In both Brazil and Argentina the governments have been repressive toward the universities, purging them of many students and professors suspected of being antigovernment. In addition, students and professors in both countries have been beaten and jailed. At the same time these governments have voiced their intentions of upgrading standards within the universities and of producing greater numbers of technically competent graduates. It is questionable, however, whether it is possible to produce a high level of technical training in institutional settings in which political concerns are suppressed and the carriers of visionary politics purged or feel compelled to leave. Often it is these students and professors who are among the most qualified in their fields. Given the shortage of highly qualified professors in Latin America, especially in the natural sciences, their removal from the universities can only have a significant negative impact upon any attempt to upgrade the standards of teaching and research.

The issue of depoliticizing the university while improving academic and scientific quality transcends the expulsion of politically suspect people from the institutions of higher education. In such a political milieu there are subjects or areas which cannot be safely explored without fear of political reprisal. The stifling of dissent inhibits innovations in such crucial features of university life as academic reform, new directions in research, and new modes of professional training. This should not imply that Latin American universities have been in the absence of repressive governments, innovative institutions; for clearly, as we have earlier indicated, this generally has not been the case. The relevant point here, however, is that some universities were moving toward becoming more creative institutions − a movement which was abruptly halted by political acts of the Argentine and Brazilian military governments. Such policies undermine the attempts to create more innovative institutions. Governments, and not only those in Latin America, cannot impose political restrictions on their universities and expect them to function as true and enduring centers of learning and professional training. Despite the lip service paid to grave national problems by the current national leaders in Brazil and Argentina or their expression of concern with improved educational standards, it is difficult to see how universities in these two countries can make significant contributions to their respective societies when student visionaries and respected professors are purged or feel the atmosphere to be incompatible with serious scholarly effort.

We have raised a number of questions in this conclusion, not the least of which concerns the most productive relationship among students, universities, and national governments. How can student visionaries constructively contribute to solving serious and chronic economic and social problems? From our perspective this can best be done in a national setting in which governmental policy is fundamentally committed to meeting the needs of the still marginal millions of Latin Americans. This kind of policy commitment, of necessity, demands certain changes within universities such as updating curricula, greater emphasis on research and innovative teaching, a more balanced distribution of students among facultads, and a greater willingness on the part of students, professors, and administrators to experiment with internal political and structural arrangements. It also perforce obliges students, universities, and governments to coordinate closely their activities and interim objectives. These types of changes seem minimal if students and universities are to be important participants along with governments in working toward the solutions to major societal problems. Student opposition, as well as apathy, can be transformed into support and their political and professional roles fused within the context of meaningful national efforts to improve the lives of tens of millions of Latin Americans and eradicate serious social inequities.

At the same time, however, it is necessary that both students and professors maintain a significant degree of independence from their governments, regardless of how committed or worthy these governments may be. This independence is important for the overall effort at national problem solving for it affords the university community the leeway and opportunity to constructively criticize government policies and programs as well as propose its own or amended programs. Admittedly, this type of independence is extremely difficult to maintain during periods of national mobilization. However, if such independence is not attained and protected, negative consequences will follow both for the students and their universities and for the national regimes and their goals. The interaction between free universities and committed governments, while indeed rarely devoid of difficulties for both parties, can at the same time produce optimum conditions for solving the grave and enduring problems of Latin America. History has shown that student visionaries, those who most closely resemble the ideal typical Latin American students, cannot by themselves bring about the changes and reforms that they so fervently desire. At the same time, history has also revealed that such students are a perennial regenerative force, consistently infusing the body politic with democratic and progressive ideals. Through their deeds, as well as their ideals, these students have been instrumental in the overthrow of dictatorships while also building vital support and acceptance for more progressive regimes.

Finally, we would like to conclude our discussion of Latin American university students with an insightful statement by Kalman Silvert, a social scientist long concerned with the study of Latin America. His statement summarizes our feelings and thoughts about the complex phenomena called Latin American university students:

A complex mythology of the Latin American student has grown up in the United States, in large measure a result of the excited findings of observers scurrying to make up for irrevocably lost time. We hear that the Latin American student is a radical, uninterested in study, the pawn of professional agitators, the persecutor of his professors, and the bane of responsible university administrators. Some students are all these things. Others are serious and questioning young people working well and serenely in rapidly improving faculties and departments . . . They form the reservior of modern men and women upon whom the nation can draw for its development, susceptible to national leadership and willing to take the risks demanded when societies break from one world of thought and action into another.[5]

Appendix A: Methods

The data that are the basis for chapters 2, 3, 4, and 5 are derived from surveys of university students in Colombia, Puerto Rico, Mexico, Paraguay, Uruguay, and Panama conducted in 1964 and 1965 under the auspices of Seymour Martin Lipset, Director of the Comparative National Development Project. These five countries and the Commonwealth of Puerto Rico were chosen for several reasons. There was a desire for a diverse representation of Latin American societies and at the same time a concern for the practical problem of completing the research within the limits of budget, personnel, and other meaningful considerations.

Politics and national sensitivities were also considerations before, during, and after the survey was completed. As several of the contributors in this volume can acknowledge from firsthand experience, a survey of student politics has to be carried out with the greatest of care. Americans studying Latin American students and their politics, even when native personnel are making the face to face contact, represent a potentially combustible mixture. Fortunately for the researchers and the study, politics had only one appreciable affect upon the survey and that was in only one country, Panama. There, the students decided beforehand not to answer any question dealing with their politics despite the assurances of anonymity that were given to all student respondents. Thus, whenever political items are used in any analysis or comparison of the students from the various countries, the Panamanian students are not included.

The survey instrument that was used was developed and pretested at the Institute of International Studies, University of California at Berkeley. For purposes of comparative analysis, the same basic instrument was used in each of the six societies. However, when the content of a particular item was relevant only to the respondent of a given country such as the names of towns, cities, political parties, and political figures, the item involved was reworded to ensure both its applicability and its comparability.

In each of the six societies, full-time students enrolled at the largest and most prestigeous university constituted the universe from which the sample was drawn. These were the most influential universities in the particular countries and were the ones which are considered the national universities, analogous to a major state university in the United States. In all cases this university was a public one situated in or adjacent to the capital city. However, with respect to Mexico and Colombia, the two largest countries among the six, students from additional universities were included in the statistical universe. In Mexico, the total number of universities utilized for the study was two while for Colombia the number was five. In Colombia, the country which has the largest proportion of private and Catholic universities, students from a private and a Catholic university were also included and represent the only students in the entire study who did not attend a public university.

The universities according to country included in this study together with the number of students in each university responding are:

(1)	Puerto Rico	Universidad de Puerto Rico (577)
(2)	Uruguay	Universidad de la República (469)
(3)	Paraguay	Universidad Nacional de Asunción (417)
(4)	Panama	Universidad Nacional de Panama (1027)
(5)	Mexico	Universidad Nacional Autonoma de México (682)
		Universidad de Guanajuato (148)
(6)	Colombia	Universidad Nacional de Colombia (347)
		Universidad de los Andes (631)
		Universidad Libre de Colombia (159)
		Universidad Pontificia Javeriana (209)
		Universidad del Cauca (Popayán) (149)

The general procedure followed with respect to seeking cooperation of specific universities in the six societies had two key elements. First, an intial letter of inquiry from the project director to the rector of university was followed up by an in-person visit of a staff member or subcontractor having command of Spanish and some sort of "interpersonal roots" on the local scenes. The field directors in most of the countries had many personal friends or acquaintances, often in high positions, in the universities being considered for study. Thus, in most of the countries in the sample, the standard line of legitimate authority was carefully followed in seeking permission and cooperation for the study. A second important aspect of seeking cooperation from the universities in each country involved offering the local officials and cooperating social scientists a copy of the coded and punched data, codebooks, and preliminary marginals for their own use. Such an approach permitted the interested officials in each country to obtain some useful information for their *own* purposes, in addition to cooperating with a more abstract scientific ideal of inquiry and discovery.

Once the universities had been selected and some form of cooperation secured, the basic design called for a systematic random sample in each university, stratified by *facultad* (the equivalent of "school" in United States universities). This meant that the standard procedure was to obtain the list of students enrolled full-time in each school within the selected universities and then to select every nth name from these lists. The interval used between every nth name varied from school to school, according to its size. The aim here was to secure reliable samples of even the small schools while avoiding the possibility of being overwhelmed with cases from an especially large school within the university. In very small schools, a total sample was usually attempted. As an additional constraint, some attempt was made to limit the samples to those schools within a university that were similar to schools in other universities, in order to facilitate comparative analysis.

Circumstances forced modifications in the basic sampling design in certain countries. Officials at the Universidad de los Andes, for instance, limited the survey to all students present in classes on a particular day. And where the total university enrollment was too small to provide an adequate number of respondents in the various schools, as in Libre and Javeriana in Colombia, a nonstratified, systematic random sample of 10 percent was taken from the university as a whole. Such smaller universities tended to have a smaller array of schools, in addition. In Uruguay and to a lesser extent in Paraguay, official limitations as well as communication problems with subcontractors doing the actual sampling resulted in nonproportional sampling by faculty. In Puerto Rico, students at the School of Medicine were uncooperative and completed and returned only 13 questionnaires. Therefore, the total sample obtained is not proportional to the actual numbers of persons in either universities or schools within universities. The results can be seen in Table 32 where all the students in the sample are divided according to country, university, and school or facultad.

Once specific names had been chosen from each school in a university, each student falling into the intended sample was sent a letter requesting his cooperation, stating the purpose of the questionnaire, the identity of the institutions conducting and sponsoring the study, the estimated time required to complete the questionnaire, and where and when the questionnaire would be administered. In most countries the questionnaire was administered to groups of students. Students who did not take the questionnaire at the first session were requested to complete it at a subsequent session. In cases where there was still no response, an attempt was made to obtain the required data by mail, by giving the student a questionnaire to fill out at home, or by personal interview. In Paraguay, the entire data collection process was performed by means of personal interviews rather than group administration. Students who were selected as part of the intended sample but who refused to respond to the questionnaire after one or more follow-up attempts were replaced in the intended sample by another name randomly drawn from the appropriate list. (The usual procedure was to select the next name in the list after the name of the nonresponding student.)

The field directors generally reported high completion and low refusal rates. However, owing to administrative and communications problems, a precise description of nonresponse rates and the number of substituted names in the final sample was, in general, not kept. The most accurate records seem to have been kept in Colombia, where a median completion rate of roughly 90 percent was reported. The lack of complete records on this matter of nonrespondents and sampling substitutions, together with the highly variable proportion of students sampled from each school (and, in Mexico and Colombia, university) within a given country, preclude any claim that the present samples are representative in a strict statistical sense of university students either in the six

Table 32. Percentages of students responding to questionnaire in each faculty by university and by country

									Colombia				
Faculty	Puerto Rico	Mexico	UNAM	Guan.	Panama	Uruguay	Paraguay	Total	L.A.	Jav.	U.N.	L.	C.
Engineering	71	320	237	83	90	49	46	519	319	45	65	12	78
Humanities	49	60	60		316	50	40	133	78	42	13		54
Medicine	13	62	62		28	50	73	205	61	45	45		
Pharm. and natural sci.	50	72	55	17	273		51	77	32		45	79	17
Law	96	217	169	48	30	50	41	211	70	26	89		
Economics		99	99			50	59	94			24	68	
Education	95							96			27		
Architecture					41	46	47	62	62	51	38		
Social science	73							98	9				
Social service					249								
Business adm.	70					50	24						
Veterinary sci.						50	24						
Agronomy						50	24						
Dentistry						24							
Gen. studies	60												
N	(557)	(830)	(682)	(148)	(1027)	(469)	(417)	(1495)	(631)	(209)	(347)	(159)	(149)

selected countries as a whole or in the specific universities with which we are dealing in each country.

At a more basic level, however, there is good reason to accept the validity of the data, irrespective of its representativeness. A great deal of care was taken by the field director in each country to assure than the study and its questionnaire were taken seriously. In cases where there was any reasonable doubt as to the validity of a questionnaire or interview, the case was discarded. Such a procedure led to discarding over one hundred cases in the six countries and probably further contributed to biases in the sampling, although the result is a more valid and reliable set of data.

The present samples of students could be weighted in such a way that they are more nearly representative of their universities, schools, and countries. However, such a weighting has not been attempted in the present analysis for three main reasons. First, such a weighting procedure makes the analysis and the kinds of statistics used much more complex, as well as being tedious, costly, time-consuming, and in the present case quite difficult to perform because of the size of the samples, the number of countries and universities involved, and the number of schools involved. Still, it could be done. Second, the lack of precise records on the quality of the data collection (nonresponses, substitutions, and so forth) makes it quite possible (likely?) that even after the complex and expensive weighting process, the resulting weighted samples would still not be representative of the universities involved, let alone representative of all university students in the six societies or *all* Latin American university students. Among other problems, lack of data from certain schools and universities in each country would be critical stumbling blocks. Third, most of the analysis to be performed here does not hinge critically on the representativeness of the sample. In a few instances, we attempt to make an inference about proportions of certain characteristics in the broader university student population. However, in most instances we are primarily interested in understanding the workings of important *processes. We look mainly at the relationships between or among variables, rather than at the absolute frequency of specific kinds of behavior*. For the latter kind of analysis to be interesting and important, it is not strictly necessary that samples be perfectly representative of any particular universe. What is vital is that one's sample include a fairly broad range of cases in terms of the phenomena being investigated. With a truly diverse sample, however representative, the phenomena of importance and the relationships among variables that characterize these phenomena may be validly and reliably investigated.

No additional points regarding the nature of the present data require explanation. By way of putting the present study in context, it should be pointed out that this was the first large scale, consciously cross-cultural, comparative survey research study performed on Latin American university students (or university students from other countries) from as many as six countries using the same basic instrument. The basic design sought representative samples at first, but then practical exigencies and problems of numerous kinds led to deviations from the ideal design. When one considers the type of respondents, the nature of the institutions involved, the number of countries, certain aspects of the subject matter (especially the many political attitude and value questions), political conditions in the universities and in the countries, as well as the problems of supervising various data collection teams and agencies with varying levels of training, expertise, and local connections, the quality and quantity of the present data seem to indicate a success.

The final point to be made is probably the most telling one. Unlike most studies, whether dealing with students or any other topic or type of respondent in the social sciences, the present study has built into its design a very important and substantial amount of *replication*. For any given relationship, we are generally able to report not merely what one country's data show, but what is shown by six sets of data gathered completely independently of each other. In a very real sense, therefore, *we are reporting here on six different studies that all have similar kinds of respondents and a nearly identical research instrument, to which have been applied identical analytical and statistical techniques.* Clearly, any relationships that turn out to be consistently significant across the data for all six countries deserve very special attention from both social scientists and practitioners. On the other hand, relationships that are inconsistent across the six countries — especially if they are statistically significant in opposing directions — must be viewed as more culture-specific or more culture-sensitive. The latter sort of relationships may be very important indeed for the people of a given country, but they will stand in a different role to social scientific knowledge from those relationships which seem to hold consistently across countries. It should also be noted in this connection that, from the standpoint of scientific knowledge, a relationship that is found to be *consistent though weak* in six countries will very likely be more important than a relationship that is found to be inconsistent across the six countries though strong in one or two. And, finally, although our samples may not be very representative, they are self-replicating — a virtue that far outweighs the value of representativeness.

Appendix B: Latin American University Student Questionnaire (English Version)

This is a scientific study of public opinion concerning the problems of the university in general and of student life in particular. The study is essentially a comparative one, including more than 15 universities in several Latin American nations, among them Brazil, Colombia, Mexico and Panama. A central focus of the study is the adequacy of educational structures for fulfilling the needs of developing nations. The present study concentrates on a description by university students of their problems, both educational and other. By this means we hope to obtain a clear picture of university life, including its social, economic, political and psychological aspects. The study is absolutely anonymous, and for this reason we request that you do not write in your name or any other indication of your identity as an individual. We are interested solely in frequencies and statistical tendencies, not in individual cases.

We request that you draw a circle around the number corresponding to your answer to each question, (except for cases where a written answer is appropriate.) Thus, in the first question, if you are 20 years old, circle the number 2, as below:

1. How old are you?

Less than 18	1
19 to 20	②
21 to 22	3
etc.	

We request that you answer all the questions. There will be some in which the alternative answers provided do not precisely correspond to your opinion. In these cases, circle the response closest to your opinion, adding your comments on the reverse side of the page. The responses will be transferred to IBM cards and statistical tables will be developed from them. The results of the study will be widely published in sociological journals.

1. How old are you?

18 or younger	1
19 to 20	2

20 to 21	3
22 to 23	4
24 to 25	5
26 to 30	6
31 to 35	7
36 to 40	8
more than 40	9

2. Are you male or female?

male	1
female	2

3. What is the highest level of education your father, mother and father's father received?

	father	mother	father's father
primary school (complete or incomplete), or no education	1	1	1
secondary school, general or *bachillerato* (complete or incomplete)	2	2	2
secondary technical school (complete or incomplete)	3	3	3
normal school (complete or incomplete)	4	4	4
industrial or commercial institute (complete or incomplete)	5	5	5
agricultural school	6	6	6
other school at the secondary school level	7	7	7
university, incomplete	8	8	8
university, complete	9	9	9
don't know	0	0	0

4. If your father, mother or father's father attended university, whether or not they completed their studies, what was their field of specialization? (If more than one, indicate the most important.)

	father	mother	father's father
did not attend university	Y	Y	Y
law	1	1	1
medicine or other medical special-ties (dentistry, veterinary medicine, nursing, etc.)	2	2	2
social sciences (sociology, psychology, economy, etc.)	3	3	3
humanities and fine arts (philosophy, literature, etc.)	4	4	4
natural sciences (geology, agronomy, chemistry, etc.)	5	5	5
exact sciences (mathematics, physics)	6	6	6
engineering (civil, chemical, electric, etc.)	7	7	7
sciences of education (pedagogy, etc.)	8	8	8
other	0	0	0
don't know	X	X	X

5. Where did you live the major part of the time between the ages of seven and fifteen, and where did your father live the major part of the time up to the age of 25?

	you lived from 7 to 15 years of age in:	your father lived up to the age of 25 in:
largest city (of nation)	1	1
2nd largest city	2	2
3rd largest city	3	3
4th largest city	4	4
another city of more than 100,000 inhabitants	5	5
city of more than 20,000 and less than 100,000 inhabitants	6	6
a city of less than 20,000 inhabitants	7	7
a town, farm, or rural zone	8	8

a) In what department was it located (where you lived)? _____

b) In what department was it located (where your father lived)? _____

6. What is your marital status?

single	1
engaged	2
married	3
other (separated,	
divorced, widowed)	4

7. Do you have a job?

a) How many hours a week do you work?

I don't have a job	1
40 hours a week or more	2
20 to 39 hours per week	3
less than 20 hours per week	4

b) If you have a job, in what occupation do you work? (Please provide details, including the level of specialization, level of responsibility, etc. Write freely in the space below. For example, "I operate a grocery store, with four employees under my supervision."

c) Give a description of your work during an ordinary, typical workday.

d) Do you have subordinates, or persons that work under your direction? How many?

none	1
less than 5	2
from 6 to 10	3
from 11 to 20	4
from 21 to 100	5
more than 100	6

e) For whom do you work?

the government	1
a nationally owned private enterprise	2
a foreign-owned private enterprise	3
for myself	4
in an educational or research institution	5
other (which): _____	6

8. What is your father's occupation? (If your father is not living, what was his occupation during the major part of his life? Please give details of his work, including his level of specialization, level of responsibility, etc. Write freely in the space below. For example, "science teacher in public secondary school.")

a) Write a brief description of his work, during an ordinary, typical workday.

b) Does (or did) you father have subordinates, or people who work (or worked) under his direction? How many?

none	1
less than 5	2
6 to 10	3
11 to 20	4
21 to 100	5
more than 100	6

c) For whom does he (or did he) work?

the government	1
a nationally-owned private enterprise	2
a foreign-owned private enterprise	3
for himself	4
in an educational or research institution	5
other (which): _____	6

9. How many brothers and sisters do you have?

	brothers	sisters
none	1	1
one	2	2
two	3	3
three	4	4
four	5	5
more than four	6	6

10. How many *older* brothers or sisters do you have?

	brothers	sisters
none	1	1
one	2	2
two	3	3
three or more	4	4

11. With whom do you live, and where?

with parents	1
with other relatives or older friends of your parents	2
in a boarding house for students	3
in a boarding house (pension) not exclusively for students	4
in a house or apartment with friend(s)	5
in a house or apartment, alone	6
in a university dormitory or other university residence	7
with husband or wife	8

12. There is a lot of talk these days about social classes, and different people use different terms for referring to social classes. Below there is a list of terms that are commonly used. Indicate which one you consider to be most applicable to your family (your parents), which one you consider will apply to you ten years after completing your studies, and which one you consider most applicable to those who have completed their studies in your *facultad* (school or department).

	your family	yourself, ten years after graduation	the majority of those who have graduated in your *facultad*
upper or wealthy class	1	1	1
upper middle class	2	2	2
lower middle class	3	3	3
working class (*trabajadora*)	4	4	4
poorer class (*obrera*)	5	5	5
peasant class	6	6	6

13. What type of secondary school course did you have?

scientific	1
humanities	2
industrial	3
commercial	4
agricultural	5
other	6

14. During secondary school, in which subject did you do best, and in which did you have the most difficulty?

a) your best subject: _____

b) your worst subject: _____

15. What type of student were you during secondary school?

excellent	1
good	2
average	3
poor	4
very poor	5

16. In what year did you first enter the university?

1964	1
1963	2
1962	3
1961	4
1960	5
1959	6
1955–1958	7
1954 or before	8

17. In what year of your university career are you enrolled?

first	1
second	2
third	3
fourth	4
fifth	5
sixth	6
post-graduate work	7

18. In what *facultad* or school are you enrolled? (for example: law, medicine, etc.) _____

19. What is your specialization within your *facultad*? (for example, in engineering: civil engineering, electrical engineering, etc.)?

_____

20. Have you changed your field of study since beginning your university studies? (If you have changed more than once, note only the most recent one.)

no	1
yes, I previously studied _____	2

21. If you could begin your university studies over again, would you enroll in your present *facultad*?

yes	1
no	2

22. How important is it to you to *complete* your university studies?

very important	1
rather important	2
more or less important	3
of little importance	4

23. If you could go to a foreign country to complete your studies or to do specialized studies, to what country would you most like to go?

name of the country: _____

24. Which of the following languages can you read? How easily can you read the literature of your specialty in these languages? Please mark the number corresponding to the degree of difficulty you have in reading these languages.

I can read:	very well	fairly well	with some difficulty	with much difficulty	I cannot read
English	1	2	3	4	5
French	1	2	3	4	5
another language (which):					
_____	1	2	3	4	5

25. When did you first consider seriously the career which you have chosen?

before primary school	1
during primary school	2
after finishing primary school and before beginning secondary school	3
during secondary school	4
after finishing secondary school and before entering university	5
after entering university	6
I have not yet decided on a career	7

26. Many factors influence the choice of a career. Which factors most influenced your career choice? (Write your answer in the space provided below):

_____
_____
_____
_____
_____

27. In what occupation do you *plan* to work after graduating? Write in the name of the occupation and answer the additional questions about the occupational situation in which you expect to work.

Name of the occupation: _____

I plan to work:
for the government	1
in a nationally-owned private enterprise	2
in a foreign-owned private enterprise	3
for myself	4
in an educational or research institution	5
other (which):_____	6

28. How likely is it that you will work in this occupation after graduating?

very likely	1
rather likely	2
not very likely	3

29. Considering the average person graduated from your *facultad*, how much do you think he will earn five years after graduation? And how about the average graduate in engineering and law, how much do you think they will earn five years after graduation? (If your *facultad* is engineering or law, do not answer for that one, but only for "*your facultad*.")

	your facultad	engineering	law
less than double the minimum salary*	1	1	1
2 to 3 times the minimum	2	2	2
4 to 6 times the minimum	3	3	3
6 to 10 times the minimum	4	4	4
10 to 15 times the minimum	5	5	5
15 to 20 times the minimum	6	6	6
20 to 30 times the minimum	7	7	7
30 to 50 times the minimum	8	8	8
more than 50 times the minimum	9	9	9

*[These terms to be translated into national currency, "minimum salary" refers to a legally prescribed minimum for salaried or hourly employees, or if there is none, to a figure representing a comparable salary.]

30. How would you compare yourself with other students in your class (year) with respect to general academic performance? Would you say that you are in:

the upper quarter of your class	1
the upper half of your class	2
the lower half of your class	3
the lowest quarter of your class	4

31. What was your average grade in secondary school and what is it now in university? (If you don't know the exact grade, make an approximation):

    a) in secondary school: _____

    b) in university: _____

32. Do you have any courses to make up (repeat)?

no	1
yes, one	2
yes, two	3
yes, three or more	4

33. How do you think your standard of living, five years after graduation will compare with your family's present standard of living?

I expect that mine will be:

much higher	1
a little higher	2
more or less the same	3
a little lower	4
much lower	5

34. What do you think is the most important factor for success in this country?

competence	1
luck	2
personal contacts or family situation	3

35. What quality among the following would you most prefer in a professor of your *facultad*?

to be a good lecturer	1
to know his material well	2
to be a good researcher (investigator)	3

36. There are various opinions concerning the qualities necessary for success in various university careers.

a) Considering a person who is very intelligent but not very studious, in which of the following two types of careers do you think he would have the most success?

law or philosophy   1
engineering or physics   2

b) And a person who is very studious but not very intelligent, in which type of career do you think he would be most successful?

law or philosophy   1
engineering or physics   2

37. Of the following, which is the *more* important function of the university?

to provide a general education to students   1
to prepare students for professional life   2

38. How satisfied are you with your life as a student, including all aspects — professors, courses, facilities, examinations, etc.?

very satisfied   1
satisfied   2
unsatisfied   3
very unsatisfied   4

39. How would you evaluate your professors in general, taking into account their knowledge of material, lectures, assignments, examinations, etc.?

the majority are excellent   1
few or none are excellent   2

40. How desirable is it that professors in your *facultad* be active in politics?

very desirable   1
desirable   2
undesirable   3
very undesirable   4

41. To what extent do you think of yourself as belonging to each of the following categories of persons? For example, do you think of yourself as an intellectual most of the time, often, rarely, or never?

	most of the time	often	rarely	never
an intellectual	1	2	3	4
a scientist	1	2	3	4
a professional	1	2	3	4

42. If you had to define yourself in these terms, would you say that you are more an intellectual, a scientist, or a professional? (Choose one only.)

intellectual   1
scientist   2
professional   3

43. How often do you discuss the following topics with fellow students?

	every day	every two or three days	at least once a week	less than once a week, but at least once a month	less than once a month
personal problems	1	2	3	4	5
academic and career problems	1	2	3	4	5
art and literature	1	2	3	4	5
national politics	1	2	3	4	5
international politics	1	2	3	4	5
student politics in your *facultad* or school	1	2	3	4	5
student politics in general	1	2	3	4	5

44. If you had to choose between being an academic person, for example, a professor or researcher, and being a politician, for example, a deputy or senator, which would you choose?

professor or researcher   1
deputy or senator   2

45. There is talk of a proposal to organize university careers so that students would not choose their field of specialization (*facultad*) until their third year, taking courses in several fields during their first two years of study. Some favor this new proposal, and others prefer the present system. What is your opinion?

favorable to the proposal   1
opposed to the proposal   2

46. In many Latin American universities there are differences of opinion concerning the role to be played by university student government. Which of the following alternatives do you prefer?

University student government should express student views concerning national and international politics   1

University student government should be concerned solely with student and academic affairs   2

47. Do most of your friends belong to:

your *facultad*	1
other *facultades*	2
or:	
most of them are not university students	3

48. Which of the changes listed below would you like to have in your *facultad*? Indicate only the *one* which you consider *most* important.

improvement of recreational activities (sports, cultural activities, etc.)	1
improvement of educational facilities (library, laboratory, etc.)	2
more courses oriented toward practical application	3
more freedom to teach (*libertad de catedra*)	4
more student participation in *facultad* and university government	5

49. In general, do your friends agree with you on political issues?

all agree	1
most agree	2
few agree	3
none agree	4

50. How active are you in university affairs? For example, did you vote in the last elections of your *facultad* or school? Have you attended a meeting of the student council in your *facultad* or of the university in the past six months?

a) voted in the last elections of school or *facultad*

yes	1
no	2

b) attended a meeting of a student council

yes	1
no	2

51. Some people believe that the decisions of university student leaders should not be influenced by their affiliations with political parties outside the university, while others believe that such influence is all right. What is your opinion?

It is all right for student leaders to represent the interests and ideologies of national political parties in student politics	1
Student leaders should have nothing to do with the interests and ideologies of national political parties	2

52. There are considerable differences of opinion among students concerning the kinds of problems that would justify the student strike as an expression of student sentiments. Without considering the particular *content* of problems that might be involved in a particular strike, what is your general opinion with respect to the use of the strike in the following *types* of problems:

	strikes are justified	strikes are *not* justified
a) university issues	1	2
b) national or international political issues	1	2

53. With respect to your own experience, in how many strikes or demonstrations have you participated *actively*?

none	1
one	2
two	3
three	4
four or more	5

54. Which of the following kinds of organizations do you belong to? (Indicate as many as apply.)

	yes	no
a) national political party or organization	1	2
b) student political party	1	2
c) cultural organization (those concerned with presenting plays, concerts, art expositions, literary meetings, etc.)	1	2
d) religious association	1	2
e) social or sports organization (sports club, club that presents social events, dances, fiestas, etc.)	1	2
f) professional or scientific association (those concerned with the interests and problems of the members of a career or field of study)	1	2
g) other type (which): _____	1	2

55. Do you now occupy, or have you occupied in the past year, a position of formal responsibility (e.g., elective or appointive position) within one or more student organizations?

yes	1
no	2

56. How much interest do you have in questions of student politics?

a lot	1
some	2
little	3
none	4

57. How much interest do you have in the next national elections?

a lot	1
some	2
a little	3
none	4

58. Below you will find a list of the most important parties that have competed in, or been influential in, national elections within the last ten years. Indicate which one of these you, your father (or guardian), and your best friend *most* prefer. In case you consider none of these as preferable, indicate the one which you would prefer, in general.

	you	your father	your best friend
	1	2	3

[a list of the appropriate political parties and groups should be provided here]

59. If you had to make a choice among the following three things, which do you think is most important for this country?

political democracy	1
economic development	2
social and economic equality	3

60. What do you think about this country joining the Latin American Free Trade Association?

strongly favorable	1
favorable	2
opposed	3
strongly opposed	4

61. There is a lot of talk today about agrarian reform. How do you feel about it with respect to this country?

a) Are you for or against it?

for	1
against	2

b) If you are in favor of agrarian reform, which form of compensation to landowners do you consider adequate?

none	1
cash in full	2
cash and bonds	3
bonds	4
other (which?): _____	5

c) Assuming that agrarian reform is carried out, what type of land tenure do you favor?

small private plots	1
cooperative farms (one large farm owned by a number of families)	2
state-owned farms	3
other (which?): _____	4

62. What is your opinion concerning the Alliance for Progress as it affects *this* country? Would you say that it is:

very beneficial	1
moderately beneficial	2
has no effect on the country	3
somewhat harmful	4
very harmful	5

63. The Cuban Revolution has aroused a great deal of interest. Some people approve of the changes that have taken place there and others do not. Speaking generally about the form of government, the economy, and other changes, what is your opinion of the Cuban Revolution?

very favorable	1
favorable	2
unfavorable	3
very unfavorable	4

64. With which one of the following statements are you most in agreement?

the government should not intervene in the economic life of the country, but should leave economic affairs in the hands of private parties	1
the government should not own economic enterprises, but should control some aspects of their conduct	2
the government should control some aspects of the conduct of enterprises and industries, and should own the basic industries	3
the government should own all industries and control the total economic life of the country	4

65. With which of the following statements are you most in agreement?

foreign capital brings only benefits to the nation	1
foreign capital has more good than bad effects on the nation	2
foreign capital has more bad than good effects on the nation	3
foreign capital is harmful to the nation	4

66. Below are the names of some national and foreign statesmen and politicians. Indicate the degree to which you are favorable or unfavorable to the ideas and actions of these men.

	strongly approve	approve more than disapprove	disapprove more than approve	strongly disapprove
Fidel Castro	1	2	3	4
John F. Kennedy	1	2	3	4
Nasser	1	2	3	4
Khruschev	1	2	3	4

[four or five names of national leaders of different tendencies should be included with the above.]

67. Among the following fields of intellectual specialization, how would you classify the relative development of France, the United States, the Soviet Union, and [this country]. (In each field, mark an X for the country you consider the most developed.)

	Physics and Mathematics	Philosophy and History	Art and Literature	Social Sciences
[name of this country]				
France	_____	_____	_____	_____
U.S.S.R.	_____	_____	_____	_____
U.S.A.	_____	_____	_____	_____

68. Now we would like to ask your opinion about specific aspects of various countries. Draw a circle around the name of the country that you think is highest in each of the following characteristics

a) standard of living	USSR	USA	France	Red China	Sweden
b) economic development	USSR	USA	France	Red China	Sweden
c) individual liberty	USSR	USA	France	Red China	Sweden
d) equal distribution of wealth	USSR	USA	France	Red China	Sweden
e) all things considered, the country toward which you have the most favorable feelings	USSR	USA	France	Red China	Sweden

f) all things considered,
the country with the
greatest future   USSR   USA   France   Red China   Sweden

69. Now some questions about statements that people often hear. Many persons are totally in accord with these expressions, others are somewhat in agreement, and others totally disagree. Indicate your own response to each of the following:

	agree strongly	agree somewhat	disagree somewhat	disagree strongly
1) In order to be happy, one should conduct himself as others wish, even if this means keeping his own ideas to himself.	1	2	3	4
2) The son of a laboring man does not have a very good chance of entering the liberal professions.	1	2	3	4
3) The city is not a very friendly place; people can make friends only among others similar to themselves.	1	2	3	4
4) When choosing a job, one should arrange to work near his parents, even if this means losing a good opportunity.	1	2	3	4
5) People in a big city are cold and impersonal; it is hard to make new friends.	1	2	3	4
6) Making plans only brings unhappiness, because the plans are hard to fulfill.	1	2	3	4
7) The saints intercede and pray for us.	1	2	3	4
8) If you have a chance to hire an assistant in your work, it is always better to hire a relative instead of a stranger.	1	2	3	4

	agree strongly	agree somewhat	disagree somewhat	disagree strongly
9) With things as they are today, an intelligent person ought to think only about the present, without worrying about what is going to happen tomorrow.	1	2	3	4
10) Religion impedes the progress of the country.	1	2	3	4
11) It makes little difference if people choose one or another candidate for political office, because nothing or very little will change	1	2	3	4
12) Human nature being what it is, there will always be wars and conflicts.	1	2	3	4
13) There are two kinds of people in the world: the strong and the weak.	1	2	3	4
14) In spite of everything one hears, political corruption has decreased in [this country] in recent years.	1	2	3	4
15) The most important thing a child should learn is to obey his parents.	1	2	3	4
16) The only way to understand our present confused world is to listen to the leaders and other trustworthy persons.	1	2	3	4
17) All religions should have the same rights before the law.	1	2	3	4
18) In spite of everything the majority of politicians are still honest.	1	2	3	4
19) [Nationals, e.g., Mexicans] can do anything better than a foreigner.	1	2	3	4

	agree strongly	agree somewhat	disagree somewhat	disagree strongly
20) People should devote them- selves to their friends and comrades and not pardon their enemies and adversaries.	1	2	3	4
21) The health of a [National, e.g., Mexican] is of greater value than the life of a foreigner.	1	2	3	4
22) One should not talk to people who have ideas opposed to his own.	1	2	3	4
23) Every politician is a thief and the ones who are not will become thieves if they are elected to office.	1	2	3	4
24) A person can have confidence in people only if he knows them well.	1	2	3	4
25) A person can be both a Communist and a good Catholic.	1	2	3	4
26) Science and religion have basically opposed ways of seeing the world; these ways are inherently irreconcilable.	1	2	3	4
27) A rapid increase in economic development would require substantial limitations on individual freedom.	1	2	3	4
28) A rapid increase in economic development would require a much stronger, national government than we now have.	1	2	3	4
29) Differences in income among the various occupations should be reduced.	1	2	3	4

70. Many people say that some groups have too much power in this country and some have too little; but they often disagree on which groups have too much or too little. For each of the following groups of people in this country, please indicate whether they have more or less power than you think they should.

	have more power than they should	have less power than they should
The wealthy	1	2
Large corporations	1	2
Jews	1	2
Labor unions	1	2
The Church	1	2

71. Compared with most other students in the university, would you say that your general political position is:

much more left than most students	1
more left than most students	2
about the same as most students	3
more right than most students	4
much more right than most students	5

72. What is your religion? your father's? your mother's?

	yourself	father	mother
Baptist	1	1	1
Other Protestant sects	2	2	2
Jewish	3	3	3
Catholic, practicing	4	4	4
Catholic, but non-practicing	5	5	5
Spiritualist	6	6	6
Other	7	7	7
I have no religion, but I believe in God	8	8	8
Atheist or agnostic	9	9	9

73. Do you consider yourself:

very religious	1
moderately religious	2
slightly religious	3
not religious at all	4

74. How often do you attend church, temple, synagogue, etc.? and your father? and your mother?

	yourself	father	mother
never	1	1	1
almost never	2	2	2
once a year or more often, but less than once a month	3	3	3
once or twice a month	4	4	4
once a week	5	5	5
more than once a week	6	6	6

75. Would you say that your religious sentiments have changed since entering the university?

No, I am just as religious as before	1
I have never been religious	2
Now I am more religious	3
Now I am less religious	4

76. Concerning divorce, with which of the following statements do you most agree?

divorce should be permitted for anyone who wishes it	1
divorce should be allowed only in special cases	2
divorce should not be permitted to anyone	3

77. With regard to married women working outside the home, what is your opinion?

fully approve	1
more in favor than opposed	2
more opposed than favorable	3
fully opposed	4

78. In your own case, when you are married (or if you are already married) how important is it to you to remain faithful to your spouse?

very important	1
rather important	2
of little importance	3
not important	4

79. In your own case, would you say that it is difficult to remain faithful to your spouse (or that it will be difficult when you are married)?

very difficult	1
rather difficult	2
somewhat difficult	3
not difficult at all	4

80. If you were to enter a game between two teams which had already begun playing, (a soccer game, for example), in which of the following situations would you most prefer to play?

I would most like to play:

with a team which was ahead by a large margin	1
with a team which was ahead by a small margin	2
in a game in which both teams were tied	3
with a team which was behind by a small margin	4
with a team which was behind by a large margin	5

81. When you have a difficult problem of any kind to solve, do you prefer to solve it yourself, without the help of anyone else?

always	1
usually	2
rarely	3
never	4

82. In general, would you say that you are a person who is:

very happy	1
moderately happy	2
somewhat happy	3
unhappy	4

83. How much do you enjoy reading serious literature?

a great deal	1
a moderate amount	2
some, but not much	3
not at all	4

84. How much do you enjoy listening to classical music?

a great deal	1
a moderate amount	2
some, but not much	3
not at all	4

85. Do you ever think about the problems of the country, analyzing them and elaborating plans in your imagination to resolve them?

frequently	1
sometimes	2
seldom	3
never	4

86. Would you say that during your childhood and adolescence you were generally:

very happy	1
rather happy	2
rather unhappy	3
very unhappy	4

87. Have you ever found yourself daydreaming, imagining yourself in situations in which you played an important role?

frequently	1
fairly often	2
rarely	3
never	4

Now, some questions concerning your health during the past two years.

88. Have you been bothered by nausea or stomach pains?

frequently	1
fairly often	2
rarely	3
never	4

89. Have you experienced headaches?

frequently	1
fairly often	2
rarely	3
never	4

90. Have you had feelings of dizziness?

frequently	1
fairly often	2
rarely	3
never	4

Finally, some questions concerning your mental health. Answer these with respect to the last two years:

91. Have you had difficulties getting to sleep, either because you were thinking about something or for other reasons?

frequently	1
fairly often	2

rarely   3
never   4

92. Do you chew your fingernails?

frequently   1
fairly often   2
rarely   3
never   4

93. Do you have nightmares?

frequently   1
fairly often   2
rarely   3
never   4

94. Do you have feelings of fear or anxiety at night, during sleep?

frequently   1
fairly often   2
rarely   3
never   4

95. Do your palms sweat?

frequently   1
fairly often   2
rarely   3
never   4

96. Have you experienced cold perspiration?

frequently   1
fairly often   2
rarely   3
never   4

97. Have you felt depressed and sad?

frequently   1
fairly often   2
rarely   3
never   4

98. In general, how would you rate your mental health, and that of your father and mother?

	you	father	mother
excellent	1	2	3
good	1	2	3
average	1	2	3
poor	1	2	3
very poor	1	2	3

MANY THANKS FOR YOUR KIND COOPERATION. IS THERE ANYTHING YOU WOULD LIKE TO ADD? PLEASE WRITE ANY COMMENTS ON THE FOLLOWING PAGE.

Notes

1. UNIVERSITIES, UNIVERSITY REFORM, AND STUDENT POLITICS IN LATIN AMERICA: A HISTORICAL OVERVIEW

1. John Tate Lanning, *Academic Culture in the Spanish Colonies* (New York, Oxford University Press, 1940), pp. 14–38; C. H. Haring, *The Spanish Empire in America* (New York, Oxford University Press, 1947), pp. 229–232; and Hubert Herring, *A History of Latin America: From the Beginnings to the Present*, 2nd ed., rev. (New York, Alfred A. Knopf, 1965), pp. 209–211.

2. Lanning, *Academic Culture*, pp. 55–56, and Roberto Mac-Lean y Estenos, *La crisis universitaria en Hispano-América* (Mexico City, Biblioteca de Ensayos Sociológicos, Universidad Nacional, 1956), pp. 89–92.

3. Lanning, *Academic Culture*, pp. 61–74, and Haring, *The Spanish Empire*, pp. 231–233.

4. Lanning, *Academic Culture*, p. 64.

5. *Ibid.*, pp. 38–42, 61–89; Roland D. Hussey, "Traces of French Enlightenment in Colonial Hispanic America," in Arthur P. Whitaker, ed., *Latin America and the Enlightenment* (New York, Appleton-Century, 1942), pp. 33–42 (hereafter referred to as *Enlightenment*); John Tate Lanning, "The Reception of the Enlightenment in Latin America," in Whitaker, ed., *Enlightenment*, pp. 77–88; Alexander Marchant, "Aspects of the Enlightenment in Brazil," in Whitaker, ed., *Enlightenment*, pp. 109–115; Laurence Gale, *Education and Development in Latin America* (London, Routledge and Kegan Paul, 1969), pp. 65–67; and Harold R. W. Benjamin, *Higher Education in the American Republics* (New York, McGraw-Hill, 1965), p. 16.

6. Social Progress Trust Fund, *Socio-Economic Progress in Latin America*, Seventh Annual Report, 1967 (Washington, D.C., 1968), pp. 318, 323, 327, 328; Benjamin, *Higher Education in the American Republics*, pp. 16–31, 50.

7. J. Fred Rippy, *Latin America: A Modern History* (Ann Arbor, University of Michigan Press, 1958), pp. 302–305; Benjamin, *Higher Education in the American Republics*, pp. 30–31; and Valdemar Rodriguez, *National University of Mexico: Rebirth and Role of the Universitarios (1910–1957)*, (Ph.D. diss., University of Texas, 1958), pp. 1–8.

8. Social Progress Trust Fund, *Socio-Economic Progress*, pp. 318, 323, 327–328, 341; Benjamin, *Higher Education in the American Republics*, pp. 16–31; and Frank Bowles, *Access to Higher Education* (Paris, United Nations Educational, Scientific and Cultural Organization and the International Association of Universities, 1965), I, 113.

9. Gabriel del Mazo, "What Reform Means," in International Student Conference, *University Reform in Latin America: Analyses and Documents* (Leiden, Netherlands, 1959), p. 24. Gabriel del Mazo, a former student leader of the Reform Movement, has become the Movement's principal historian. Among his works on University Reform are: *El movimiento de la reforma universitaria en América Latina: Cinco conferencias* (Lima, Peru, Universidad Nacional Federico Villarreal, 1967); *La reforma universitaria y la universidad latino-americana* (Resistencia, Argentina, Universidad Nacional del Nordeste, 1957); *Reforma universitaria y cultura nacional* (Buenos Aires, Editorial Raigal, 1955); *Estudiantes y gobierno universitario* (Buenos Aires, Libreria "El Ateneo" Editorial, 1956).

10. Benjamin, *Higher Education in the American Republics*, pp. 15-16; Lanning, *Academic Culture*, pp. 39, 40, 49; Gale, *Education and Development*, pp. 66-67; Robert J. Havighurst, "Latin American and North American Higher Education," *Comparative Education Review*, 4 (February 1961), 175.

11. José Medina Echavarría, "A Sociologist's View," in José Medina Echavarría and Benjamin Higgins, eds., *Social Aspects of Development in Latin America* (Paris, UNESCO, 1963), II, 46-48, and Arthur Liebman, *The Politics of Puerto Rican University Students* (Austin, Texas, University of Texas Press, 1970), p. 9; Havighurst, "Latin American and North American Higher Education," p. 175.

12. Mark Van Aken, "The Militants: A Portrait of the Uruguayan Student Movement," mimeographed (1964), on deposit at the Center for International Affairs, Harvard University, Cambridge, Mass., chap. 2, pp. 16-29.

13. Van Aken, "The Militants," pp. 27-29, and Frank Bonilla and Myron Glazer, *Student Politics in Chile* (New York, Basic Books, 1970), p. 33 (hereafter referred to as *Chilean Students*).

14. Del Mazo, *La reforma universitaria y la universidad latino-americana*, pp. 12-14.

15. Richard J. Walter, *Student Politics in Argentina: The University Reform and Its Effects, 1918-1964* (New York, Basic Books, 1968), pp. 33-35, 40-51 (hereafter referred to as *Argentine Students*).

16. Del Mazo, *El movimiento de la reforma*, pp. 16-24, and Carlos Cossio, *La reforma universitaria* (Buenos Aires, Espasa-Calpe, 1927), pp. 119-173.

17. "Córdoba Manifesto" in International Student Conference, *University Reform in Latin America*, pp. 8-12.

18. Del Mazo, "What Reform Means," pp. 19-20.

19. Walter, *Argentine Students*, pp. 40-55.

20. Del Mazo, *El movimiento de la reforma*, pp. 18-24.

21. Del Mazo, "What Reform Means," pp. 21-24, and Del Mazo, *El movimiento de la reforma*, pp. 22-24.

22. Walter, *Argentine Students*, pp. 50-51.

23. Hubert Herring, *A History of Latin America* pp. 543-544, 590-591, 664-668, 702-706; Van Aken, "The Militants," chap. 2, pp. 31-35; Walter, *Argentine Students*, pp. 23-35; and Bonilla and Glazer, *Chilean Students*, pp. 25-33.

24. Gino Germani, "Social and Political Consequences of Mobility," in Neil J. Smelser and Seymour Martin Lipset, eds., *Social Structure and Mobility in Economic Development* (Chicago, Aldine, 1966), pp. 384-387.

25. *Ibid.*, p. 373.

26. Walter, *Argentine Students*, p. 27.

27. Bonilla and Glazer, *Chilean Students*, p. 38.

28. Victor Raul Haya de la Torre, "Latin America's Student Revolution," *The Living Age*, 331 (October 1926), 104–106; Harry Kantor, *The Ideology and Program of the Peruvian Aprista Movement* (New York, Octagon, 1966), pp. 7–10 (hereafter referred to as *Peruvian Aprista Movement*). Robert N. Schwartz, *Peru: Country in Search of a Nation* (Los Angeles, Inter-American, 1970), pp. 117–119; and James C. Carey, *Peru and the United States, 1900-1962* (Notre Dame, Indiana, University of Notre Dame Press, 1964), pp. 32–50.

29. Kantor, *Peruvian Aprista Movement*, pp. 10–11.

30. *Ibid.*, pp. 10–13, and Haya de la Torre, "Latin America's Student Revolution," pp. 105–106.

31. Jaime Suchlicki, *University Students and Revolution in Cuba, 1920-1968* (Coral Gables, Fla., University of Miami Press, 1969), pp. 19–37 (hereafter referred to as *Cuban Students*).

32. Quoted in John Duncan Powell, *Political Mobilization of the Venezuelan Peasant* (Cambridge, Mass., Harvard University Press, 1971), p. 29.

33. *Ibid.*, pp. 18–32; John D. Martz, "Venezuela's 'Generation of '28': The Genesis of Political Democracy," *Journal of Inter-American Studies*, 6 (January 1964), 17–20; and Daniel H. Levine, "Political Development in Venezuela: Conflict, Conciliation, and Exclusion," mimeographed (Ann Arbor, Mich., 1971), pp. 5–9.

34. Vernon Lee Fluharty, *Dance of the Millions: Military and the Social Revolution in Colombia, 1930-1956* (Pittsburgh, University of Pittsburgh Press, 1957), p. 191.

35. Robert H. Dix, *Colombia: The Political Dimensions of Change* (New Haven, Yale University Press, 1967), pp. 42–63, 77–91, 341–351; Kenneth N. Walker, "A Comparison of the University Reform Movements in Argentina and Colombia," in Seymour Martin Lipset, ed., *Student Politics* (New York, Basic Books, 1967), pp. 304–314; and Fluharty, *Dance of the Millions*, pp. 27–49, 183–191.

36. Kevin Lyonette, "Student Organizations in Latin America," *International Affairs*, 42 (October 1966), 657.

37. Del Mazo, "What Reform Means," p. 25; Leon Cortiñas Pelaez, "Autonomy and Student Co-Government in the University of Uruguay," *Comparative Education Review*, 7 (October 1963), 171.

38. Lyonette, "Student Organizations," 656–657; Kalman H. Silvert, "The University Student," in John J. Johnson, ed., *Continuity and Change in Latin America* (Stanford, Stanford University Press, 1964), pp. 221–224; and John H. Petersen, "Recent Research on Latin American University Students," *Latin American Research Review*, 5 (Spring 1970), 37.

39. Walter, *Argentine Students*, pp. 87–151, and Luigi Einaudi, "University Autonomy and Academic Freedom in Latin America," in The United States National Student Association, *Readings On: Latin American Student Movement and The Rise of the Latin American Left* (Philadelphia, 1965), pp. 4–5.

40. Suchlicki, *Cuban Students*, pp. 24–81.

41. Harrison, "Learning and Politics," pp. 330–333; S. Walter Washington, "The Political Activity of Latin American Students," in Robert D. Tomasek, ed., *Latin American Politics* (Garden City, Doubleday, 1966), p. 115.

42. Bonilla and Glazer, *Chilean Students*, p. 107.

43. Ted Goertzel, *Student Politics in Brazil* (Ph.D. diss., University of Oregon, 1969), p. 164 (hereafter referred to as *Brazilian Students*).

44. "Resolutions of the Third Latin American Student Congress," in International Student Conference, *University Reform in Latin America*, pp. 135–139.

45. Benjamin, *Higher Education in the American Republics*, pp. 52–55, 88–92, 111–118; Gale, *Education and Development*, pp. 77–79; Havighurst, "Latin American and North American Higher Education," pp. 178–179; Cortiñas Pelaez, "Autonomy and Student Co-Government in the University of Uruguay," pp. 169–172.

46. David Spencer, "The Impact of the Cuban Revolution on Latin American Student Politics," in David Spencer, ed., *Student Politics in Latin America* (Philadelphia, United States National Student Association, 1965), pp. 91–95.

47. Richard Gott, *Guerrilla Movements in Latin America* (London, Thomas Nelson, 1970), pp. 9–27, 357–366.

48. Spencer, "The Impact of the Cuban Revolution," p. 95.

49. Goertzel, *Brazilian Students*, pp. 158–242.

50. *Ibid.*, p. 184.

51. *New York Times*, December 13, 1970.

52. A Latin American Correspondent, "Coping with a Coup," in Bruce Douglas, ed., *Reflections on Protest: Student Presence in Political Conflict* (Richmond, Va., John Knox, 1967), pp. 111–119.

53. Institut International d'Etudes sur l'Education, *Bulletin*, June 23, 1971.

54. Robert Alexander, "Evolution of Student Politics in Latin America," in U.S. N. S. A., *Readings on: Latin American Student Movement*, p. 34, and Silvert, "The University Student," in Johnson, ed., *Continuity and Change*, pp. 225–226.

55. "Cordoba Manifesto," in *University Reform*, p. 10.

2. SOCIAL CHARACTERISTICS AND CAREER ORIENTATIONS OF CONTEMPORARY UNIVERSITY STUDENTS IN LATIN AMERICA

1. Social Progress Trust Fund, *Socio-Economic Progress in Latin America*, 7th Annual Report, 1967 (Washington, D.C., 1968), p. 370.

2. Arthur Liebman, "West European Student Politics," mimeographed (Cambridge, Mass., Center for International Affairs, Harvard University), p. 8.

3. Social Progress Trust Fund, *Socio-Economic Progress*, p. 411.

4. Organization of American States, *Provisional Report of the Conference on Education and Economic and Social Development in Latin America* (Washington, D.C., 1962), p. 23.

5. Social Progress Trust Fund, *Socio-Economic Progress in Latin America*, Fifth Annual Report, 1965 (Washington, D.C., 1966) p. 79. For some individual country data in the mid-1960s see Organization of American States, *América en Cifras*, 1967 (Washington, D.C., 1969), pp. 87–90.

6. United States Department of Health, Education and Welfare, Office of Education, *Digest of Educational Statistics, 1965* (Washington, D.C., Government Printing Office, 1966), p. 124.

7. Pan American Union, "Final Report of the Special Commission for Programming and Developing of Education, Science and Culture in Latin America," mimeographed (Washington, D.C., 1963), p. 33.

8. United Nations, Economic Commission for Latin America, *Human Resources of Central America, Panama and Mexico, 1950–1980, in Relation to Some Aspects for Economic Development*, prepared by L. J. Ducoff (New

York, 1960), p. 23, and Richard Jolly, "Education," in Dudley Seers, ed., *Cuba: The Economic and Social Revolution* (Chapel Hill, University of North Carolina Press, 1964), p. 170.

9. Oscar Vera, "The Educational Situation and Requirements in Latin America," in Egbert De Vries and José Medina Echavarría, eds., *Social Aspects of Economic Development in Latin America*, I (Paris, United Nations Educational, Scientific and Cultural Organization, 1963), p. 291, and OAS, *América en Cifras*, p. 87.

10. Morris A. Horowitz, "High Level Manpower in the Economic Development of Argentina," in Frederick Harbison and Charles A. Myers, eds., *Manpower and Education* (New York, McGraw-Hill, 1965), pp. 19–20.

11. Arthur Liebman, *The Politics of Puerto Rican University Students* (Austin, University of Texas Press, 1970), p. 73.

12. Quoted in Kalman Silvert, "The University Student," in John J. Johnson, ed., *Continuity and Change in Latin America* (Stanford, Stanford University Press, 1964), pp. 213–214.

13. Aldo Solari, "Secondary Education and the Development of Elites," in Seymour M. Lipset and Aldo Solari, eds., *Elites in Latin America* (New York, Oxford University Press, 1967), p. 462.

14. OAS, *Provisional Report*, p. 25.

15. U.S. Department of Health, Education and Welfare, Office of Education, *The Development of Education in Venezuela* (Washington, D.C., Government Printing Office, 1963), pp. 103–104.

16. Charles N. Myers, *Education and National Development in Mexico* (Princeton, Industrial Relations Section, Department of Economics, Princeton University, 1965), p. 55.

17. Frank Bowles, *Access to Higher Education* (Paris, UNESCO and the International Association of Universities, 1965), II, 38–39.

18. Melvin Tumin, *Social Class and Social Change in Puerto Rico* (Princeton, Princeton University Press, 1961), pp. 118–119.

19. Solari, "Secondary Education," p. 460.

20. OAS, *Provisional Report*, p. 29; Vera, "Educational Situation," p. 295, Social Progress Trust Fund, *Socio-Economic Progress*, 5th Annual Report, p. 80; Frank Bonilla, "Brazil," in James S. Coleman, ed., *Education and Political Development* (Princeton, Princeton University Press, 1965), p. 200.

21. Meyers, *Education*, pp. 53–54; Vera, "Educational Situation," p. 298; OAS, *Provisional Report*, pp. 21–24.

22. Social Progress Trust Fund, *Socio-Economic Progress*, 7th Annual Report, pp. 341, 376–393.

23. Universidad Nacional Autonoma de México, *Anuraio Estadístico, 1964,* (Mexico City, 1966), p. 198.

24. Universidad de Buenos Aires, *Censo de Alumnos, 1964*, (Buenos Aires, 1965), p. 3.

25. Liebman, *Puerto Rican Students*, p. 70.

26. A. H. Halsey, "The Changing Functions of Universities," in A. H. Halsey, Jean Floud, and C. Arnold Anderson, eds., *Education, Economy, and Society* (New York, Free Press, 1961), p. 457.

27. U.S. Bureau of the Census, *School Enrollment: October 1968 and 1967* (Washington, D.C., Government Printing Office, 1969), p. 57 (Current Population Reports, series P-20, no. 190).

28. U.S. Bureau of the Census, *Characteristics of Students and Their Colleges, October, 1966* (Washington, D.C., Government Printing Office, 1969), p. 2 (Current Population Reports, series P-20, no. 183).

29. UNAM, *Anuario Estadístico, 1964*, pp. 304–306.

30. Universidad de Buenos Aires, *Censo de Alumnos, 1964*, p. 79.

31. Jean Labbens, "Las universidades latinoamericanos y la movilidad social," in Aldo Solari, ed., *Estudiantes y política en America Latina* (Caracas, Monte Avila Editores, 1968), p. 124.

32. Liebman, *Puerto Rican Students*, pp. 79–80.

33. Liebman, "West European Student Politics," p. 15.

34. Aldo Solari, "Introducción," in Solari, ed., *Estudiantes*, p. 35.

35. Latin American Center, University of California, *Statistical Abstract of Latin America, 1965*, 9th ed. (Los Angeles, 1966), pp. 54–55.

36. Richard J. Walter, *Student Politics in Argentina: The University Reform and Its Effects, 1918-1964* (New York, Basic Books, 1968), pp. 132–133, 149, and Institut International d'Etudes sur l'Education, *Monthly Survey* (February 1970).

37. Jolly, "Education," pp. 257, 259.

38. Aldo Solari, "La universidad en transición en una sociedad estancada: El caso de Uruguay," in Solari, ed., *Estudiantes*, p. 164.

39. Luis Nieves Falcón, *Recruitment to Higher Education in Puerto Rico, 1940-1960* (San Juan, Editorial Universitaria, 1965), p. 83.

40. UNAM, *Anuario Estadístico*, pp. 304–306.

41. Universidad de Buenos Aires, *Censo de Alumnos*, p. 79.

42. Economic Commission for Latin America, "The Training of Human Resources in the Economic and Social Development of Latin America," *Economic Bulletin for Latin America*, 11 (October 1966), p. 22, and Vera, "Educational Situation," p. 303.

43. William Mangin, "Latin American Squatter Settlements: A Problem and a Solution," *Latin American Research Review*, 2 (Summer 1967), pp. 84–85.

44. Tumin, *Social Class*, p. 108.

45. Oscar Lewis, *Children of Sanchez* (New York, Vintage Books, 1961), p. 98.

46. OAS, *Provisional Report*, p. 24; Social Progress Trust Fund, *Socio-Economic Progress*, 5th Annual Report, p. 7.

47. Solari, "Secondary Education," pp. 462–464.

48. Christopher Jenks and David Riesman, *The Academic Revolution* (Garden City, Doubleday, 1968), p. 96.

49. Nieves Falcón, *Recruitment*, p. 83.

50. Social Progress Trust Fund, *Socio-Economic Progress*, 7th Annual Report, p. 324; Vera, "Educational Situation," p. 298.

51. Leila Sussman, "High School to University in Puerto Rico," mimeographed (San Juan, 1965), p. 85.

52. Frank Bowles, *Access to Higher Education*, I, 147–148.

53. Bowles, *Access to Higher Education*, II, 22.

54. Solari, "Secondary Education," pp. 474–476.

55. *Ibid.*, pp. 470–471.

56. Bowles, *Access to Higher Education*, p. 113.

57. Tumin, *Social Class*, p. 108

58. UNESCO, *Statistical Yearbook, 1965* (Paris, 1966), pp. 109–110.

59. UNESCO, *World Survey of Education, Higher Education*, (New York, 1966), IV, 1356.

60. Social Progress Trust Fund, *Socio-Economic Progress*, 7th Annual Report, p. 324, and Harold R. W. Benjamin, *Higher Education in the American Republics* (New York, McGraw-Hill, 1965), pp. 67, 69–70.

61. Bowles, *Access to Higher Education*, I, 147.

62. Bowles, *Access to Higher Education*, II, 30.

63. Bowles, *Access to Higher Education*, I, 150.

64. U.S. Department of Health, Education and Welfare, Office of Education, *The Current Situation in Latin American Education*, Bulletin 1963, 21 (Washington, D.C., Government Printing Office, 1962), p. 26, and Social Progress Trust Fund, *Socio-Economic Progress*, 7th Annual Report, pp. 321–323.

65. Bowles, *Access to Higher Education*, I, 144, 151; II, 35; and Timothy F. Harding, *The University, Politics and Development in Contemporary Latin America*, Latin American Research Program, Research Seminar Series No. 3, June 1968, University of California, Riverside, p. 8.

66. Ted Goertzel, *Student Politics in Brazil* (Ph.D. diss., University of Oregon, 1970), pp. 199–222.

67. *Ibid*, p. 203.

68. OAS, *Provisional Report*, p. 214.

69. Horowitz, "High Level Manpower," p. 6.

70. Reported in Social Progress Trust Fund, *Socio-Economic Progress*, 7th Annual Report, p. 349.

71. Robert F. Arnove, *The Impact of University Social Structure on Student Alienation: A Venezuelan Study* (Stanford, California, Stanford International Development Education Center, School of Education, Stanford University, 1970), p. 17.

72. Jolly, "Education," pp. 255–257.

73. Institut International d'Etudes sur l'Education, *Monthly Survey*, March 1970.

74. For the impact of United States' values on Puerto Rico see Liebman, *Puerto Rican Students*, pp. 15–18.

75. Daniel Goldrich, *Sons of the Elite* (Chicago, Rand McNally, 1966), pp. 12–26.

76. Seymour M. Lipset presents a different interpretation. He maintains that preindustrial values prevail in Uruguay partly because of the rural social structure that persists. Thus, the country is not yet achievement-oriented, and this partially accounts for the relatively small percentage of students selecting competence as the prime factor in future professional success ("Values, Education and Entrepreneurship," in Lipset and Solari, eds., *Elites in Latin America*, p. 9).

77. Mark J. Van Aken, "The Militants: A Portrait of the Uruguayan Student Movement," mimeographed (1964), on deposit at Center for International Affairs, Harvard University, Cambridge, Mass., chapters 8 and 12.

78. Unless specified otherwise, whenever social status is used as a variable pertaining to the survey data, it will indicate the employment of our social status scale. The component items for this scale include questions 3, 8, and 12 in the questionnaire (see Appendix B).

79. Horowitz, "High Level Manpower," pp. 12–13, and Lipset, "Values, Education and Entrepreneurship," pp. 13–14.

80. According to Merle Kling's analysis, political instability in Latin America in large part stems from the fact that the governmental structure relative to the business sector is more open, fluid, and accessible to individuals and strata without family connections. Thus, mobility aspirations and competitive drives are concentrated and fought out primarily within the governmental system. See Merle Kling, "Toward A Theory of Power and Political Instability in Latin America," in John H. Kautsky, ed., *Political Change in Underdeveloped Countries* (New York, John Wiley and Sons, 1962), p. 130.

81. U.S. Bureau of the Census, *Characteristics of Students*, p. 18; UNESCO, *World Survey of Education, Higher Education*, pp. 1355, 1356, 477, 480, 165, 166, 407, 518, 549, 614, 673, 867, 1056.

3. UNIVERSITY PROBLEMS AND STUDENTS' ATTITUDES TOWARD HIGHER EDUCATION

1. For the emphasis on the need for high-level manpower see Frederick Harbison and Charles A. Myers, *Education, Manpower, and Economic Growth* (New York, McGraw-Hill, 1964). For the emphasis on broad-based education see the work of Wilbert Moore including *"Learning" and the Creation of New Social Roles and Types*, Round-Table Conference on the Social Prerequisities of Industrialization, UNESCO House, Place de Fontenoy, Paris, 12–15 September 1961, Working Paper No. 1/7, p. 4. Also, Moore, "Requirements for Rapid Economic and Social Development: The Strategy of Fostering Performance and Responsibility" (unpublished paper, sponsored by UNESCO), p. 8.

2. The essence of this type of period has been very well captured by Rollo May. "When a culture is caught in the profound convulsions of a transitional period, the individuals in the society understandably suffer spiritual and emotional upheaval; and finding that the accepted mores and ways of thought no longer yield security, they tend either to sink into Dogmatism and conformism, giving up awareness, or are forced to strive for a heightened self-consciousness by which to become aware of their existence with new conviction and on new bases . . . this approach is understandably more apt to appear in ages of transition, when one age is dying and the new one not yet born, and the individual is either homeless and lost or achieves a new self-consciousness (*Existence* [New York, Basic Books, 1958], p. 17).

3. H. Moyses Nussensveig, "Migration of Scientists from Latin America," *Science*, 1965 (September 26, 1969), pp. 1328–1329.

4. Harold R. W. Benjamin, *Higher Education in the American Republics* (New York, McGraw-Hill, 1965), pp. 59–63; Darcy Ribeiro, "Universities and Social Development," in Seymour Martin Lipset and Aldo E. Solari, eds., *Elites in Latin America* (New York, Oxford University Press, 1967), pp. 363–366; and Gino Germani, "O Profesor e a Cátedra," *América Latina*, 13 (January–March, 1970), 83–87.

5. Laurence Gale, *Education and Development in Latin America* (London, Routledge and Kegan Paul, 1969), pp. 78–79; Germani, "O Profesor," p. 87.

6. I. H. Simpson, "Patterns of Socialization into Professions: The Case of the Student Nurses," Paper presented at the Meetings of the American Sociological Association, New York, Aug. 30, 1960.

7. For a discussion of such patterns in Colombian education, see R. Morse, R. Wickham, A. Wolf, "Education in Colombia," mimeographed Ford Founda-

tion Mission to Colombia, June, 1960. Similar findings in Mexico and Colombia are reported by E. Wight Bakke, "Students on the March: The Cases of Mexico and Colombia," *Sociology of Education*, 37 (Spring, 1964). See also Gale, *Education and Development*, pp. 84–85.

8. Rudolph P. Atcon, *The Latin American University* (Bogotá, ECO Revista de la Cultura Occidente, 1966), pp. 27, 87–88.

9. Frank Bonilla and Myron Glazer, *Student Politics in Chile* (New York, Basic Books, 1970), pp. 269–271.

10. David Nasatir, "Education and Social Change: The Argentine Case," *Sociology of Education*, 39 (Spring 1966), 169–173.

11. Rose K. Goldsen, Morris Rosenberg, Robin Williams, Jr., and Edward Suchman, *What College Students Think* (Princeton, Van Nostrand, 1960), p. 103.

12. Kalman H. Silvert, *The Conflict Society: Reaction and Revolution in Latin America* (New Orleans, Tulane University Press, 1961), pp. 64–65.

13. Bakke, "Students on the March," p. 214.

14. Ribeiro, "Universities and Social Development," pp. 359–360.

15. For further discussion of this point see Myron Glazer, "Chile," in Donald K. Emmerson, ed., *Students and Politics in Developing Countries* (New York, Praeger, 1968), pp. 294–303.

16. Glaucio A. D. Soares, "Intellectual Identity and Political Ideology Among University Students," in Lipset and Solari, eds., *Elites in Latin America*, p. 433.

17. Kalman H. Silvert, "The University Student," in John J. Johnson, ed., *Continuity and Change in Latin America* (Stanford, Stanford University Press, 1964), p. 219.

18. Germani, "O Profesor," 83–101; Gale, *Education and Development*, pp. 66, 71–72, 76, 84–85, 154–155; J. Fred Rippy, *Latin America: A Modern History* (Ann Arbor, University of Michigan Press, 1958), pp. 303–305; Valdemar Rodriguez, *National University of Mexico: Rebirth and Role of the Universitarios (1910–1957)* (Ph.D. diss., University of Texas, 1958), pp. 1–6; Ismael Rodriguez Bou, "Significant Factors in the Development of Education in Puerto Rico," Selected Backround Studies Prepared for the United States–Puerto Rico Commission on the Status of Puerto Rico, *Status of Puerto Rico* (Washington, D.C., 1966), pp. 239–247; and James H. Street, "Social Science Research in Paraguay: Current Status and Future Opportunities," in Richard N. Adams, ed., *Responsibilities of the Foreign Scholar to the Local Scholarly Community* (Washington, D.C., The Council on Educational Cooperation with Latin America, Education and World Affairs and Latin American Studies Association, 1969), pp. 97–98.

19. Silvert, "University Student," pp. 208, 214; Gale, *Education and Development*, p. 84; Jean Labbens, "Tradition et modernisme: L'Université au Chili," *América Latina*, 13 (January-March, 1970), p. 80; Jorge Graciarena, "La deserción y el retraso en los estudios universitarios en Uruguay," *América Latina,* 13 (January-March, 1970), p. 50; and Rodriguez Bou, "Education in Puerto Rico," p. 302.

20. R. Ames Cobián, "Cooperación Popular Universitaria and the Transformation of the University," in David Spencer, ed., *Student Politics in Latin America* (Philadelphia, United States National Student Association, 1965), p. 46.

21. Gale, *Education and Development*, 84–85; Charles N. Myers, *U.S. University Activity Abroad: Implications of the Mexican Case* (New York, Educa-

tion and World Affairs, 1968), pp. 11–14; and Street, "Social Science Research in Paraguay," pp. 95, 97–98.

22. David Nasatir, "Student Action in Latin America," *Trans-Action*, 2 (March-April, 1965), p. 10.

23. Bonilla and Glazer, *Chilean Students*, p. 245.

24. William K. Knowles, "Manpower and Education in Puerto Rico," in Harbison and Myers, eds. *Manpower and Education*, p. 132.

25. Gale, *Education and Development*, pp. 70–73; H. E. Enarson, "University Education in Central America," *Journal of Higher Education*, 34 (April 1963), p. 202; Robert F. Arnove, *The Impact of University Social Structure on Student Alienation: A Venezuelan Study* (Stanford, Stanford International Development Center, School of Education, Stanford University, 1970), pp. 17–19; and Labbens, "Tradition et modernisme," 66–79.

26. Bonilla and Glazer, *Chilean Students*, pp. 207–286, 301–312.

27. "The Brazilian Universities Under the Castelo Branco Regime," *Minerva*, 3 (Summer 1965), 58.

28. Quoted in *A Report to the American Community on the Present Argentine University Situation*, Special Publication of the Latin American Studies Association (Austin, Texas, 1967), p. 37.

29. Domingo M. Rivarola, "Universidad y estudiantes en una sociedad tradicional," *Aportes*, 12 (April 1969), 53–58, 62–66.

30. Richard J. Walter, *Student Politics in Argentina* (New York, Basic Books, 1968), pp. 135–138.

31. "Suspension of University Autonomy," *Minerva*, 5 (Summer 1966), 97; and interview by Arthur Liebman with eminent former Argentine professor, December 18, 1970.

32. "The Brazilian Universities," 555–558; Institut International d'Etudes sur l'Education, *Monthly Survey*, April 1970. For an insightful account of the Brazilian universities under a military regime from 1964 to 1968, see Ted Goertzel, *Student Politics in Brazil* (Ph.D. diss., University of Oregon, 1970), pp. 158–242.

33. Benjamin, *Higher Education*, pp. 63–66; Gale, *Education and Development*, p. 86.

34. Germani, "O Profesor," p. 97; Union de Universidades de América, *Censo Universitario Latinoamericano, 1962-1965* (Mexico City, 1967), pp. 35–36, 281, 616, 651.

35. Gale, *Education and Development*, p. 86; Germani, "O Profesor," 93–94; and Goertzel, p. 211.

36. Bakke, "Students on the March," p. 216.

37. Germani, "O Profesor," pp. 88–93.

38. Gale, *Education and Development*, pp. 86–87; G. H. Waggoner, "Problems in the Professionalization of the University Teaching Career in Central America," *Journal of Inter-American Studies*, 8 (April 1966), 193–213.

39. Germani, "O Profesor," pp. 83–101.

40. J. P. Harrison, "The Confrontation with the Political University," in Spencer, ed., *Student Politics in Latin America*, p. 34.

41. We are indebted to Dr. Orlando Albórnoz for this observation.

42. Germani, "O Profesor," p. 91.

43. Bonilla and Glazer, *Chilean Students*, p. 244. For an interesting discussion of the importance of professors in reducing student alienation, see Arnove, *Venezuelan Students*, pp. 57–69.

44. The principle discussions of the relationship between student activism and the quality of higher education in Latin America include: Atcon, *The Latin American University*, pp. 82–91; Orlando Albórnoz, "Academic Freedom and Higher Education in Latin America," in Seymour Martin Lipset, ed., *Student Politics* (New York, Basic Books, 1967), pp. 283–292; Luigi Einaudi, "University Autonomy and Academic Freedom in Latin America," *Law and Contemporary Problems*, 28 (Summer 1963), 636–646; Timothy F. Harding, *The University, Politics, and Development in Contemporary Latin America* (Riverside, California, Research Seminar Series No. 3, Latin American Research Program, University of California at Riverside, 1968), pp. 1–32; John P. Harrison, "The Confrontation with the Political University," *Annals of the American Academy of Political and Social Sciences*, 334 (March 1961), 74–83; and Alistair Hennessy, "University Students in National Politics," in Claudio Veliz, ed., *The Politics of Conformity in Latin America* (New York, Oxford University Press, 1967), pp. 119–157.

45. See William S. Stokes, "Violence as a Power Factor in Latin American Politics," in Robert D. Tomasek, ed., *Latin American Politics: 24 Studies of the Contemporary Scene* (Garden City, Anchor, 1966), pp. 223–252, and D. P. Bwy, "Political Instability in Latin America: The Cross-Cultural Test of A Causal Model," *Latin American Research Review*, 3 (Spring 1968), 17–66.

46. The negative case has been most clearly stated by Atcon, *The Latin American University*, pp. 82–91; Albórnoz, "Academic Freedom and Higher Education in Latin America," pp. 283–292; and Harrison, "The Confrontation with the Political University," 74–83.

47. John Tate Lanning contends that the students' right to participate in the selection of professors was withdrawn from them in the colonial era because "Professors were . . . prone to succumb to the temptation to popularize and cater to the student's plebian tastes" (John Tate Lanning, *Academic Culture in the Spanish Colonies* [New York, Oxford University Press, 1940] , p. 56). In the present time Orlando Albórnoz cites two examples in which student power has had a distinctly negative impact on the Latin American universities: "In one case . . . the student members of a special body which awarded scholarships did so only to those students who agreed to 'kick back' part of the scholarship stipend to student political leaders." In the other case, that of a Peruvian university, he quotes from the *The* [London] *Economist* (January 29, 1966, p. 405): "power granted to students has led to a system of bribery, both with money and with high marks, by faculty members. 'I am now correcting exam papers,' said one Cuzco professor," and at least half of these poor bastards deserve to fail. They don't know anything and they don't come to class. But if I failed them they would fire me. Believe me, I take a great risk in flunking 10 per cent of my students which few other professors would dare to do.' " Albórnoz, "Academic Freedom and Higher Education in Latin America," pp. 288–289.

48. Frank Bonilla's critique of Brazilian higher education in the early 1960s was incisive in regard to this issue. See Frank Bonilla, "Brazil," in James·S. Coleman, ed., *Education and Political Development* (Princeton, Princeton University Press, 1965), p. 204. A highly personalized account bears testimony to Bonilla's observations on the relationships among students and professors; see An Academic Missionary, "On Being 'Academic' Abroad," *AAUP Bulletin*, 52 (September 1966), 334–340.

49. Arthur P. Whitaker, *The United States and Argentina* (Cambridge, Mass., Harvard University Press, 1954), p. 74.

50. Bonilla and Glazer, *Chilean Students*, p. 94.

51. *Ibid.*, pp. 301–312.

52. *Ibid.*, pp. 260–286; Goertzel, *Brazilian Students*, p. 24?; and Arnove, *Venezuelan Students*, pp. 129–171.

53. Camilo Torres, "The Crisis in the University," in John Gerassi, ed., *Revolutionary Priest* (New York, Vintage Books, 1971), pp. 158–160.

54. Interview with eminent former Latin American professor by Arthur Liebman, December 18, 1971; Bonilla and Glazer, *Chilean Students*, pp. 301–312.

55. Quoted in Leon Cortiñas Pelaez, "Autonomy and Student Co-Government in the University of Uruguay," *Comparative Education Review*, 7 (October 1963), 171.

4. FAMILY BACKGROUND, UNIVERSITY EXPERIENCE, AND STUDENT POLITICS

1. John H. Petersen, "Recent Research on Latin American Students," *Latin American Research Review*, 5 (Spring 1970), 51.

2. Information on the formal structure of university government in Latin American universities may be found in chapter 1 and in Harold R. W. Benjamin, *Higher Education in the American Republics* (New York, McGraw-Hill, 1965). For Colombia, see pp. 90–92; for Mexico, pp. 117–118; for Uruguay and Paraguay, pp. 52–56.

3. Aldo Solari, "La universidad en transición en una sociedad estancada: El caso del Uruguay," *Aportes*, 2 (October 1966), 5.

4. The significance of politics was clear in our study. Panamanian students refused to answer any political questions. For a discussion of the play of politics in the selection of rectors, or presidents, of Latin American universities, which may account in part for the frequent demand for their resignation by student political activists, see Rudolph P. Atcon, *The Latin American University* (Bogota, Ediciones de Eco, 1966), pp. 46–47.

5. See chapter 6, this volume, for extensive discussion of Puerto Rican students and the developments that have occurred since the survey data were collected. Also, for a critical analysis of the University of Puerto Rico, including a discussion of the restriction on political activities imposed following the 1948 student strike, see Arthur Liebman, *Politics of Puerto Rican University Students* (Austin, University of Texas Press, 1970).

6. Karl M. Schmitt and David D. Burks, *Evolution or Chaos: Dynamics of Latin American Government and Politics* (New York, Praeger, 1963), pp. 180–181.

7. See Robert W. Anderson, *Party Politics in Puerto Rico* (Stanford, Stanford University Press, 1965), pp. 18–31, for a discussion of constitutional and legal issues concerning parties and electoral procedures in Puerto Rico.

8. See Andrew H. Whiteford, *Two Cities of Latin America* (New York, Doubleday Anchor, 1964), for a description of Popayán, the city in which the University of Cauca is situated.

9. Editorial, "Revista de la Universidad Libre," *Epoca*, 4 (May-June, 1953), 1.

10. For a discussion of structural features associated with the prevalence of part-time teaching in Latin American universities, see chapter 3 of this volume.

11. See Russell H. Fitzgibbon and Kenneth F. Johnson, "Measurement of Latin

American Political Change," in Robert D. Tomasek, ed., *Latin American Politics* (Garden City, Anchor, 1966), pp. 4-22.

12. Schmitt and Burks, *Evolution or Chaos*, pp. 181-185. For a student view, see Miguelangel Ferrara, "University Reform in Paraguay," in International Student Conference, *University Reform in Latin America*, pp. 131-134. For a comprehensive analysis of the current student political situation in Paraguay, see Domingo M. Rivarola, "Universidad y estudiantes en una sociedad tradicional," *Aportes*, 12 (April 1969), 47-84.

13. James H. Street, "Social Science Research in Paraguay: Current Status and Future Opportunities," in Richard N. Adams, ed., *Responsibilities of the Foreign Scholar to the Local Scholarly Community: Studies of U.S. Research in Guatemala, Chile, and Paraguay* (Washington, D.C., The Council on Educational Cooperation with Latin America, Education and World Affairs and the Latin American Studies Association, 1969), pp. 97-99.

14. See Philip B. Taylor, Jr., *Government and Politics of Uruguay*, Tulane Studies in Political Science, vol. 7 (New Orleans, Tulane University, 1960); and Philip B. Taylor, Jr., "Uruguay's Dysfunctional Political System," in Tomasek, ed., *Latin American Politics*, pp. 514-542.

15. For a classic case study of the impact of the liberal ideology of professors upon students in a small residential liberal arts college, see Theodore M. Newcomb, *Personality and Social Change: Attitude Formation in a Student Community* (New York, Holt, Rinehart and Winston, 1957).

16. To simplify the presentation of findings, scales composed of combined questions are used in most instances. The original, nine-category scales have been combined into three categories. For example, the items for all scales were originally coded into three scores, then the mean scores for all the items in the scale were computed, and finally the means were converted into coded means, ranging from zero to nine. Instead of examining the pattern of responses in terms of coded means, we put these mean scores into three categories, as follows: 0-3 = low (or high); 4-6 = intermediate; 7-9 = high (or low). This combining tends to reduce some of the variation in the response patterns, but it also simplifies the analysis and permits focus on the upper or lower thirds of the scale, thus avoiding the necessity of interpreting small variations along the full range of nine scale scores.

For the benefit of the reader we have provided correlation of these scales in each country. These correlations provide insight into the interrelation between political attitude and behavior. As the accompanying table reveals, student and national political activity are relatively highly correlated in each country, ranging from a correlation of 0.359 in Uruguay to 0.557 in Puerto Rico. The scales of political ideology and student political involvement also show rather high correlations, ranging from 0.250 in Paraguay to 0.514 in Colombia. (A positive correlation here means that "leftism" and "activism" go together.) The correlations between national political involvement and political ideology are somewhat lower, ranging from 0.313 in Paraguay to 0.391 in Colombia. The scale of political normlessness, however, reveals rather low correlations with all of the other measures. It is most highly correlated with the scale of political ideology, revealing that leftists tend to believe that politicians are corrupt and that elections do not change things, but this correlation exceeds the 0.100 level only in Colombia, Puerto Rico, and Uruguay. (It has a low negative correlation with national political involvement in Mexico, Uruguay, and Paraguay, and with

Intercorrelation of political orientation scales by country[a]

Scale title	Student political involvement	Political ideology	National political involvement
Colombia			
Political ideology	0.514		
National political involvement	.531	0.391	
Political normlessness	.134	.349	0.006
Puerto Rico			
Political ideology	.387		
National political involvement	.557	.353	
Political normlessness	.070	.231	.077
Mexico			
Political ideology	.297		
National political involvement	.415	.356	
Political normlessness	.009	.071	−.090
Uruguay			
Political ideology	.318		
National political involvement	.359	.328	
Political normlessness	.044	.173	−.098
Paraguay			
Political ideology	.250		
National political involvement	.495	.313	
Political normlessness	−.121	.090	−.206

[a]The values in the table are product-moment correlation coefficients.

student political involvement in Paraguay.) Political normlessness, then, does not appear to be closely linked to the active-radical syndrome revealed by the other scale correlations and is presumably related to somewhat different factors from political activism and ideology.

The following scales were examined in this analysis:
(a) Political Normlessness − the component items include the following questions from Appendix B: 70 (11), 70 (18), 70 (23);
(b) Left/Right Scale − the component items include the following questions from Appendix B: 63, 64, 65, 66, 67, 71, 72;
(c) Student Political Involvement Scale − the component items include the following questions from Appendix B: 44 (student politics of his school), 44 (general student politics), 51, 54, 55 (b), 57;

(d) National Political Involvement – the component items include the following questions from Appendix B: 44 (national politics), 44 (international politics), 53, 55 (a), 58, 88.

17. Gabriel A. Almond and Sidney Verba, *The Civic Culture* (Princeton, Princeton University Press, 1963), pp. 387–401. A study of Brazilian students which compared males and females with respect to political orientations also found no significant differences between the sexes. Ted Goertzel, "Student Politics in Brazil" (Ph.D. diss., University of Oregon, 1970), p. 130.

18. For component items of social status scale refer to note 78, chapter 2.

19. "Political office, from the presidency on down, is sought for the power it brings, chiefly through the opportunities to bestow patronage. Since the Colorado party is presently in power, it is expected that the economic opportunities that arise will go to Colorados rather than to Liberals," (Frederick Hicks, "Politics, Power and the Role of the Village Priest in Paraguay," *Journal of Inter-American Studies*, 9 [April 1967], 275).

20. See John Martz, *Colombia: A Contemporary Political Survey* (Chapel Hill, University of North Carolina Press, 1962); W. O. Galbraith, *Colombia: A General Survey*, 2nd ed. (London, Royal Institute of International Affairs, 1966), pp. 45–48; J. Lloyd Mecham, *Church and State in Latin America*, rev. ed. (Chapel Hill, University of North Carolina Press, 1966), pp. 115–138.

21. See Anderson, *Party Politics in Puerto Rico*, especially chapter 11, pp. 219–237, for a discussion of the character and formation of Puerto Rican parties. Also, with respect to Puerto Rico, see Henry Wells, *The Modernization of Puerto Rico* (Cambridge, Mass., Harvard University Press, 1969), pp. 267–292. See Hicks, "Politics, Power," p. 275, for a discussion of the lack of religious issues in the formation of the traditional Liberal and Colorado parties in Paraguay.

22. For a discussion of factors which tend to maintain or weaken family political traditions across the generations, see Seymour Martin Lipset, *Political Man* (New York, Doubleday Anchor, 1963), pp. 279–286; and Seymour Martin Lipset and Reinhard Bendix, *Social Mobility in Industrial Society* (Berkeley, University of California Press, 1959), pp. 66–70. Peter Bachrach, "Actitud de los estudiantes hacia autoridad," *Revista de ciencias sociales*, 1 (June 1957), 321–344, presents data showing father-student party preference patterns similar to our own for the University of Puerto Rico, in 1956.

23. Seymour Martin Lipset, "University Students and Politics in Underdeveloped Countries," in Seymour Martin Lipset, ed., *Student Politics* (New York, Basic Books, 1967), pp. 13–15, discusses the tendency for the more educated in the underdeveloped societies to be especially concerned with modernization, leading to a disproportionate support among them for parties of the left.

24. Kalman H. Silvert is a major proponent of the idea of generational continuity; Kalman H. Silvert, "The Student," in John J. Johnson, ed., *Continuity and Change in Latin America* (Stanford, Stanford University Press, 1964), p. 225.

25. The Christian Democratic parties which are relatively small in most Latin American societies except Chile are interesting in this respect. They have attempted to provide a Catholic alternative to Marxism, seeking the realization of social and economic justice and political democracy without recourse to the violent revolution or radical secularization of society proposed by some Marxist parties. Although few students reported that their fathers supported these parties, the data suggest that this type of party had strong holding and recruiting

power among Uruguayan and Paraguayan students. The number of cases studied was too small to be conclusive, but the data suggest that, at least among university students, the party's blend of radical ideology guided by Catholic doctrines of social justice offers serious competition to other parties in Latin American societies faced with severe problems of economic, social, and political development. For a disucssion of the relationship between the national Christian Democratic parties and their student affiliates, see Alistair Hennessy, "University Students in National Politics," in Claudio Veliz, ed., *The Politics of Conformity in Latin America* (London, Oxford University Press, 1967), pp. 145–149.

26. On the sensitivity of students to the idea of nationality in countries which have been "in a state of political, economic or cultural dependency," see Edward Shils, "The Intellectuals and the Powers," *Comparative Studies in Society and History*, 1 (October 1958), 13.

27. A full examination would require a longitudinal study of students which would permit analysis of socializing experiences within the family and other contexts, up to and including university experiences. However, our study is taken at only one point in time, and we must extrapolate from our findings the impact of preuniversity experiences, since our measurements were taken after any modifications due to university experience had occurred. Although our conclusions will necessarily be tentative, some of the findings are sufficiently compelling and consistent to suggest that our inferences may be correct.

28. Robert E. Scott, *Mexican Government in Transition*, rev. ed. (Urbana, University of Illinois Press, 1964), pp. 163–172; see Chapter 6, this volume, for extensive discussion of Mexican politics.

29. See Chapter 6, this volume. Also, for a discussion of political democracy in Mexico, see L. Vincent Padgett, *The Mexican Political System* (Boston, Houghton Mifflin, 1966), pp. 47–86, and "Mexico's One-Party System: A Reevaluation," *American Political Science Review*, 51 (June 1957), 995–1007; Philip B. Taylor, Jr., "The Mexican Elections of 1958: Affirmation of Authoritarianism?" *Western Political Quarterly*, 13 (September 1960), 722–744; Scott, *Mexican Government*, chapter 9, pp. 294–306. Citizen attitudes toward government are discussed in Almond and Verba, *Civic Culture*, pp. 414–428.

30. This pattern appears to be changing in the United States and Canada, with increasing demands for student participation in major decisions and with favorable response to these demands in some colleges and universities.

31. The most comprehensive treatment of the Reform movement in Argentina is Richard J. Walter, *Student Politics in Argentina* (New York, Basic Books, 1968).

32. For an analysis of the important political role of secondary students in Venezuela and the link between secondary and university student politics, see Orlando Albórnoz, "Activismo político estudiantil en Venezuela," *Aportes*, 5 (July 1967), 10–41.

33. For an analysis of the organization and activities of the proindependence (FUPI) student organization at the University of Puerto Rico, see Arthur Liebman, *The Politics of Puerto Rican University Students* (Austin, University of Texas Press, 1970), pp. 141–167.

34. See Benjamin, *Higher Education* for descriptions of academic programs and their organization in Latin American universities.

35. For a summary of the results of several studies in underdeveloped societies

concerning the relations between academic field and political orientation, see Lipset, "University Students and Politics in Underdeveloped Countries," pp. 18, 45–46, n. 52. See also Myron Glazer, "The Professional and Political Attitudes of Chilean Students," in Lipset, ed., *Student Politics*, pp. 332–356; and Metta Spencer, "Professional, Scientific and Intellectual Students in India," in Lipset, ed., *Student Politics*, pp. 357–371.

36. We would like to thank Mr. Jorge I. Domínguez for making available the paper from which this data is taken and for permission to quote from it.

37. Rivarola, "Universidad y estudiantes en una sociedad tradicional," 65; and Frank Bonilla and Myron Glazer, *Student Politics in Chile* (New York, Basic Books, 1970), pp. 237–238.

38. Morris Rosenberg, *Occupations and Values* (Glencoe, Ill., Free Press, 1957), pp. 21–22, 81–83.

5. CONSERVATIVE STUDENTS

1. Seymour M. Lipset, Kalman Silvert, and Glaucio A. D. Soares are among the few who have placed student politics in Latin America in proper perspective. See Seymour M. Lipset and Philip G. Altbach, "Student Politics and Higher Education," in Seymour M. Lipset, ed., *Student Politics* (New York, Basic Books, 1967), pp. 199–252; Kalman Silvert, "The University Student," in John Johnson, ed., *Continuity and Change in Latin America* (Stanford, Stanford University Press, 1964), pp. 206–226; and Glaucio A. D. Soares, "The Active Few: Student Ideology and Participation in the Developing Countries," in Lipset, ed., *Student Politics*, pp. 124–147.

2. Unless otherwise specified, the empirical data upon which this chapter is based come from student surveys of ten universities in five countries, Uruguay, Paraguay, Colombia, Mexico, and Puerto Rico, conducted in 1964 and 1965. The Panamanian students were not included because they refused to answer any questions dealing with politics.

3. There has been an increase in student political activism in the United States from 1965 to the present, but overall the percentage increase has not been great. In June 1969 the Gallup poll estimated that 28 percent of American students had participated in demonstrations.

4. The most recent and most extensive discussion of the relationship between the government and student politics in Paraguay is Domingo M. Rivarola, "Universidad y estudiantes en una sociedad tradicional, *Aportes*, 12 (April 1969), 47–84. For interesting general discussions of Paraguay and the oppressive nature of the Stroessner regime, see John Gerassi, *The Great Fear in Latin America* (New York, Collier, 1965), pp. 121–127, and John Gunther, *Inside South America* (New York, Harper and Row, 1967), pp. 238–256.

5. See note 18 in chapter 4 for the component items of the left/right ideology scale.

6. Jeanne H. Block, Norma Haan, and M. Brewster Smith, "Activism and Apathy in Contemporary Adolescents," in James F. Adams, ed., *Understanding Adolescents: Current Developments in Adolescent Psychology* (Boston, Allyn and Bacon, 1968), p. 200.

7. Seymour M. Lipset, "The Activists: A Profile," *The Public Interest*, 13 (Fall 1968), 45.

8. Alistair Hennessy, "University Students in National Politics," in Claudio

Veliz, ed., *The Politics of Conformity in Latin America* (New York, Oxford University Press, 1967), p. 135.

9. See R. McKenzie and Allan Silver, *Angels in Marble: Working Class Conservatives in Urban England* (Chicago, University of Chicago Press, 1968) and Seymour M. Lipset, "Class Politics and Religion in Modern Society: The Dilemma of the Conservatives," in Seymour M. Lipset, ed., *Revolution and Counter-Revolution* (New York, Basic Books, 1968), pp. 160–163.

10. Soares, "The Active Few," pp. 124–143.

11. See note 16 in chapter 4 for component items of the scale of student political involvement.

12. Soares, "The Active Few," pp. 136–138.

13. Hennessy, "University Students," p. 135.

14. Seymour M. Lipset, "American Student Activism in Comparative Perspective," Seminar on Manpower Policy and Program, U.S. Dept. of Labor, May 16, 1968, pp. 28–29.

15. Arthur Liebman, *The Politics of Puerto Rican University Students* (Austin, University of Texas Press, 1970), p. 285; and Center for Intercultural Documentation, Mexico, *Movimiento*, Dossier No. 14 (Cuernavaca, Mexico: CIDOC, 1967), pp. 14–43.

16. *Ibid.*, p. 41.

17. Seymour M. Lipset, "University Students and Politics in Underdeveloped Countries," in Lipset, ed., *Student Politics*, pp. 16–17.

18. "The Cordoba Manifesto," in David Spencer, ed., *Student Politics in Latin America* (Philadelphia, U.S. National Student Association, 1965), p. 22.

19. N. B. Lyle and R. A. Calman, eds., *Statistical Abstract of Latin America, 1965* (Los Angeles, Latin American Center of the University of California, Los Angeles, 1966); and B. M. Russet, H. R. Alker, K. W. Deutsch, and H. D. Lasswell, *World Handbook of Political and Social Indicators* (New Haven, Yale University Press, 1964).

20. See Liebman, *Puerto Rican Students*, pp. 15–45. See also chapter 6, in this volume for further and more updated comments on the Puerto Rican students.

21. Philip B. Taylor, Jr., *Government and Politics in Uruguay*, Tulane Studies in Political Science, vol. 7 (New Orleans, Tulane University, 1960), pp. 43–68, 107–130, 151–159; Philip B. Taylor, Jr., "Uruguay's Dysfunctional Political System," in Robert D. Tomasek, ed., *Latin American Politics: 24 Studies of the Contemporary Scene* (Garden City, Anchor, 1966), pp. 514–542; Institute for the Comparative Study of Political Systems, *Uruguay: Election Factbook* (Washington, D.C., 1966), pp. 3–10, 15, 31–36; and Eduardo Galeano, "Uruguay: Promise and Betrayal," in James Petras and Maurice Zeitlin, eds., *Latin America: Reform or Revolution?* (Greenwich, Conn., Fawcett Premier, 1968), pp. 454–466.

22. Mark Van Aken, "The Militants: A Portrait of the Uruguayan Student Movement," mimeographed (1964), on deposit at the Center for International Affairs, Harvard University, Cambridge, Mass., chapter 6, pp. 20–30.

23. *Ibid.*, chapter 8, p. 12.

24. Marysa Gerassi, "Uruguay's Urban Guerrillas," *New Left Review*, 62 (July–August, 1970), 23–27; Alphonse Max, *Tupumaros – A Pattern for Urban Guerrilla Warfare in Latin America* (The Hague, International Documentation and Information Centre, 1970), pp. 1–16; and *New York Times*, July 7, 1971.

Marysa Gerassi and Alphonse Max, while in accord on some facts concerning the Tupumaros, hold highly divergent points of view about them. Gerassi is highly positive while Max is intensely negative. Their biases are quite evident and tend to color their interpretation of this guerrilla organization. They illustrate the difficulties and the problems of conducting "objective" research on highly emotional and political topics.

25. Rivarola, "Universidad y estudiantes en una sociedad tradicional," pp. 53-63; James H. Street, "Social Science Research in Paraguay: Current Status and Future Opportunities," in Richard N. Adams, ed., *Responsibilities of the Foreign Scholar to the Local Scholarly Community: Studies of U.S. Research in Guatemala, Chile and Paraguay* (Washington, D.C., The Council on Educational Cooperation with Latin America, Education and World Affairs and Latin American Studies Association, 1969), p. 97; and Joseph Pincus, *The Economy of Paraguay* (New York, Praeger, 1968), pp. 9-10.

From 1811 to 1840, Paraguay was ruled by a dictator, Dr. Jose Gaspar Rodríguez de Francia. During his tenure in office, he nationalized and socialized agriculture and imposed tight regulations on trade and manufacturing. As a result of his policies he virtually destroyed the hierarchical structure of colonial society and replaced it with a relatively egalitarian one. His successors from 1840 to 1870 pursued similar policies which also inhibited the development of a rigid hierarchical system of stratification. The disastrous War of the Triple Alliance (1864-1870) wreaked havoc on the Paraguayan society as the country lost about three-quarters of its population. In 1870 there were less than 29,000 males left in Paraguay. From 1870 to 1936, there was a period of economic collapse and chaos as well as a great deal of foreign control over Paraguay's economic resources. The following decades were characterized by chronic political instability and various dictatorships. All of these factors together produced a rather fluid stratification system in which the state was the primary mechanism for the allocation of resources and for social mobility (Paul H. Lewis, *The Politics of Exile: Paraguay's Febrerista Party* [Chapel Hill, University of North Carolina Press, 1968], pp. xvi-xxv, 8-63).

26. Pincus, *Economy of Paraguay*, pp. 11-12.

27. Rivarola, "Universidad y estudiantes en una sociedad tradicional," pp. 53-63.

28. See chapter 6, this volume for detailed discussion of the Mexican situation.

29. Robert H. Dix, *Colombia: The Political Dimensions of Change* (New Haven, Yale University Press, 1967), pp. 115-168, 360-386; Kenneth N. Walker, "Latin American Student Politics in Comparative Perspective" (Ph.D. diss., University of California, Berkeley, 1969), pp. 51-79.

30. Dix, *Colombia*, p. 163.

31. *Ibid.*, pp. 137-168.

32. *Ibid.*, pp. 341-351.

33. John Gerassi, "Introduction," in John Gerassi, ed., *Revolutionary Priest: The Complete Writings and Messages of Camilo Torres* (New York, Vintage, 1971), pp. 20-37.

34. *Le Monde*, June 17, 1971.

35. Institut International d'Etudes sur l'Education, *Monthly Survey* (Brussels, March 1970).

36. William Goode, *The Family* (Englewood Cliffs, N.J., Prentice-Hall, 1964), pp. 3-6; and Seymour M. Lipset, "Values, Education and Entrepreneurship,"

in Seymour M. Lipset and Aldo Solari, eds., *Elites in Latin America* (New York, Oxford University Press, 1967), pp. 39–40.

37. The component items in the family traditional scale include the following questions from Appendix B: 77, 78, 79, 80.

38. Joseph Kahl, *The Measurement of Modernism: A Study of Values in Brazil and Mexico* (Austin, University of Texas Press, 1968), p. 79.

39. Richard Flacks, "The Liberated Generation: An Exploration of the Roots of Social Protest," *Journal of Social Issues*, 23 (July 1967), 68; and Jeanne Block et al., "Activism and Apathy," pp. 207–212.

40. Samuel Lubell, "That 'Generation Gap'," *Public Interest*, 13 (Fall 1968), p. 53.

41. Richard E. Dawson and Kenneth Prewitt, *Political Socialization* (Boston, Little, Brown, 1969), pp. 112–116.

42. Westby and Braungart and Flacks note that student activists of both the left and the right are generally not rebelling against the politics of their parents as much as they are extending them. David Westby and R. G. Braungart, "Class and Politics in the Family Backgrounds of Student Political Activists," *American Sociological Review*, 31 (October 1966), 691; and Flacks, "The Liberated Generation," pp. 66–67.

43. See chapter 4, this volume, for discussion of the differences which can be attributed to particular universities within the countries in the study. In particular, see Table 7 in that chapter.

44. Karl Mannheim, "The Sociological Problem of Generations," in B. McLaughlin, ed., *Studies in Social Movements* (New York, Free Press, 1969), p. 363.

45. Seymour M. Lipset, *Political Man* (Garden City, N.Y., Doubleday, 1960), p. 267.

46. Klemens Von Klemperer, *Germany's New Conservatism* (Princeton, Princeton University Press, 1957), p. 44. Walter Laquer notes that as early as 1921, to all intents, there was no left wing in the German Youth Movement. Walter Z. Laqueur, *Young Germany* (New York, Basic Books, 1962), p. 160.

47. Rose Goldsen, Morris Rosenberg, Robin Williams, Jr., and Edward Suchman, *What College Students Think* (Princeton, D. Van Nostrand, 1960), pp. 100–101.

48. Mervin B. Freedman, "Changes in Attitudes and Values over Six Decades," in Marie Jahoda and Norman Warren, eds., *Attitudes* (Baltimore, Penguin, 1966), pp. 128–129.

49. The best general reference work on the relationship between the Roman Catholic churches of Latin America and their respective governments is J. Lloyd Mecham, *Church and State in Latin America*, rev. ed. (Chapel Hill, University of North Carolina Press, 1966). For more recent and a more analytic treatment of religious developments both inside and outside of the Church in Latin America see Ivan Vallier, "Religious Elites: Differentiations and Developments in Roman Catholicism," in Lipset and Solari, eds., *Elites in Latin America*, pp. 190–232, and Ivan Vallier, *Catholicism, Social Control, and Modernization in Latin America* (Englewood Cliffs, N.J., Prentice-Hall, 1970); and Norman Gall, "Latin America: The Church Militant," *Commentary*, 49 (April 1970), pp. 25–37.

50. Vallier, *Catholicism in Latin America*, p. 29.

51. Ted Goertzel, "Student Politics in Brazil" (Ph.D. diss., University of Oregon, 1970), p. 132.

52. See chapter 6, this volume.

53. Dix, *Colombia*, pp. 310–315; Mecham, *Church and State*, pp. 132–138.

54. Vallier, *Catholicism in Latin America*, pp. 123, 125.

55. *Le Monde*, June 17, 1971.

56. Mecham, *Church and State*, pp. 190–200; *New York Times*, May 9, 1970.

57. *Hispanic American Report*, 17 (October 1964), p. 753.

58. Liebman, *Puerto Rican Students*, pp. 9, 72–75; Robert Anderson, *Party Politics in Puerto Rico* (Stanford, Stanford University Press, 1965), pp. 111–112.

59. Goertzel, "Brazilian Students," pp. 124–128; Myron Glazer, "Chile," in Donald K. Emmerson, ed., *Student Politics in Developing Countries* (New York, Praeger, 1968), p. 299.

60. Frederic Hicks, "Interpersonal Relationship and *Caudillismo* in Paraguay," *Journal of Inter-American Studies and World Affairs*, 13 (January 1971), 94.

61. *Ibid.*, 94–95, 101–103; Lewis, *Politics of Exile*, pp. 89–119.

62. For the best general discussion of this process, see Lipset, *Political Man*, pp. 80–83.

63. E. Wight Bakke, "Students on the March: The Cases of Mexico and Colombia," *Sociology of Education*, 37 (Spring 1964), 219–221.

64. *Ibid.*, p. 221.

65. See chapter 6, this volume.

66. *New York Times*, June 12, 1971.

67. Institut International d'Etudes sur l'Education, *Bulletin*, June 23, 1971.

68. Rudolph Atcon contends that there are no truly autonomous universities in Latin America. Political control through the budget and the appointment of rectors and professors, he charges, is pervasive. Students, according to him, serve as political agents who carry out the wishes of their party leaders inside the universities (Rudolph P. Atcon, *The Latin American University* [Bogota, Colombia, ECO Revista de la Cultura de Occidente, 1966], pp. 60–69, 83–84). The phenomenon of political intervention in universities, of course, is not unique to Latin America. In the United States, state governments and prominent business interests influence curricula and the selection and dismissal of professors and administrators. The most notable example of this process in recent years has been in California, where Governor Ronald Reagan and members of the University of California Board of Regents, many of whom are Reagan's appointees, have become actively involved in the internal affairs of the University of California, seemingly motivated primarily by their political values and concerns. See James Ridgeway, *The Closed Corporation: American Universities in Crisis* (New York, Ballantine, 1968).

69. Lipset, "University Students and Politics in Underdeveloped Countries," pp. 30–31.

70. Goertzel, *Brazilian Students*, pp. 117–118.

71. This is not a hard and fast generalization because there have of course been many rightist intellectuals, particularly in the 1930s. See Lipset, *Political Man*, pp. 80–83.

72. Fred P. Ellison, "The Writer," in Johnson, ed., *Continuity and Change in Latin America*, pp. 89–96.

73. Glaucio A. D. Soares, "Intellectual Identity and Political Ideology Among University Students," in Lipset and Solari, eds., *Elites in Latin America*, pp. 432–434.

74. John Johnson, *Political Change in Latin America: The Emergence of the Middle Sectors* (Stanford, Stanford University Press, 1958).

75. Glaucio A. D. Soares in "Intellectual Identity and Political Ideology Among University Students," is a representative example in this case as he focuses virtually all of his attention on the left.

76. Taylor, *Government and Politics in Uruguay*, pp. 49–68; and Institute for the Comparative Study of Political Systems, pp. 31–36.

77. See Liebman, *Puerto Rican Students*, pp. 30–33, and chapter 6, this volume.

78. See chapter 4 in this volume which deals intensively with interuniversity differences.

79. Lipset, "University Students and Politics in Underdeveloped Countries," p. 18.

80. Arthur Liebman's interview with Isabel Pico de Hernandez, Professor of Political Science, University of Puerto Rico, Rio Piedras, Puerto Rico, June 15, 1971.

6. STUDENT POLITICS AND NATIONAL CONTEXT: THE CASES OF MEXICO AND PUERTO RICO

1. Oscar Lewis, *La Vida* (New York, Random House, 1966), pp. x–xv.

2. *Ibid.*, p. xv.

3. Junta de Planificacion, *Informe Economico al Gobernador, 1964* (San Juan, Estado Libre Asociado de Puerto Rico, 1965); Junta de Planificacion, *Indicadores Economices de Puerto Rico* (San Juan, Estado Libre Asociado de Puerto Rico, 1965); Henry Wells, *The Modernization of Puerto Rico: A Political Study of Changing Values and Institutions* (Cambridge, Mass., Harvard University Press, 1969), pp. 324–325.

4. Richard U. Miller, "Labor Legislation and Mexican Industrial Relations," *Industrial Relations*, 7 (February 1968), 172; Gilberto Loyo, "The Mexican Revolution Has Not Finished Its Task," in Stanley R. Ross, ed., *Is the Mexican Revolution Dead?* (New York, Knopf, 1966), pp. 189–190; Oscar Lewis, "Mexico Since Cárdenas," in Richard Adams, Oscar Lewis, et al., eds., *Social Change in Latin America Today* (New York, Vintage, 1961), pp. 287–289, 326–331.

5. Edmundo Flores, *Land Reform and the Alliance for Progress* (Princeton, Princeton University, Woodrow Wilson School of Public International Affairs, 1963), pp. 7–8.

6. William P. Glade, Jr., and C. W. Anderson, *The Political Economy of Mexico* (Madison, University of Wisconsin Press, 1963), p. 3.

7. Lloyd G. Reynolds and Peter Gregory, *Wages, Productivity and Industrialization in Puerto Rico* (Homewood, Illinois, Irwin, 1965), p. 38.

8. Kal Wagenheim, "Puerto Rico: Kinship or Colony," *New Leader*, 19 (May 23, 1966), 8.

9. Junta de Planificacion, *Informa Economico al Gobernador*, pp. 147–148.

10. *Ibid.*, p. 44.

11. Eleanor E. Maccoby and Frances Fielder, *Savings Among Upper-Income Families in Puerto Rico* (Rio Piedras, Puerto Rico, University of Puerto Rico Press, 1953), p. 70.

12. Lewis, *La Vida*, pp. xiv–xv.

13. Lewis, "Mexico Since Cárdenas," p. 323.

14. *Ibid.*, p. 325.

15. *Ibid.*, p. 327.

16. *Ibid.*, pp. 291–293.

17. *Ibid.*, p. 329.

18. Bo Anderson and J. D. Cockroft, "Control and Cooptation in Mexican Politics," *International Journal of Comparative Sociology*, 7 (March 1966), 23; and Rodolfo Stavenhagen, "Social Aspects of Agrarian Structure in Mexico," *Social Research*, 33 (Autumn 1966), 476, 480–481.

19. Pablo González Casanova, *Democracy in Mexico* (New York, Oxford University Press, 1970), p. 147.

20. *Ibid.*, pp. 109, 148.

21. *Ibid.*, pp. 214, 215.

22. Lewis, "Mexico Since Cárdenas," p. 305.

23. González Casanova, *Democracy in Mexico*, pp. 141–143, 211.

24. For the best single work on the politics of each society see, for Mexico, Frank Brandenburg, *The Making of Modern Mexico* (Englewood, New Jersey, Prentice-Hall, 1964); and for Puerto Rico, Robert Anderson, *Party Politics in Puerto Rico* (Stanford, Stanford University Press, 1965).

25. Anderson and Cockroft, "Control and Cooptation," p. 19.

26. Arthur Liebman, *The Politics of Puerto Rican University Students* (Austin, University of Texas Press, 1970), pp. 32–33.

27. Karl M. Schmitt, "Communism in Mexico Today," *Western Political Quarterly*, 15 (Spring 1962), 114–118; and Robert Anderson, *Party Politics in Puerto Rico*, pp. 46–47.

28. In July 1967 a plebiscite was held on the future of the island. Of those participating, in the face of campaigns for a boycott among independence oriented parties and a faction of the Republic Statehood Party, a little over 60 percent favored the present Commonwealth status; 39 percent favored statehood and .6 percent chose independence. Of the 1,067,349 registered voters, 65.8 percent voted compared to 79 percent who voted in the 1964 gubernatorial election (Robert Anderson, "Puerto Rico's Debate Goes On," *The New Leader*, 50 [August 1967], 8).

29. Robert E. Scott, *Mexican Government in Transition*, rev. ed. (Urbana, Illinois, University of Illinois Press, 1964), p. 96.

30. Seymour M. Lipset, "Values, Education and Entrepreneurship," in Seymour M. Lipset and Aldo Solari, eds., *Elites in Latin America* (New York, Oxford University Press, 1967), p. 37.

31. Pablo González Casanova, "Mexico: The Dynamics of an Agrarian and Semi-capitalist Revolution," in James Petras and Maurice Zeitlin, eds., *Latin America: Reform or Revolution?* (Greenwich, Conn., Fawcett Premier, 1968), 482.

32. Patricia Richmond, "Mexico: A Case Study of One Party Politics" (Ph.D. diss., University of California at Berkeley, 1968), p. 225.

33. Joseph Kahl, *The Measurement of Modernism: A Study of Values in Brazil and Mexico* (Austin, University of Texas Press, 1968), p. 114.

34. Gabriel A. Almond and Sidney Verba, *The Civic Culture* (Princeton, Princeton University Press, 1963), pp. 72, 77–78.

35. *Ibid.*, p. 64.

36. Kahl, *Measurement of Modernism*, p. 105.

37. Daniel Cosio Villegas, "The Mexican Revolution Then and Now," in Ross, ed., *Is the Mexican Revolution Dead?* pp. 125–126.

38. Anderson and Cockroft, "Control and Cooptation," pp. 20–21.

39. *Ibid.*, pp. 21–22.

40. E. Wight Bakke, "Students on the March: The Cases of Mexico and Colombia," *Sociology of Education*, 37 (Spring 1964), 213.

41. Quoted in Arthur Whitaker and D. C. Jordan, *Nationalism in Contemporary Latin America* (New York, Free Press, 1966), p. 51.

42. Glade and Anderson, *Political Economy of Mexico*, pp. 26–27; Richmond, "Mexico," p. 63; Robert E. Scott, "Student Political Activism in Latin America," in Seymour M. Lipset and Philip G. Altbach, eds., *Students in Revolt* (Boston, Houghton Mifflin, 1969), pp. 17, 116–117. It should be pointed out that Professor Scott believes that the political system is becoming less authoritarian and more pluralistic. See also Anderson and Cockroft, "Control and Cooptation," pp. 20–22.

43. Edwin Lieuwen, *Arms and Politics in Latin America*, rev. ed. (New York, Praeger, 1961), pp. 118–120.

44. Glade and Anderson, *Political Economy of Mexico*, pp. 26–27.

45. *Le Monde*, December 9, 1970.

46. Glade and Anderson, *Political Economy of Mexico*, p. 27.

47. Scott, *Mexican Government*, p. 192; Richmond, "Mexico," p. 311.

48. Bakke, "Students on the March," p. 219; Richmond, "Mexico," p. 317.

49. Charles N. Myers, *Education and National Development in Mexico* (Princeton, Industrial Relations Section, Department of Economics, Princeton University, 1965), p. 129.

50. Bakke, "Students on the March," p. 203.

51. William H. Knowles, "Manpower and Education in Puerto Rico," in Frederick Harbison and Charles Myers, eds., *Manpower and Education* (New York, McGraw-Hill, 1965), p. 125.

52. Myers, *Education and National Development*, p. 126; Liebman, *Puerto Rican Students*, chapter 3.

53. Eyler N. Simpson, *The Ejido: Mexico's Way Out* (Chapel Hill, University of North Carolina Press, 1937), pp. 579–580.

54. Lesley B. Simpson, *Many Mexicos* (Berkeley, University of California Press, 1967), p. 354.

55. George F. Kneller, *The Education of the Mexican Nation* (New York, Columbia University Press, 1951), p. 175; Frank Tannenbaum, *Mexico: The Struggle for Peace and Bread* (New York, Knopf, 1950), p. 171.

56. The sources for this section on the 1966 Mexican student strike are: Rafael Segovia, "Mexican Politics and the University Crisis," in Richard R. Fagen and Wayne Cornelius, Jr., eds., *Political Power in Latin America: Seven Confrontations* (Englewood Cliffs, N.J., Prentice-Hall, 1970), pp. 306–321; "Statements by the Principals," in Fagen and Cornelius, eds., *Political Power*, pp. 321–327; "Editorial Reactions to the Strike," in Fagen and Cornelius, eds., *Political Power*, pp. 328–336; and interviews with students at the UNAM campus in the summer of 1967 by Arthur Liebman.

57. John Womack, Jr., "Unfreedom in Mexico: Government Crackdown on the Universities," *New Republic*, 159 (October 12, 1968), p. 31.

58. Scott, "Student Political Activism in Latin America," pp. 88–89; Kalman Silvert, "The University Student," in John Johnson, ed., *Continuity and Change in Latin America* (Stanford, Stanford University Press, 1964), pp. 223–224.

59. Bakke, "Students on the March," p. 223.

60. The data for this section on the 1968 Mexican student movement and

student political activity during 1969 and 1970 are derived from: (1) the *New York Times* from July 1968 to August 1971; (2) the *Los Angeles Times, Boston Globe, Mexico City Excelsior, and Le Monde* (Paris) for the period from July 1968 to December 1968; (3) the *Guardian*, March 21, 1970, April 4, 1970, February 6, 1971, July 7, 1971; (4) *Latin American Digest*, October 1970; (5) *Institut International d'Etudes sur l'Education Bulletin*, November 25, 1970 and June 23, 1971; (6) North American Congress for Latin America, *Mexico, 1968* (New York, 1968), and North American Congress for Latin America, *Mexico '68: The Students Speak* (New York, 1968); (7) Jorge Carrion, Daniel Cazes, Sol Arguedas, and Fernando Carmona, *Tres Culturas en Agonia* (Mexico, D.F., Editorial Nuestro Tiempo, 1969); (8) Ramon Ramirez, *El movimiento estudantil de México, July–December 1968*, vols. I and II, (Mexico, D.F., Ediciones Era, 1969); (9) Womack, "Unfreedom in Mexico," pp. 27–31; and (10) Arthur Liebman's interviews with student participants and recent travelers from Mexico from 1968 to 1971 as well as his interviews with Mexican professors, students, intellectuals, and prominent businessmen in Mexico, February 1970; (11) Center for Latin American Studies, Arizona State University, *Latin American Digest*, 5 (May 1971), 1–2; (12) *Latin America: A Weekly Political and Economic Report*, 5 (June 11, 1971), 189–190, and 5 (June 18, 1971), 193, 194, 196; (13) *The Village Voice*, July 22, 1971; (14) Interview with James Goodsell, Foreign Affairs Editor of the *Christian Science Monitor*, June 28, 1971; *The Economist* (London), June 19, 1971.

61. The principal sources for this section on Puerto Rican students are: (1) Liebman, *Puerto Rican Students*, chapters 1 and 3; (2) *San Juan Star*, 1965, 1967; (3) *New York Times*, 1967, 1968, 1969, 1970, 1971; (4) *Palante* [the bi-weekly newspaper of the Young Lords Party], 1970 and 1971; (5) Institut International d'Etudes sur l'Education, *Monthly Survey of Youth and Educational Developments*, December 1969, January 1970, and March 1970; (6) Luis Nieves Falcon, *La Opinion Pública y las Aspiraciones de los Puertoriqueños* (Río Piedras: Centro de Investigaciones Sociales, Universidad de Puerto Rico, 1970), pp. 218–264; (7) Ismael Rodriguez Bou, "Significant Factors in the Development of Education in Puerto Rico," in *Status of Puerto Rico*, Selected Background Studies Prepared for the United States–Puerto Rico Commission on the Status of Puerto Rico (Washington, D.C., 1966), pp. 223–252; (8) *El Mundo*, April 25, 1971; (9) Jose Alberto Alvarez Febles, "La reforma universitaria: Revolucion educativa," inaugural address as President of the University Student Council delivered October 29, 1970. We are indebted to various Puerto Rican students and faculty of the UPR who shared their experiences and insights with us in Puerto Rico and the United States. We would particularly like to thank Professor Isabel Pico de Hernandez of the Political Science Department of the UPR for enlightening us about current and historic student politics and for sharing the preliminary results of her doctoral study on Puerto Rican students with us.

7. CONCLUSION

1. Marvin Leiner, "Cuba's Schools, Ten Years Later," *Saturday Review*, 53 (October 17, 1970), 59–61, 69–71; Richard Jolly, "Education," in Dudley Seers, ed., *Cuba: The Economic and Social Revolution* (Chapel Hill, University of North Carolina Press, 1964), pp. 161–263; Jaime Suchlicki, *University Stu-*

dents and Revolution in Cuba (Coral Gables, Fla., University of Miami Press, 1969), pp. 87–135; *Atlas*, June 1971.

The imprisonment and subsequent "confession" of the noted Cuban poet, Heberto Padilla, during the Spring of 1971 marked a severe break with the Castro government's policy of toleration of criticism. This event plus the increased difficulty of Cuban writers critical of the regime in having their works published in Cuba may foreshadow a shift to a more "normal" Communist state and intellectual relationship which many sympathizers of the Cuban revolution hoped that Cuba could avoid. See José Yglesias, "The Case of Heberto Padilla," *The New York Review of Books*, 16 (June 3, 1971), 3-6, 8.

2. Quoted in *The Guardian*, December 5, 1970.

3. Institut International d' Etudes sur l'Education, *Bulletin*, February 26, 1971.

4. *New York Times*, June 12, 1971.

5. Kalman H. Silvert, "The University Student," in John J. Johnson, ed., *Continuity and Change in Latin America* (Stanford, Stanford University Press, 1964), p. 225.

Index

Publications Written under the Auspices of the Center for International Affairs, Harvard University

Created in 1958, the Center for International Affairs fosters advanced study of basic world problems by scholars from various disciplines and senior officials from many countries. The research at the Center focuses on economic, social, and political development, the management of force in the modern world, the evolving roles of Western Europe and the Communist block, and the conditions of international order. Books published by Harvard University Press are listed here in the order in which they have been issued. A complete list of publications may be obtained from the Center.

BOOKS

The Soviet Bloc: Unity and Conflict, by Zbigniew K. Brzezinski (jointly with the Russian Research Center), 1960. Revised and enlarged edition, 1967.

Rift and Revolt in Hungary: Nationalism versus Communism, by Ferenc A. Vali. 1961.

The Economy of Cyprus, by A. J. Meyer, with Simos Vassiliou (jointly with the Center for Middle Eastern Studies), 1962.

Entrepreneurs of Lebanon: The Role of the Business Leader in a Developing Economy, by Yusif A. Sayigh (jointly with the Center for Middle Eastern Studies), 1962.

Communist China 1955-1959: Policy Documents with Analysis, with a foreword by Robert R. Bowie and John K. Fairbank (jointly with the East Asian Research Center), 1962.

In Search of France, by Stanley Hoffmann, Charles P. Kindleberger, Laurence W. Wylie, Jesse R. Pitts, Jean-Baptiste Duroselle, and Francois Goguel, 1963.

Somali Nationalism: International Politics and the Drive for Unity in the Horn of Africa, by Saadia Touval, 1963.

The Dilemma of Mexico's Development: The Roles of the Private and Public Sectors, by Raymond Vernon, 1963.

The Arms Debate, by Robert A. Levine, 1963.

Africans on the Land: Economic Problems of African Agricultural Development in Southern, Central, and East Africa, with Special Reference to Southern Rhodesia, by Montague Yudelman, 1964.

Public Policy and Private Enterprise in Mexico: Studies, by M. S. Wionczek, D.H. Shelton, C. P. Blair, and R. Izquierdo, edited by Raymond Vernon, 1964.

Democracy in Germany, by Fritz Erler (Jodidi Lectures), 1965.

The Rise of Nationalism in Central Africa: The Making of Malawi and Zambia, 1873–1964, by Robert I. Rotberg, 1965.

Pan-Africanism and East African Integration, by Joseph S. Nye, Jr., 1965.

Germany and the Atlantic Alliance: The Interaction of Strategy and Politics, by James L. Richardson, 1966.

Political Change in a West African State: A Study of the Modernization Process in Sierra Leone, by Martin Kilson, 1966.

Planning without Facts: Lessons in Resource Allocation from Nigeria's Development, by Wolfgang F. Stolper, 1966.

Export Instability and Economic Development, by Alasdair I. MacBean, 1966.

Europe's Postwar Growth: The Role of Labor Supply, by Charles P. Kindleberger, 1967.

Pakistan's Development: Social Goals and Private Incentives, by Gustav F. Papanek, 1967.

Strike a Blow and Die: A Narrative of Race Relations in Colonial Africa, by George Simeon Mwase, edited by Robert I. Rotberg, 1967. Second printing, with a revised introduction, 1970.

Development Policy: Theory and Practice, edited by Gustav F. Papanek, 1968.

Korea: The Politics of the Vortex, by Gregory Henderson, 1968.

The Brazilian Capital Goods Industry, 1929–1964 (jointly with the Center for Studies in Education and Development), by Nathaniel H. Leff, 1968.

The Process of Modernization: An Annotated Bibliography on the Sociocultural Aspects of Development, by John Brode, 1969.

Taxation and Development: Lessons from Colombian Experience, by Richard M. Bird, 1970.

Lord and Peasant in Peru: A Paradigm of Political and Social Change, by F. LaMond Tullis, 1970.

The Kennedy Round in American Trade Policy: The Twilight of the GATT?, by John W. Evans, 1971.

Korean Development: The Interplay of Politics and Economics, by David C. Cole and Princeton N. Lyman, 1971.

Peasants Against Politics: Rural Organization in Brittany, 1911–1967, by Suzanne Berger, 1972.

Transnational Relations and World Politics, edited by Robert O. Keohane and Joseph S. Nye, Jr., 1972.

Development Policy II – The Pakistan Experience, edited by Walter P. Falcon and Gustav F. Papanek, 1971.

Latin American University Students: A Six Nation Study, by Arthur Liebman, Kenneth N. Walker, and Myron Glazer, 1972.